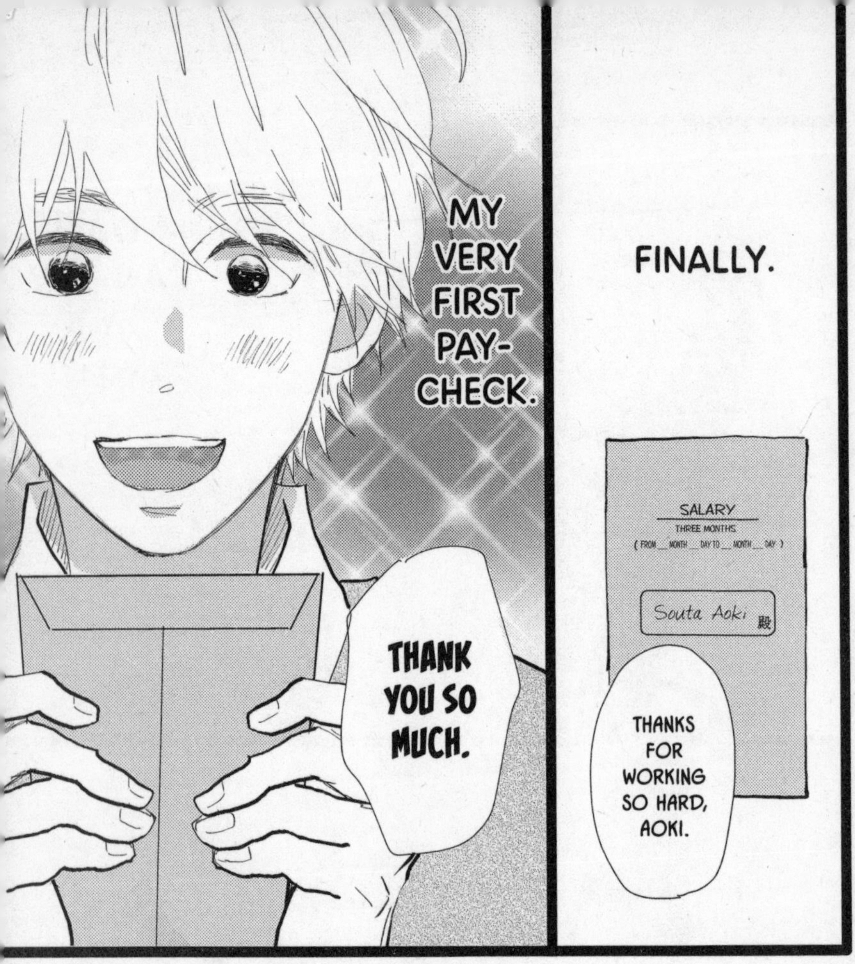

My Love Mix-Up!

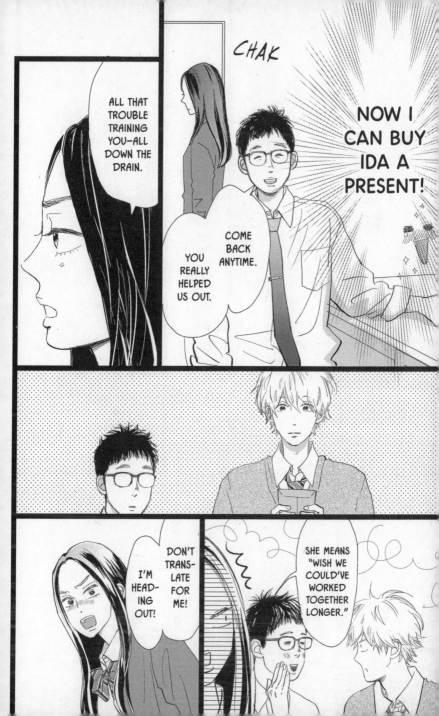

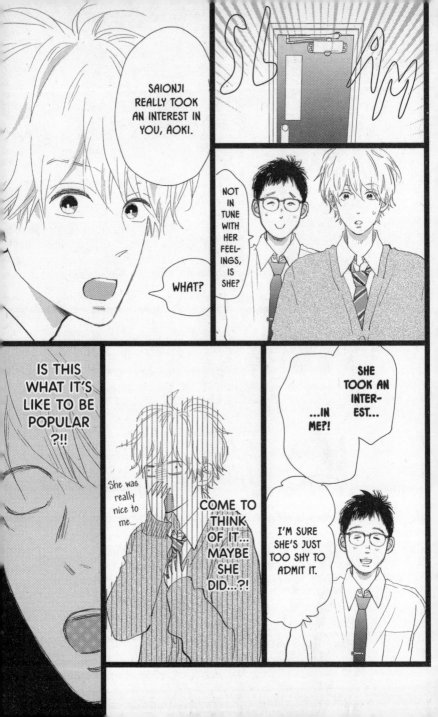

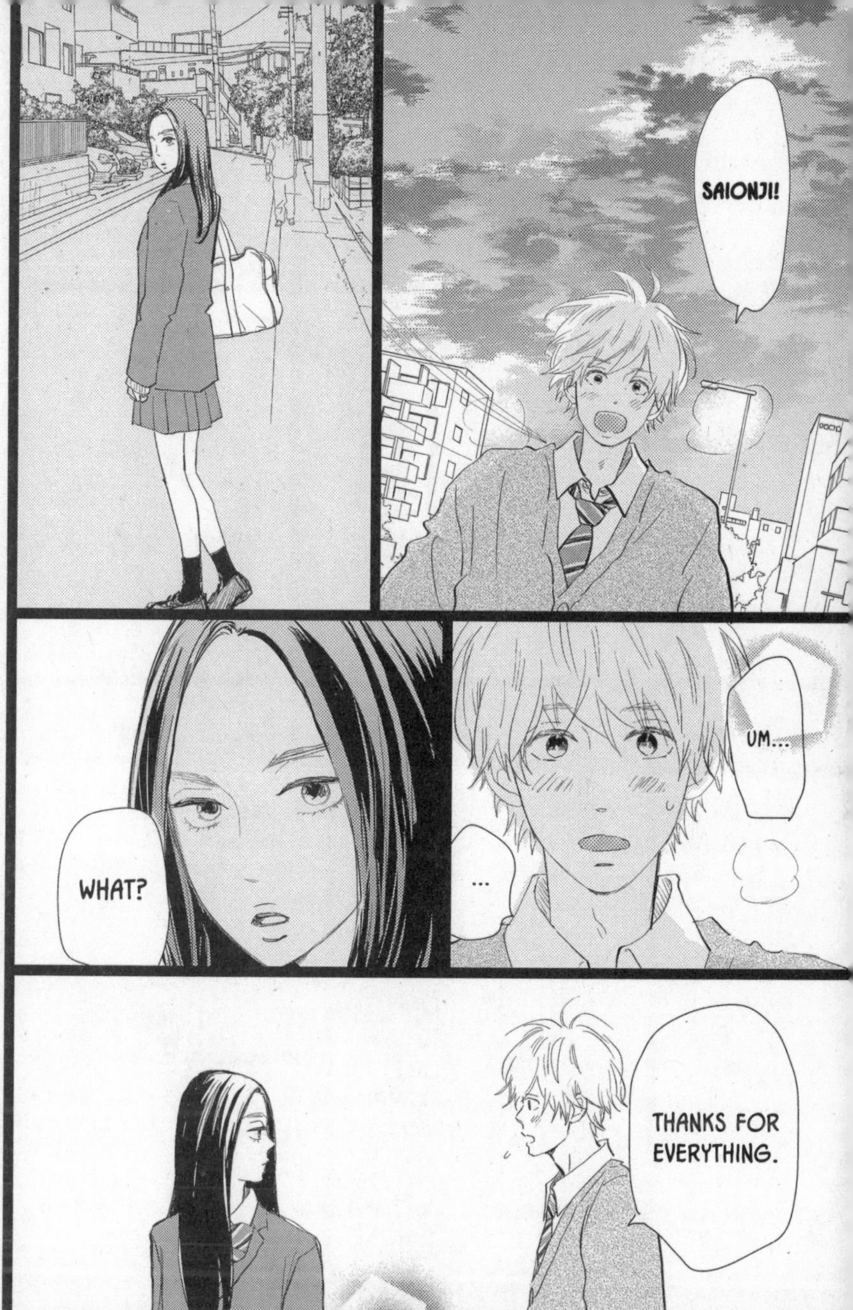
SAIONJI!
WHAT?
UM...
...
THANKS FOR EVERYTHING.

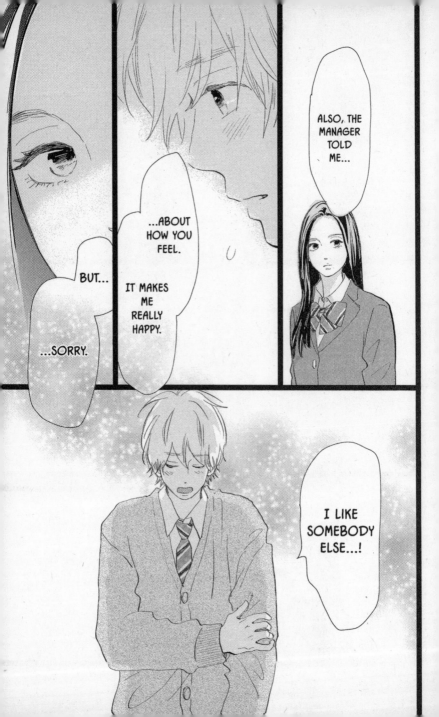

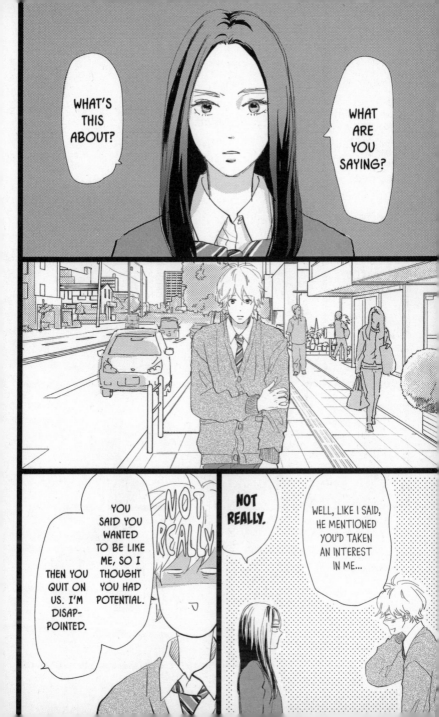

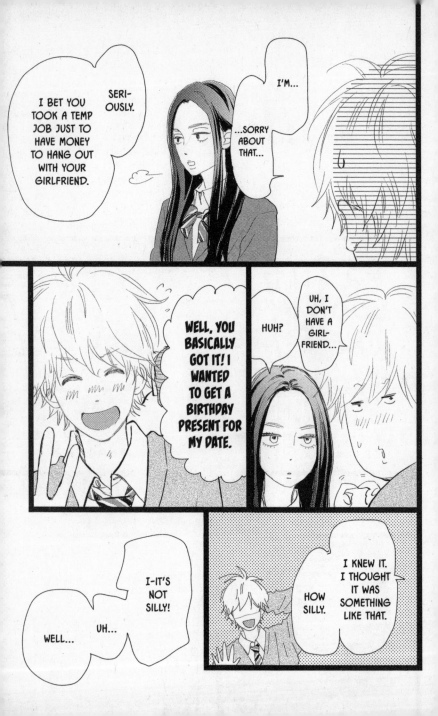

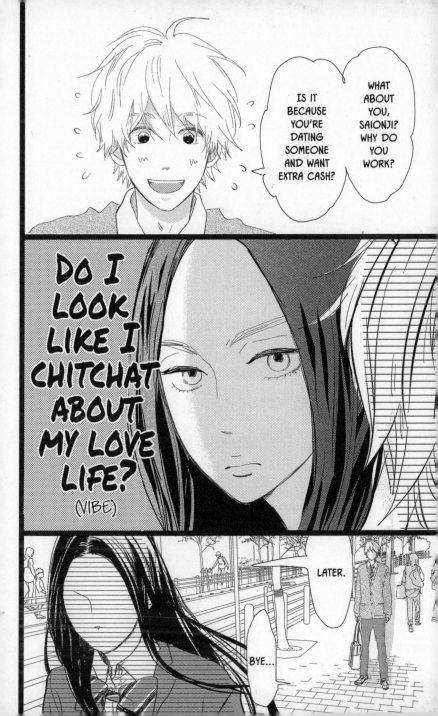

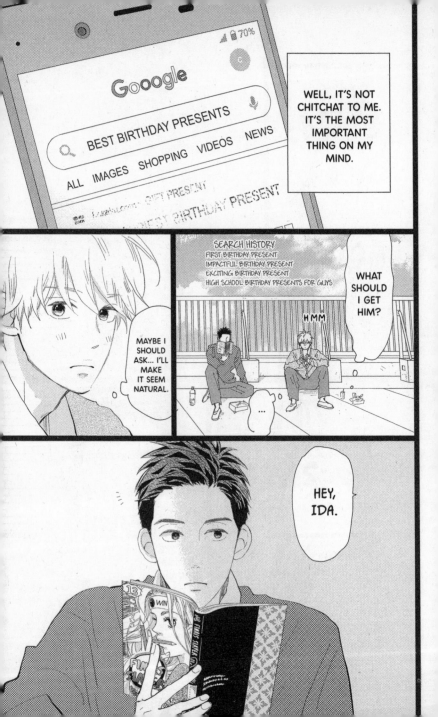

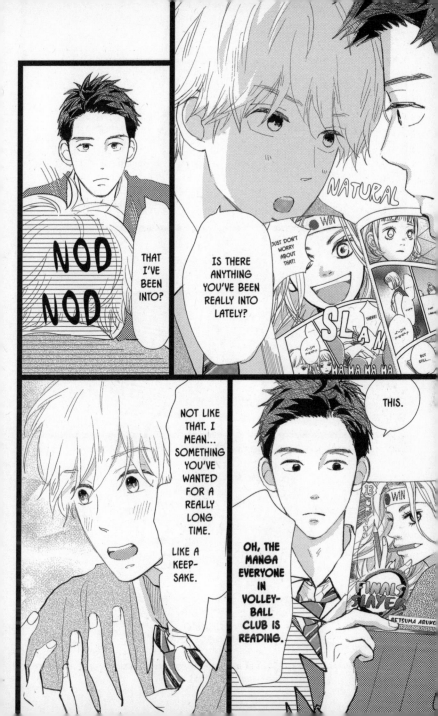

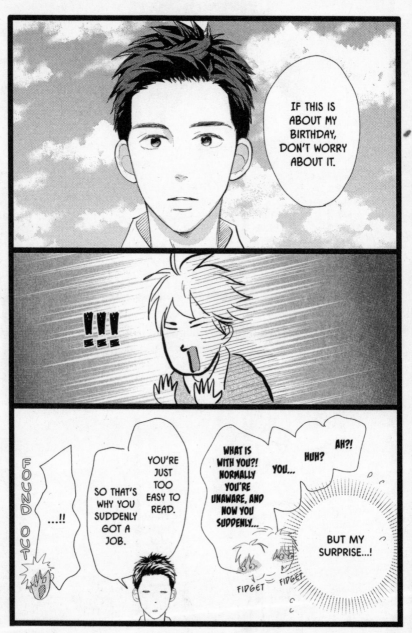

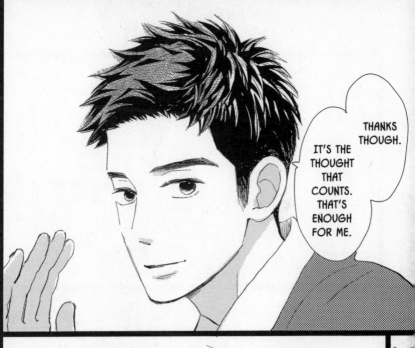

THANKS THOUGH.

IT'S THE THOUGHT THAT COUNTS. THAT'S ENOUGH FOR ME.

THE END

Don't just assume I'm going to buy something weird!

DON'T WASTE YOUR MONEY ON ANYTHING WEIRD.

I know how hard you worked for it. You should be careful how you spend it.

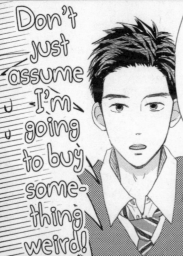

ISN'T THERE ANYTHING YOU WANT?

SERIOUSLY? YOU DON'T WANT A PRESENT?

NOPE.

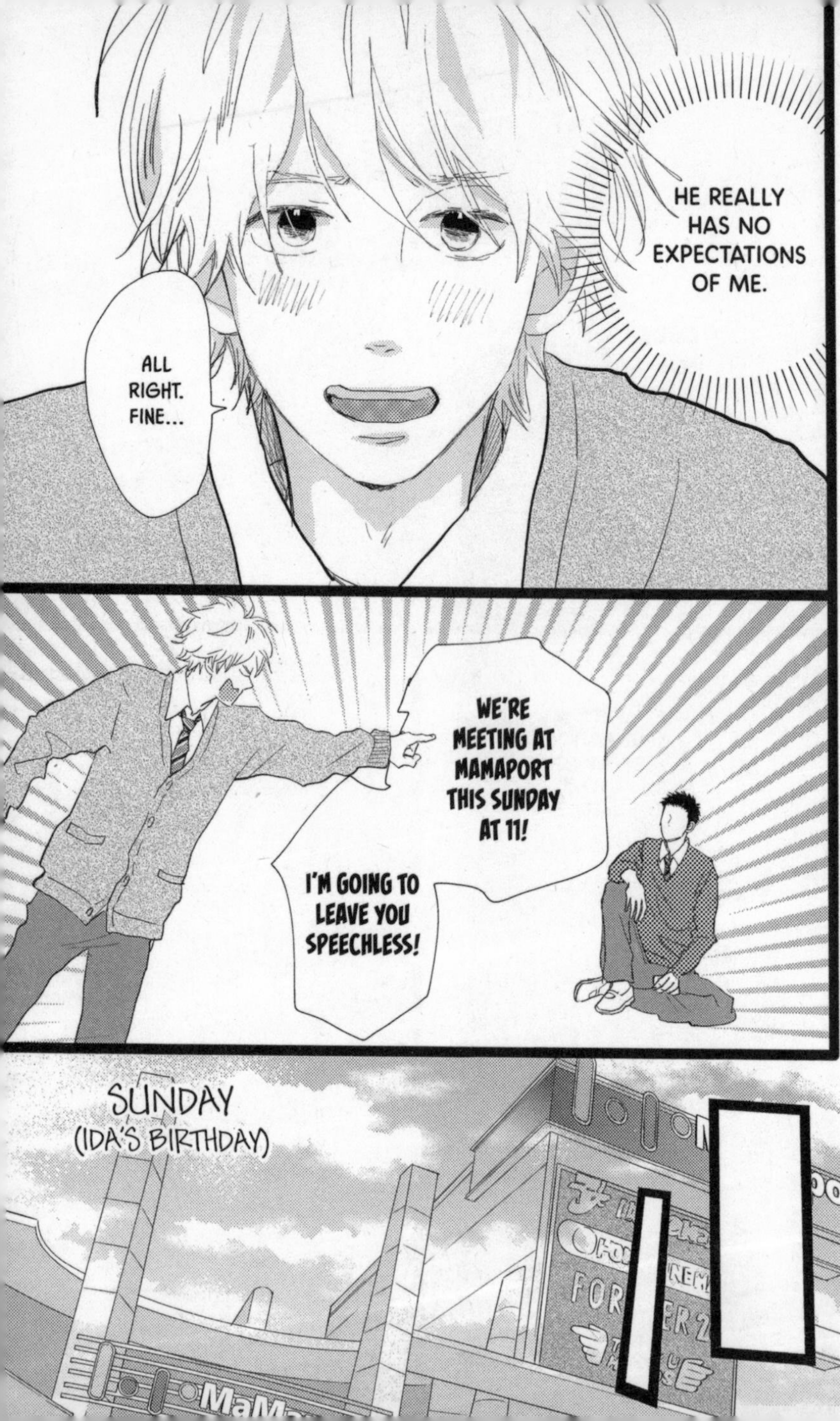
HE REALLY HAS NO EXPECTATIONS OF ME.
ALL RIGHT. FINE...
WE'RE MEETING AT MAMAPORT THIS SUNDAY AT 11!
I'M GOING TO LEAVE YOU SPEECHLESS!
SUNDAY (IDA'S BIRTHDAY)

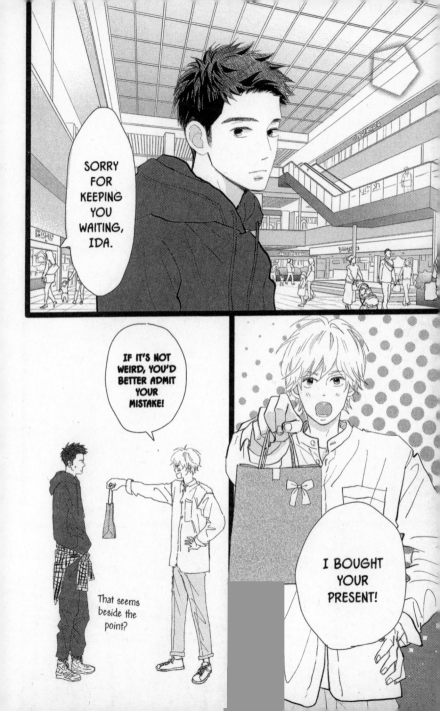

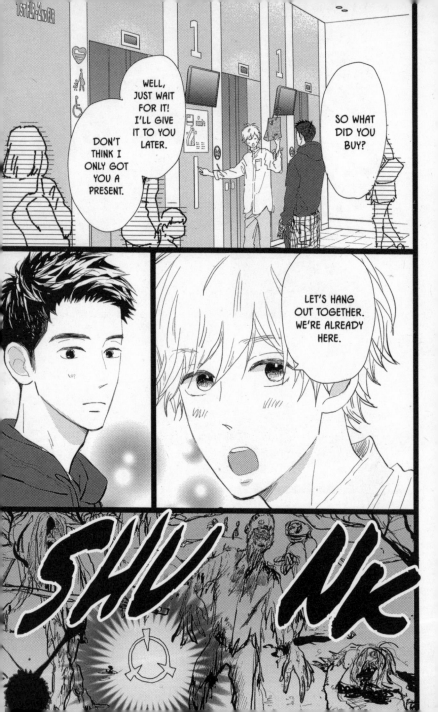

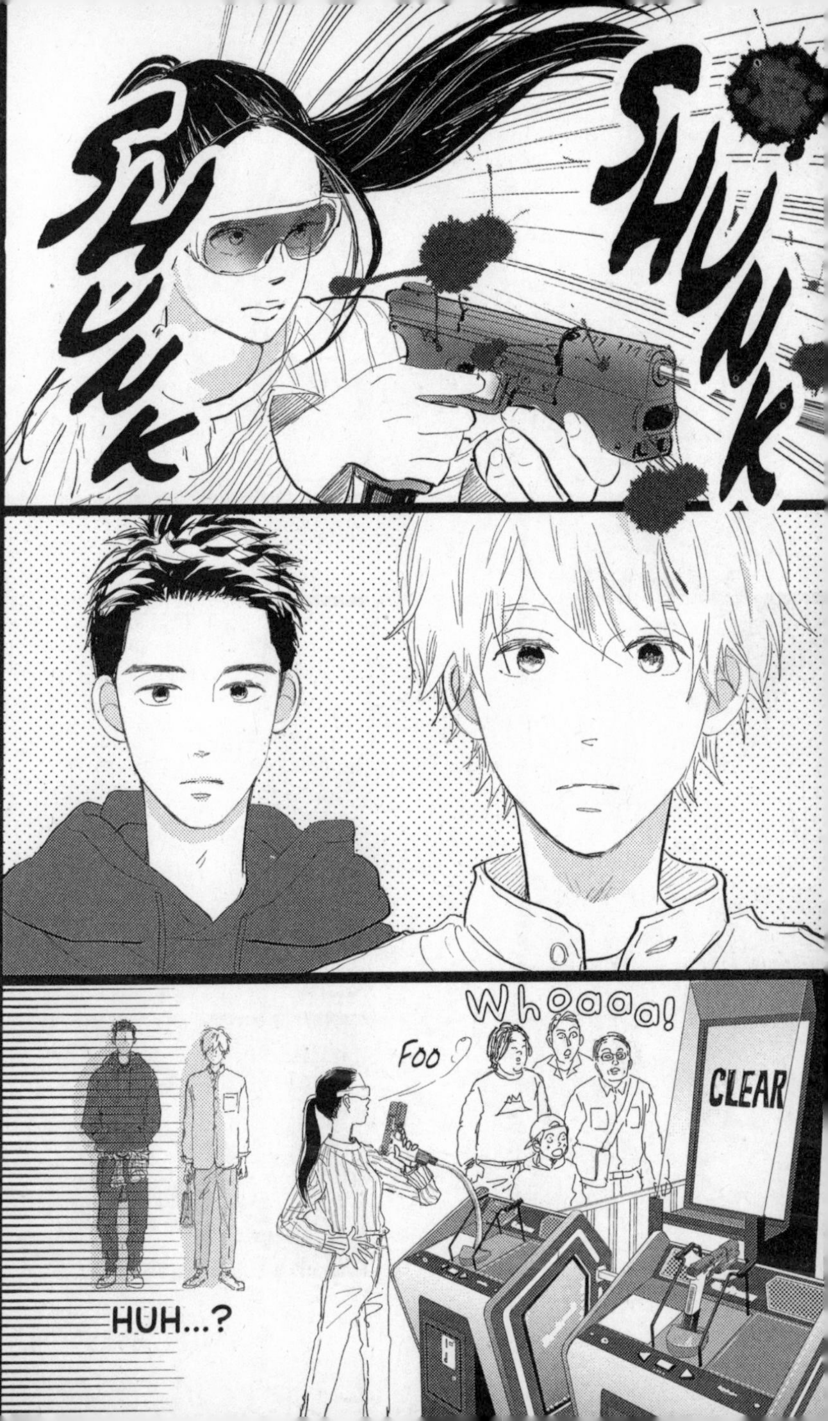
SHUNK
SHUNK
Whoaaa!
CLEAR
Foo ♡
HUH...?

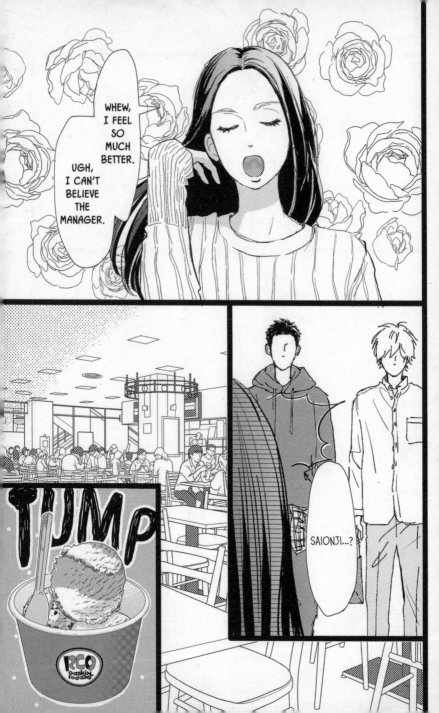

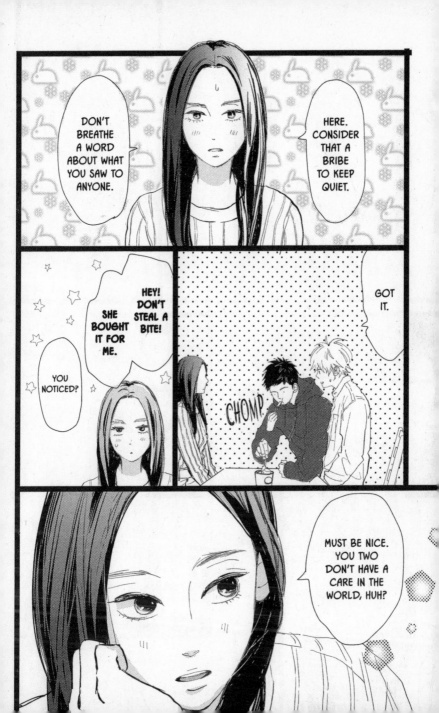

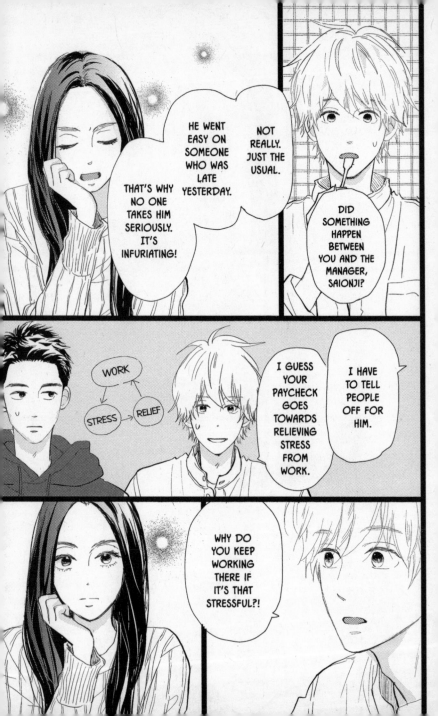

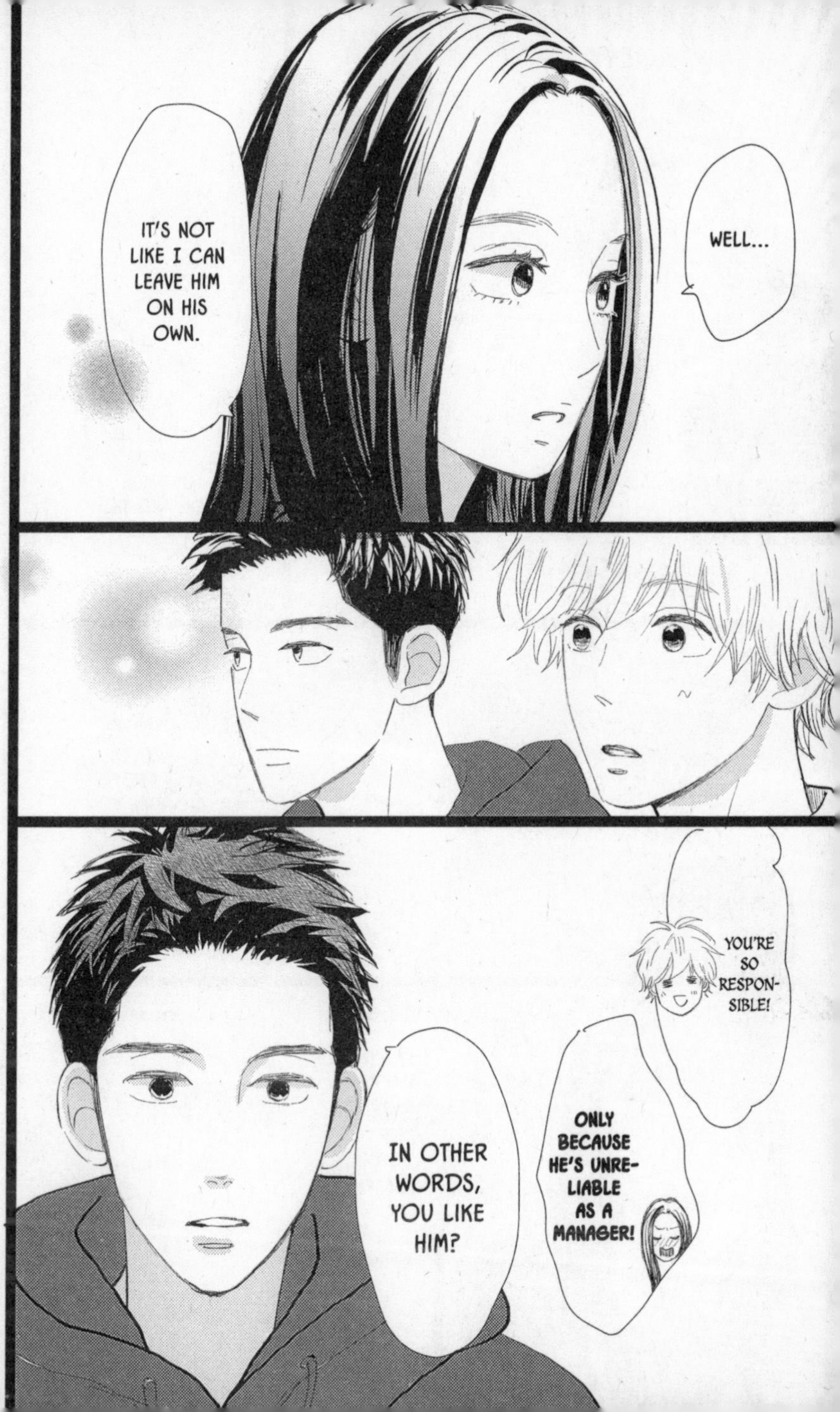
WELL...
IT'S NOT LIKE I CAN LEAVE HIM ON HIS OWN.
YOU'RE SO RESPONSIBLE!
ONLY BECAUSE HE'S UNRELIABLE AS A MANAGER!
IN OTHER WORDS, YOU LIKE HIM?

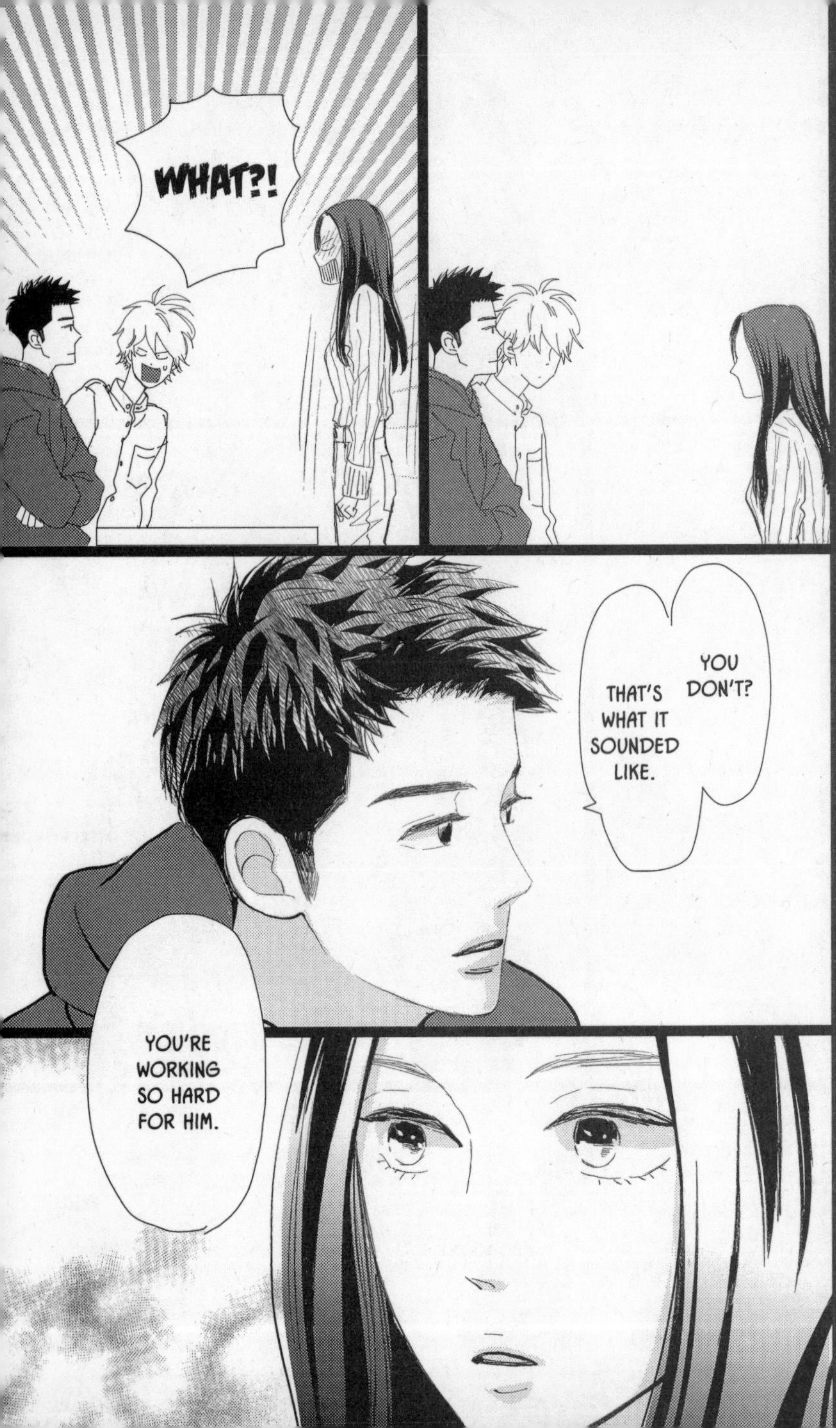
WHAT?!
YOU DON'T?
THAT'S WHAT IT SOUNDED LIKE.
YOU'RE WORKING SO HARD FOR HIM.

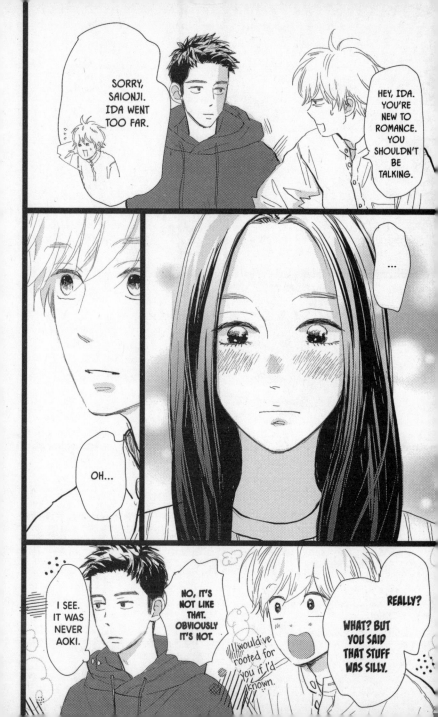

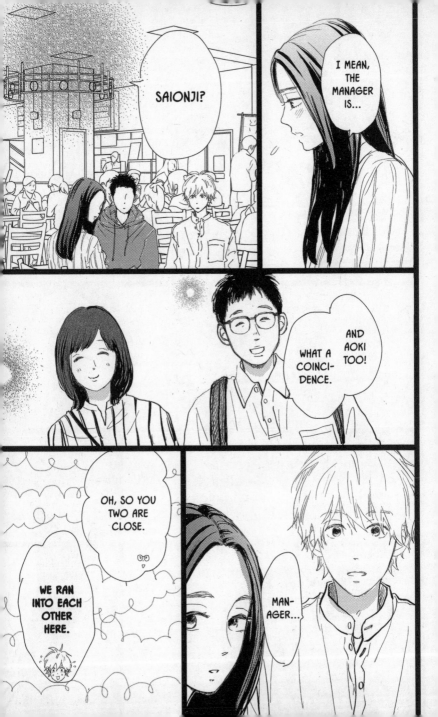

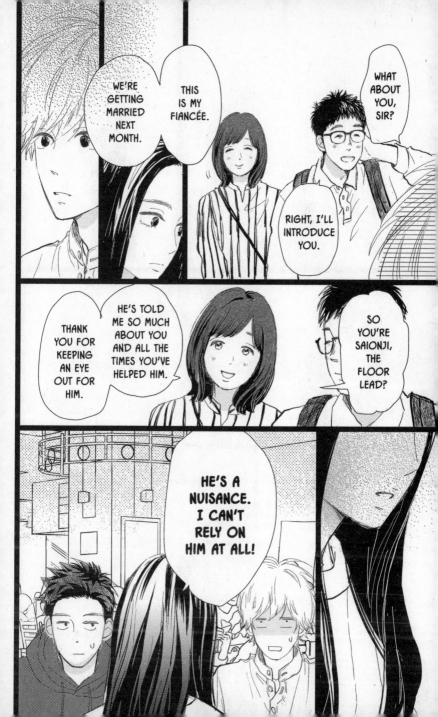

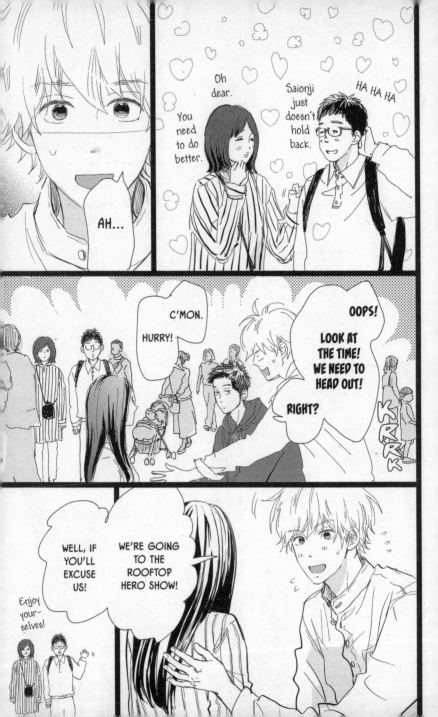

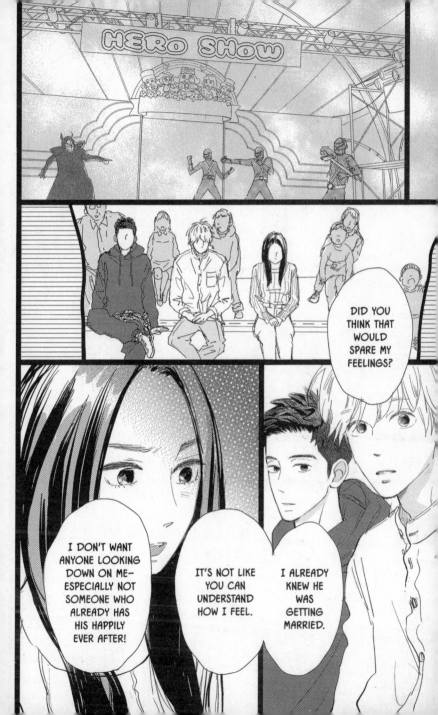

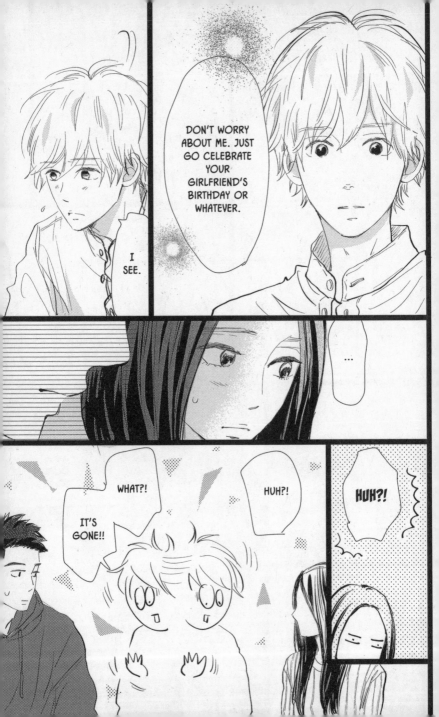

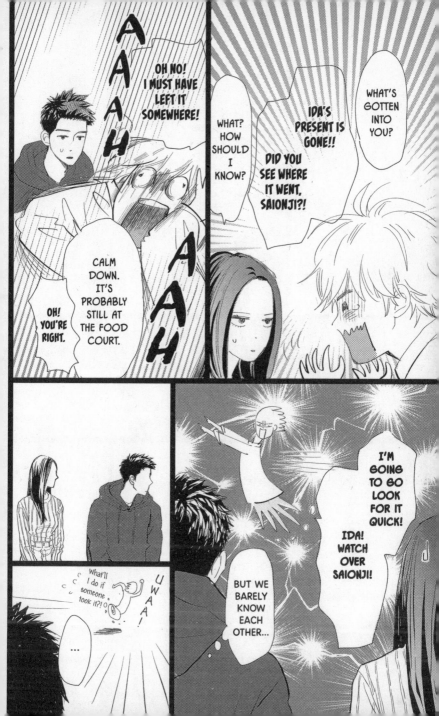

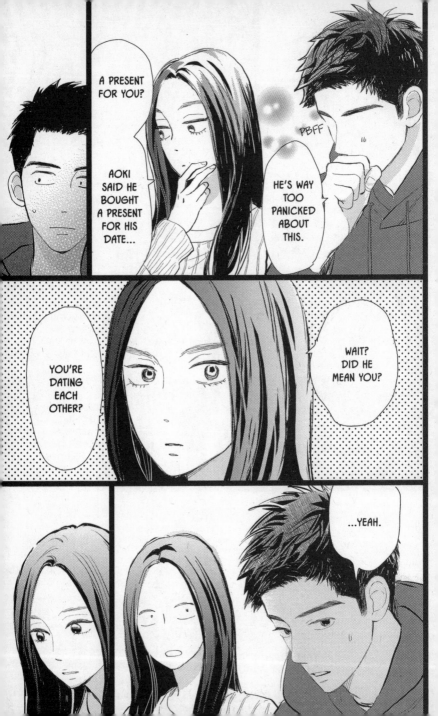

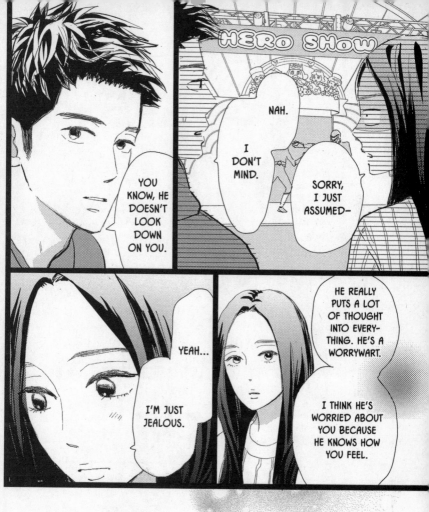

HERO SHOW

YOU KNOW, HE DOESN'T LOOK DOWN ON YOU.

NAH.

I DON'T MIND.

SORRY, I JUST ASSUMED—

HE REALLY PUTS A LOT OF THOUGHT INTO EVERY-THING. HE'S A WORRYWART.

YEAH...

I'M JUST JEALOUS.

I THINK HE'S WORRIED ABOUT YOU BECAUSE HE KNOWS HOW YOU FEEL.

...SINCE I STARTED AT THAT JOB.

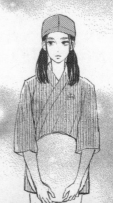

IT'S NEVER WORKED OUT FOR ME...

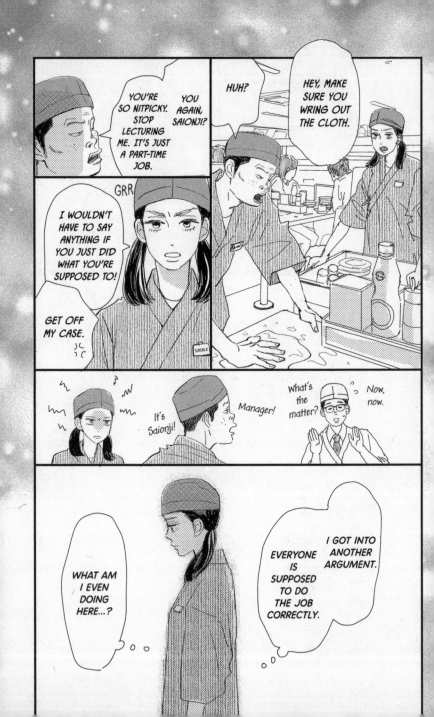

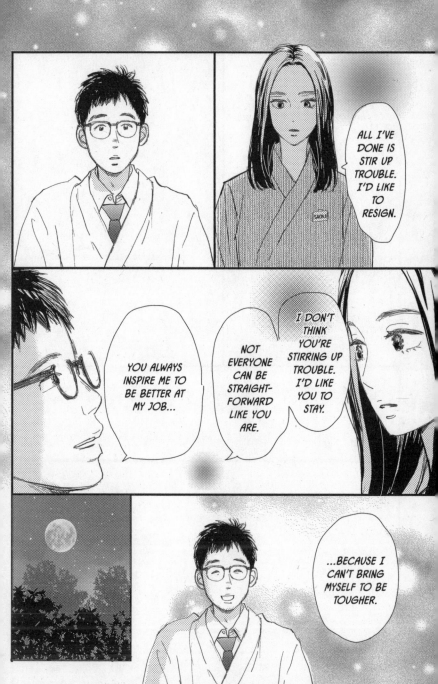

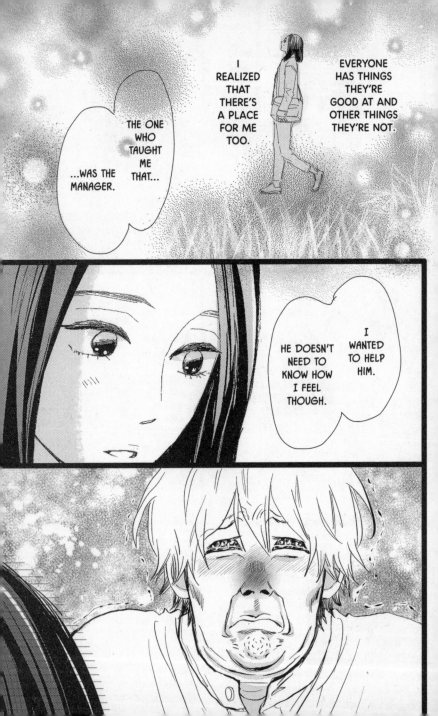

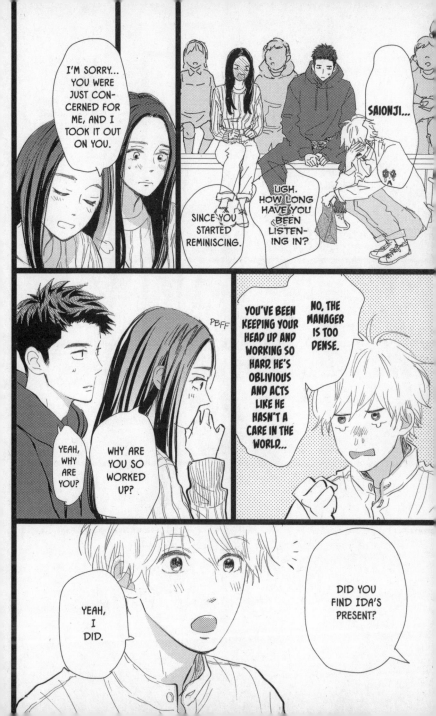

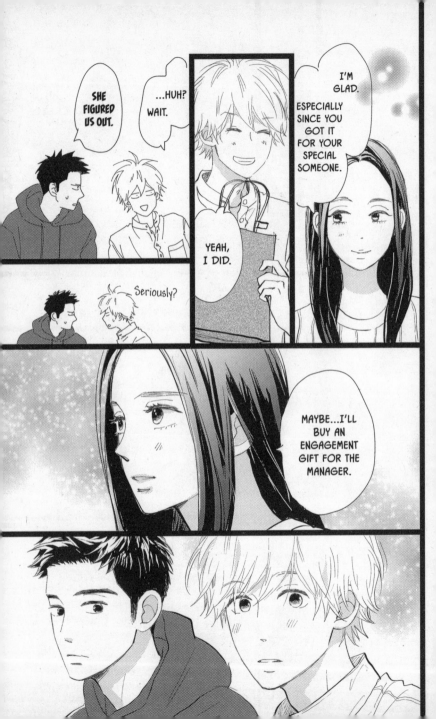

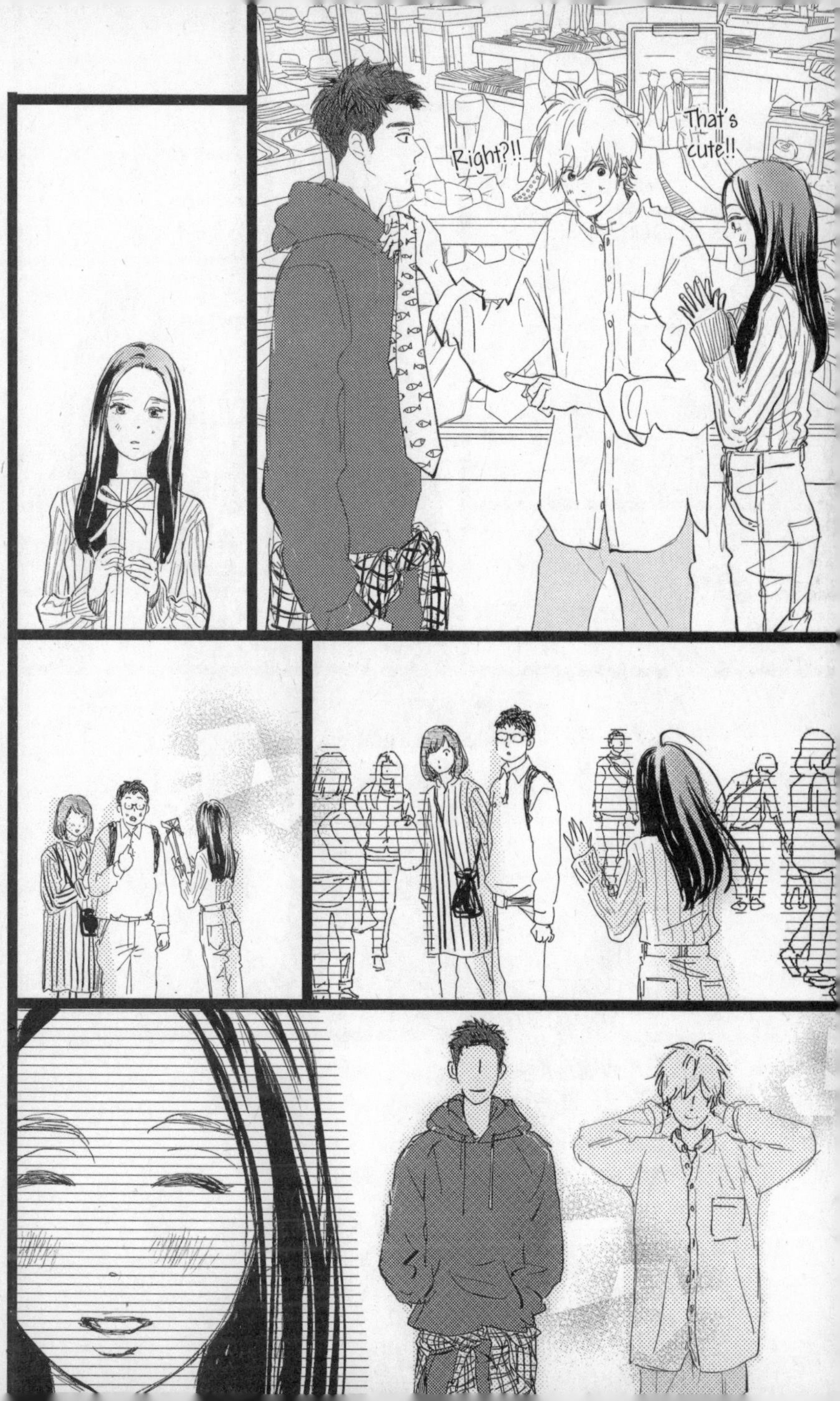
That's cute!!
Right?!!

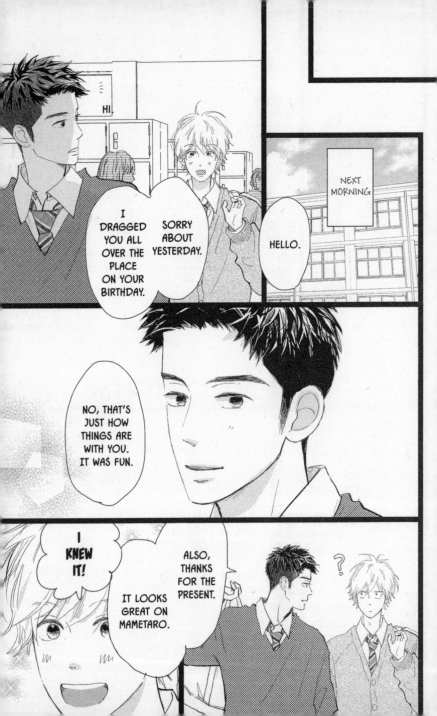

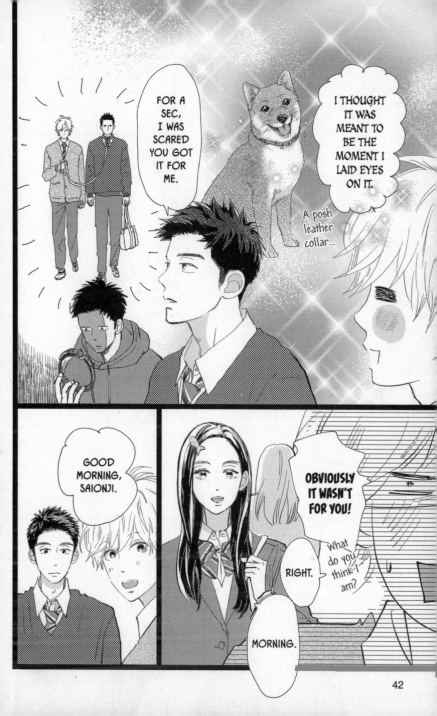

FOR A SEC, I WAS SCARED YOU GOT IT FOR ME.

I THOUGHT IT WAS MEANT TO BE THE MOMENT I LAID EYES ON IT.

A posh leather collar...

GOOD MORNING, SAIONJI.

OBVIOUSLY IT WASN'T FOR YOU!

What do you think I am?

RIGHT.

MORNING.

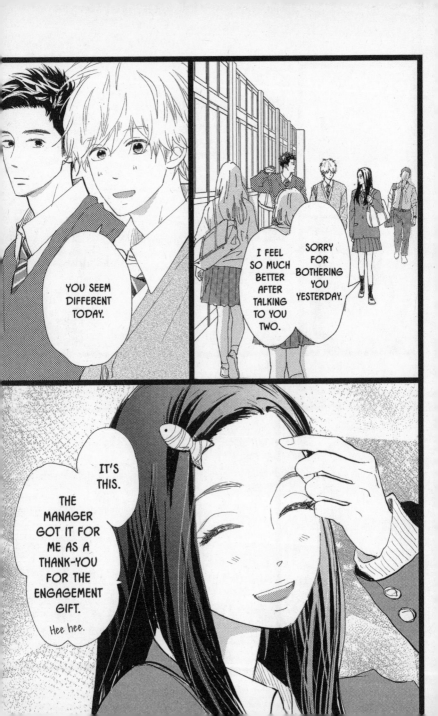

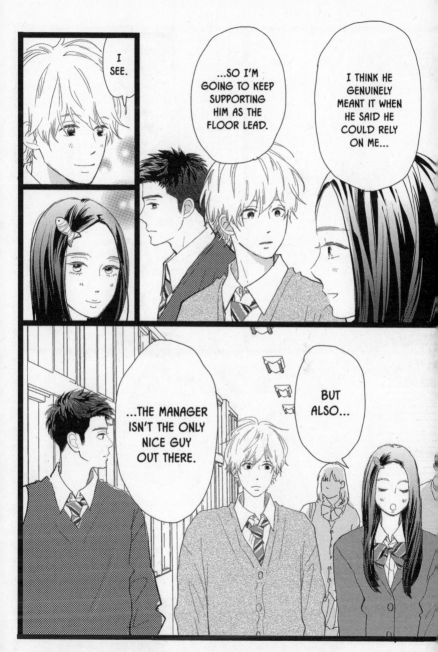

44

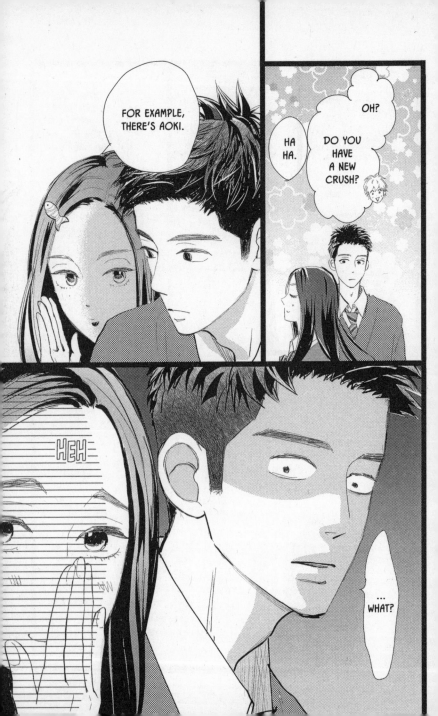

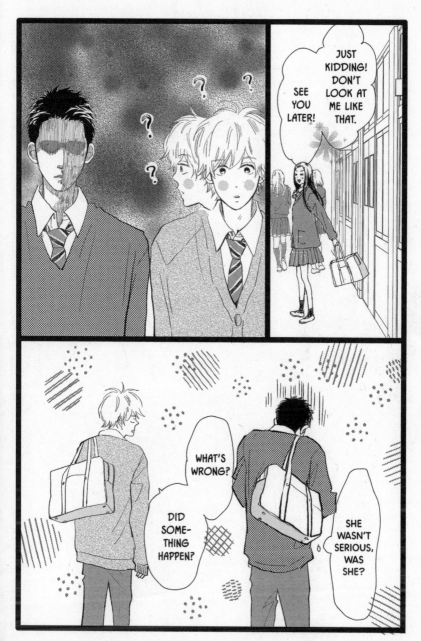

Chapter 23

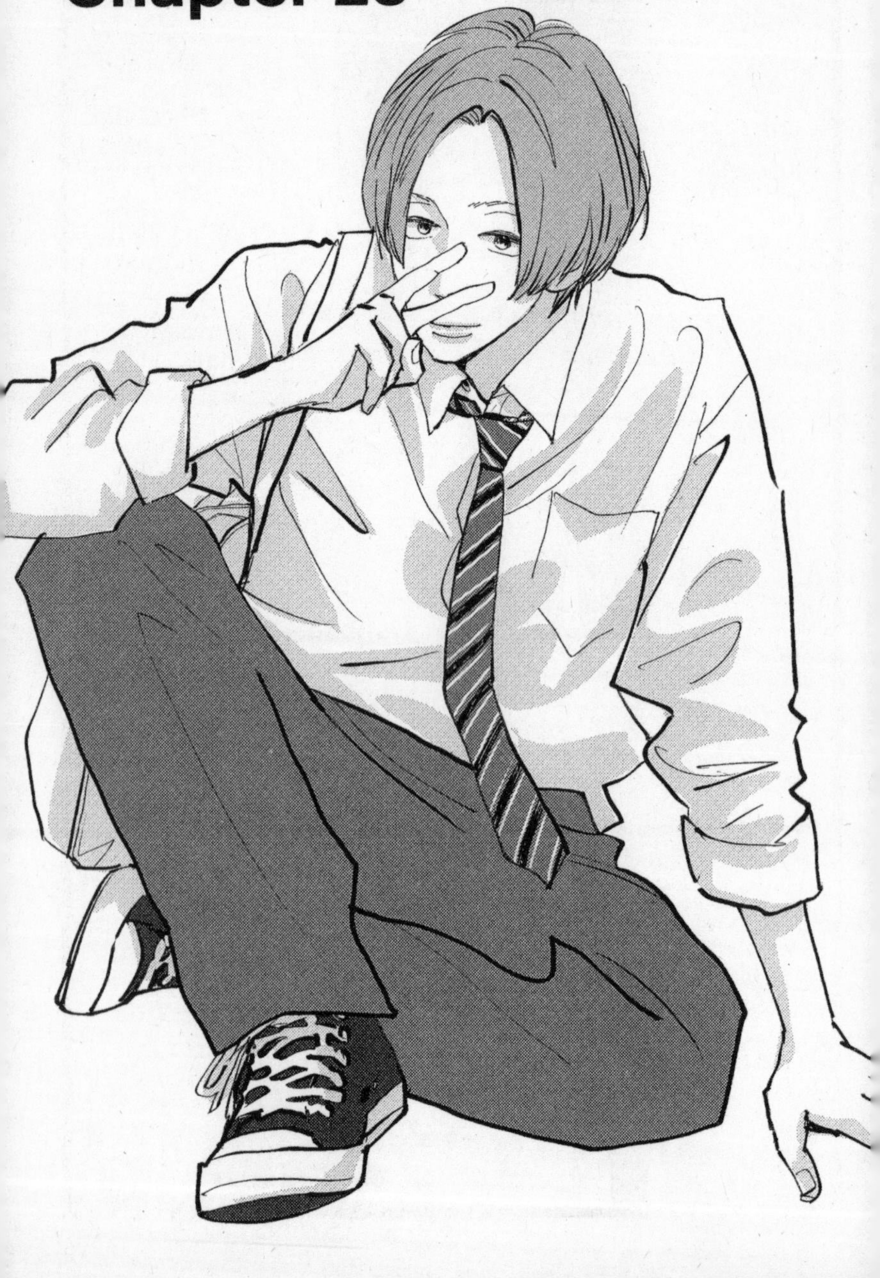

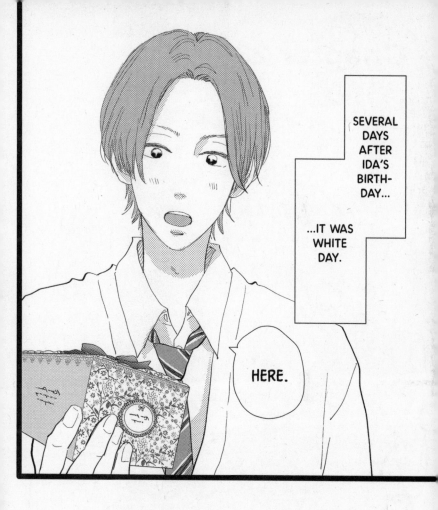

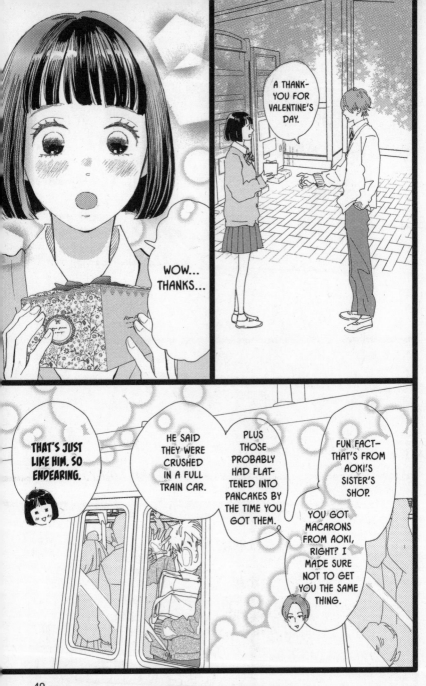

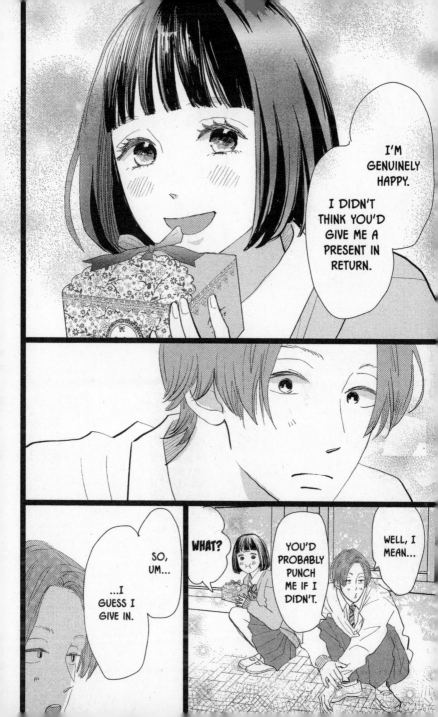

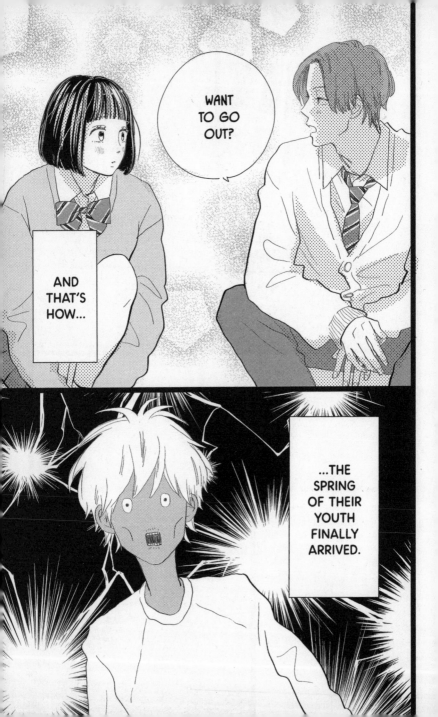

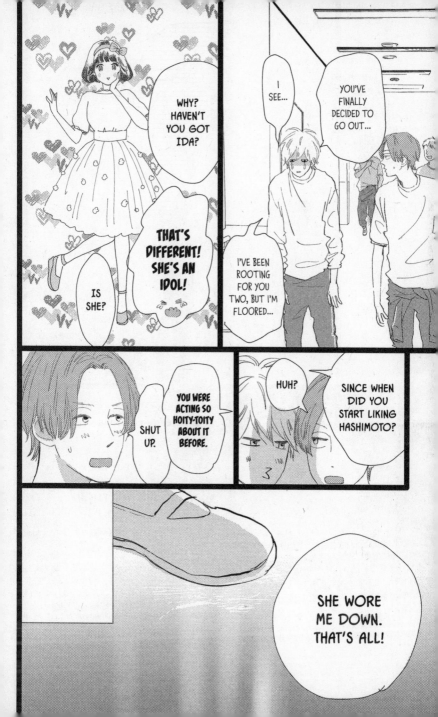

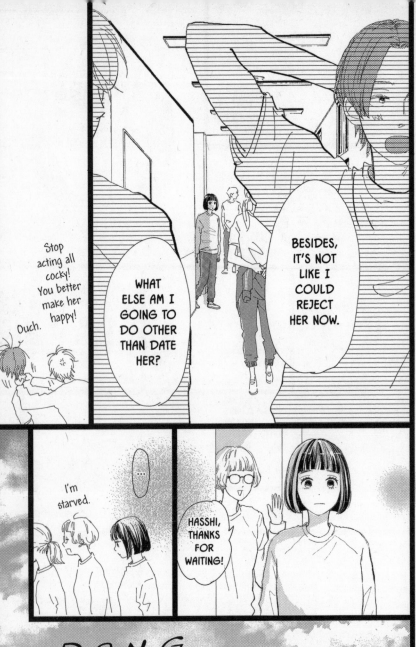

Stop acting all cocky! You better make her happy!

Ouch.

WHAT ELSE AM I GOING TO DO OTHER THAN DATE HER?

BESIDES, IT'S NOT LIKE I COULD REJECT HER NOW.

. . .

I'm starved.

HASSHI, THANKS FOR WAITING!

DONG

DONG

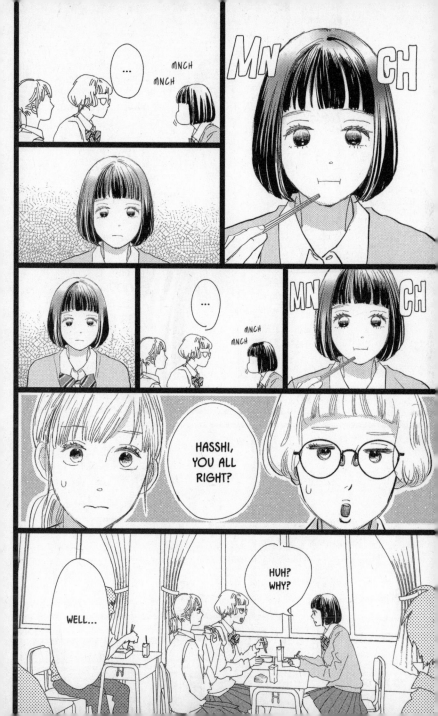

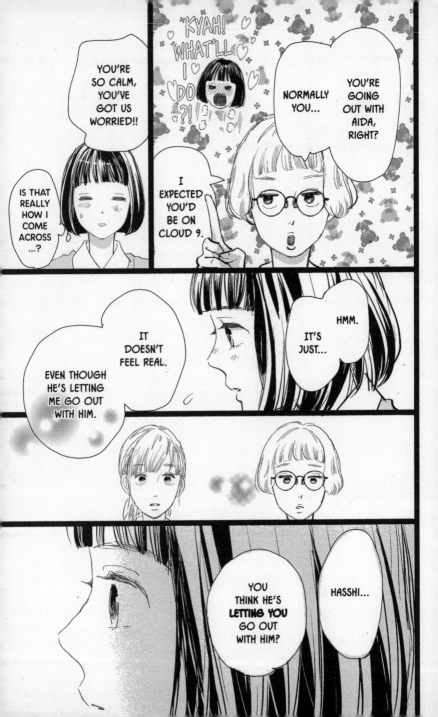

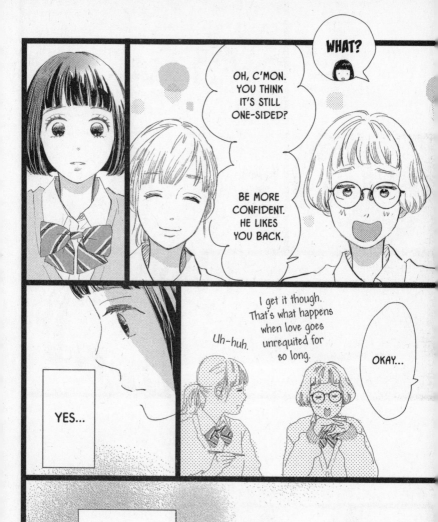

WHAT?

OH, C'MON. YOU THINK IT'S STILL ONE-SIDED?

BE MORE CONFIDENT. HE LIKES YOU BACK.

I get it though. That's what happens when love goes unrequited for so long.

Uh-huh.

OKAY...

YES...

HE'S LETTING ME DATE HIM.

BESIDES, IT'S NOT LIKE I COULD REJECT HER NOW.

SHE WORE ME DOWN. THAT'S ALL!

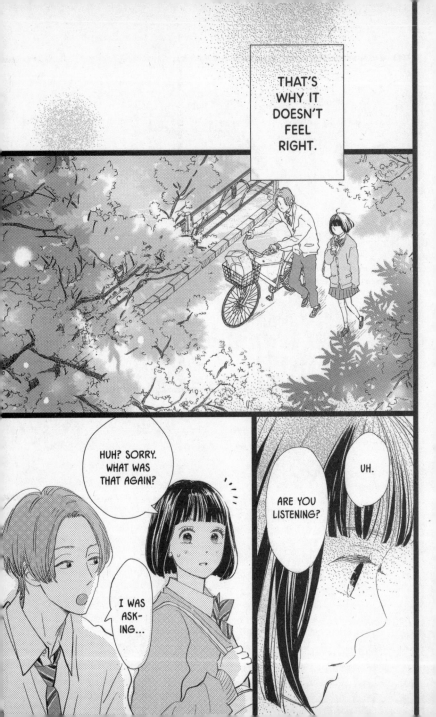

THAT'S WHY IT DOESN'T FEEL RIGHT.

HUH? SORRY. WHAT WAS THAT AGAIN?

I WAS ASK- ING...

ARE YOU LISTENING?

UH.

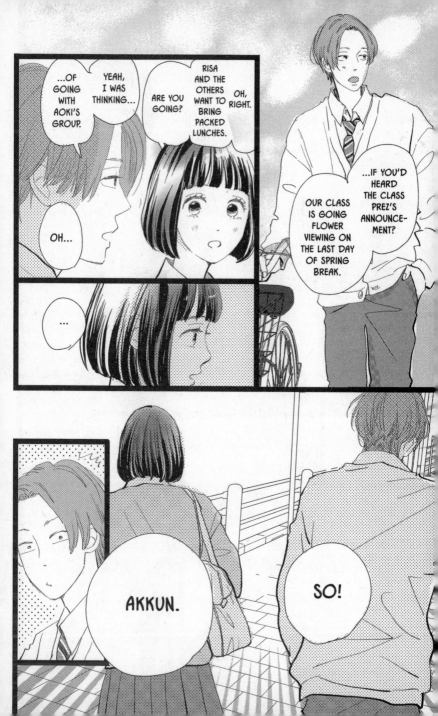

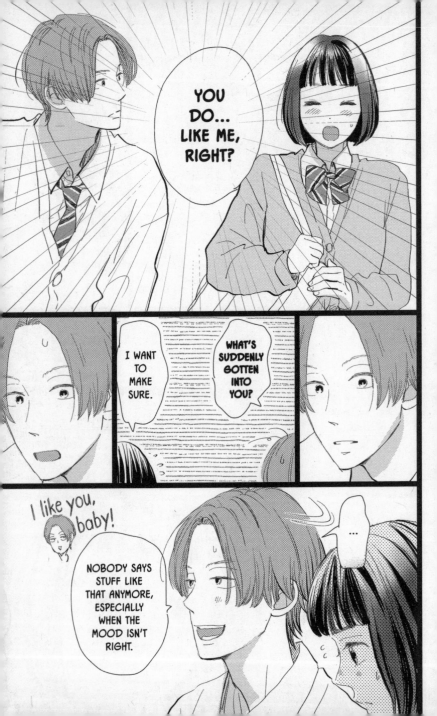

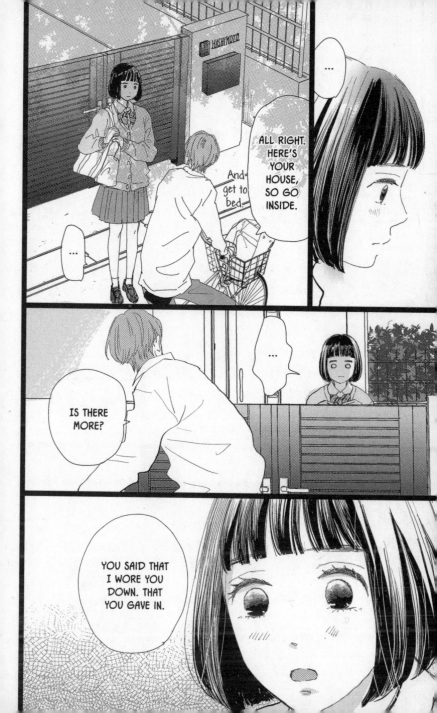

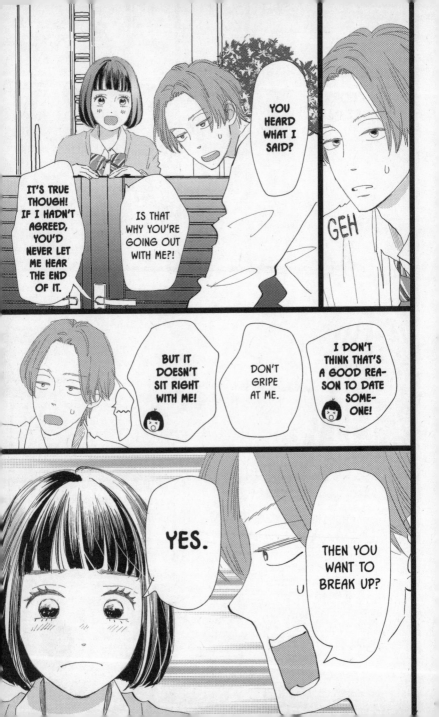

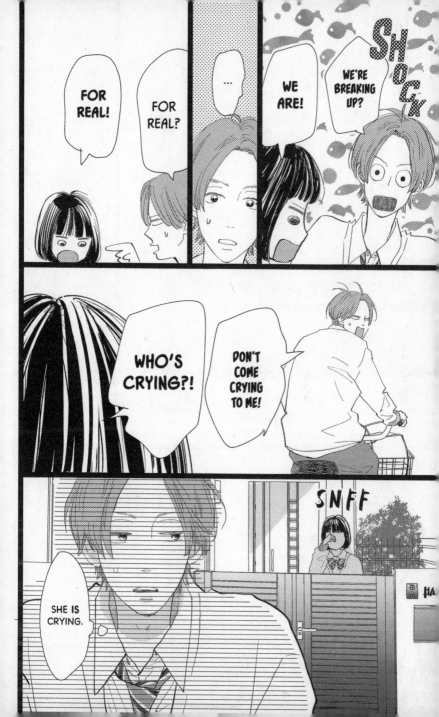

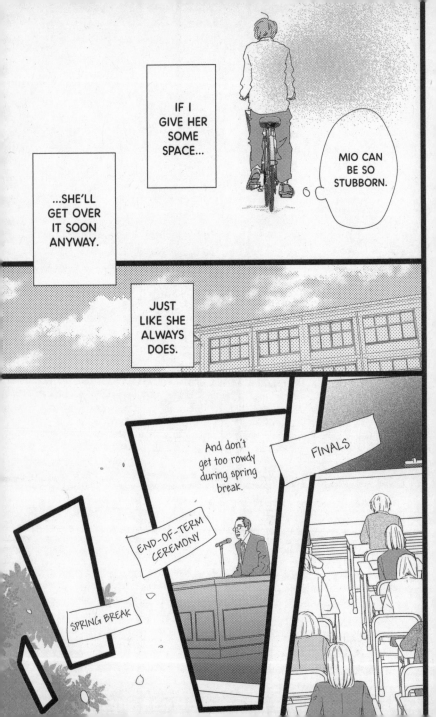

IF I GIVE HER SOME SPACE...

MIO CAN BE SO STUBBORN.

...SHE'LL GET OVER IT SOON ANYWAY.

JUST LIKE SHE ALWAYS DOES.

And don't get too rowdy during spring break.

FINALS

END-OF-TERM CEREMONY

SPRING BREAK

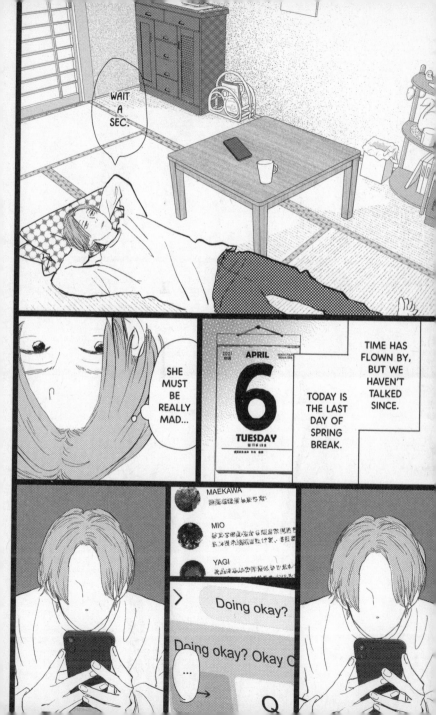

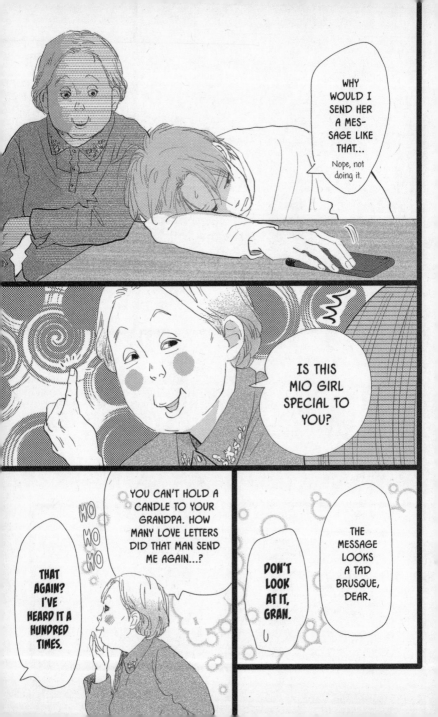

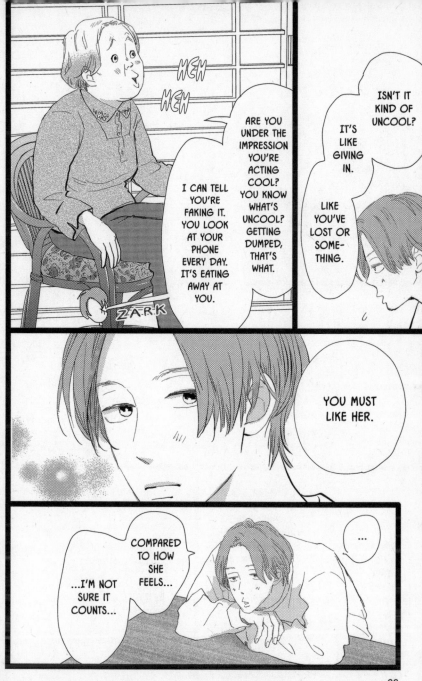

66

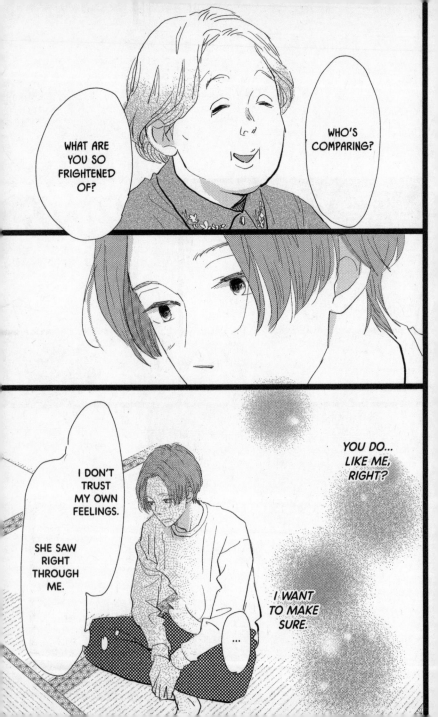

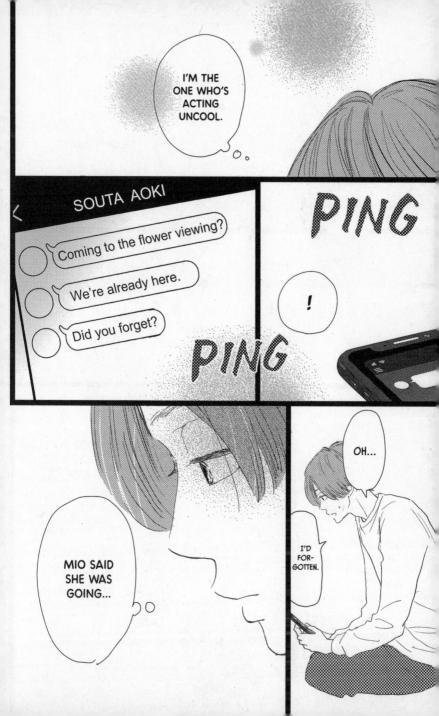

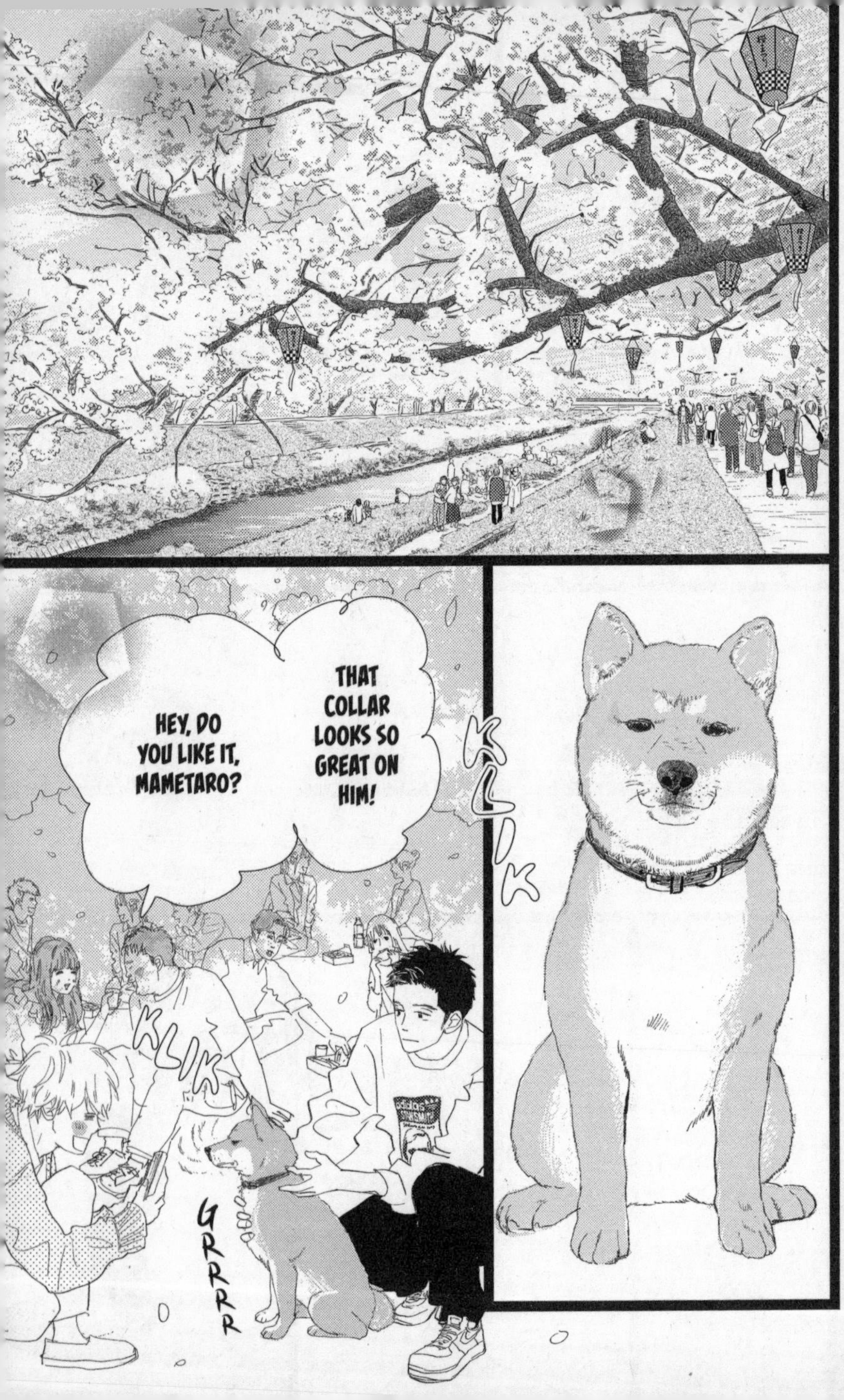
THAT COLLAR LOOKS SO GREAT ON HIM!
HEY, DO YOU LIKE IT, MAMETARO?
KLIK
KLIK
GRRRRR

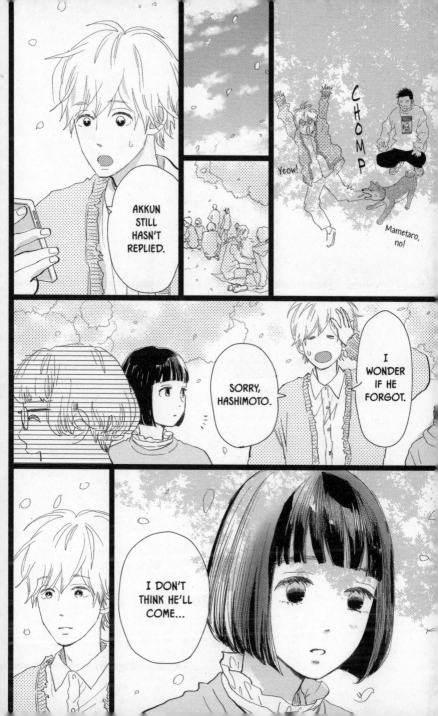

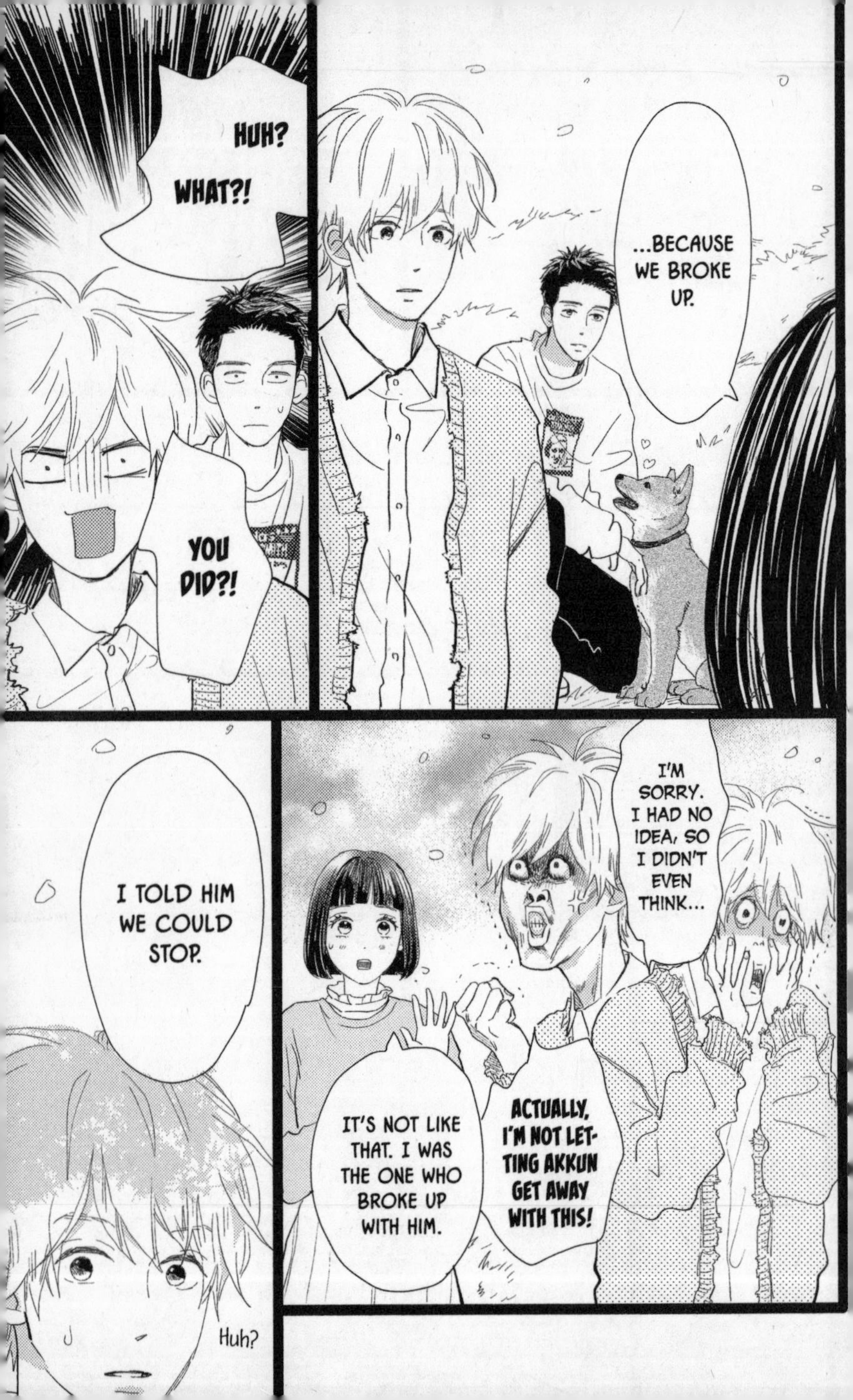
...BECAUSE WE BROKE UP.
HUH?
WHAT?!
YOU DID?!
I'M SORRY. I HAD NO IDEA, SO I DIDN'T EVEN THINK...
ACTUALLY, I'M NOT LET-TING AKKUN GET AWAY WITH THIS!
IT'S NOT LIKE THAT. I WAS THE ONE WHO BROKE UP WITH HIM.
I TOLD HIM WE COULD STOP.
Huh?

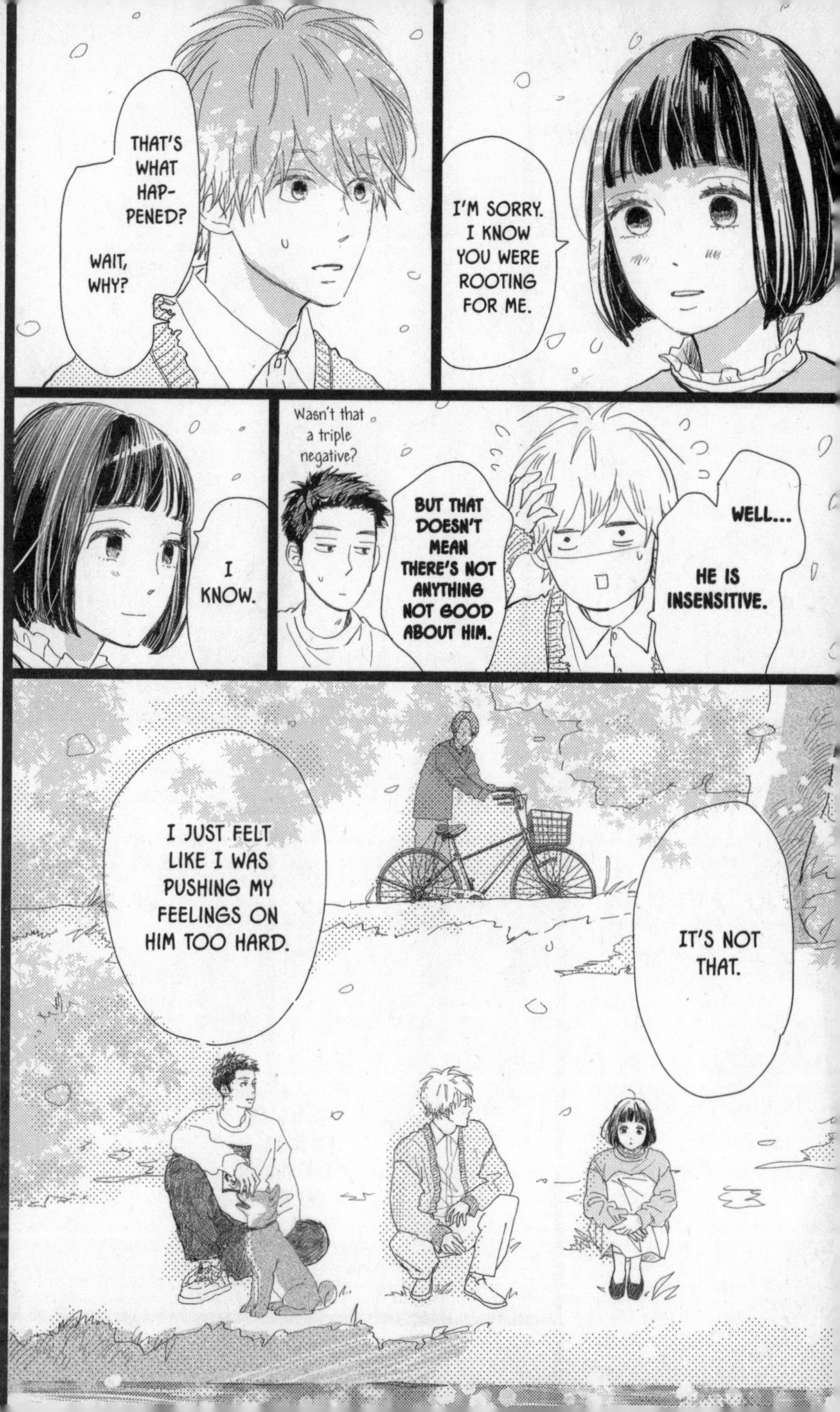
I'M SORRY. I KNOW YOU WERE ROOTING FOR ME.
THAT'S WHAT HAP-PENED?
WAIT, WHY?
WELL...
HE IS INSENSITIVE.
BUT THAT DOESN'T MEAN THERE'S NOT ANYTHING NOT GOOD ABOUT HIM.
Wasn't that a triple negative?
I KNOW.
IT'S NOT THAT.
I JUST FELT LIKE I WAS PUSHING MY FEELINGS ON HIM TOO HARD.

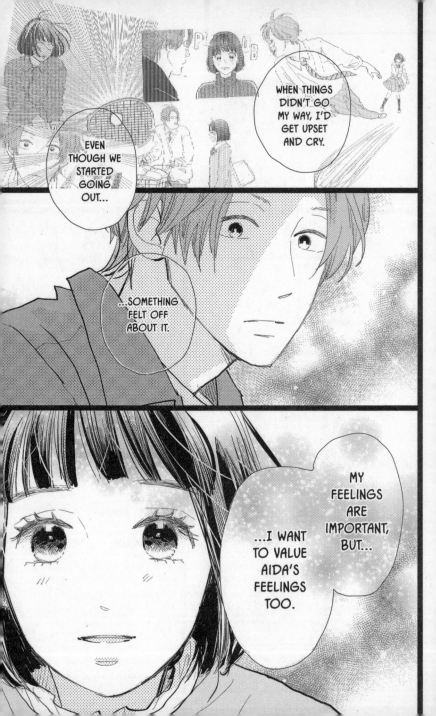

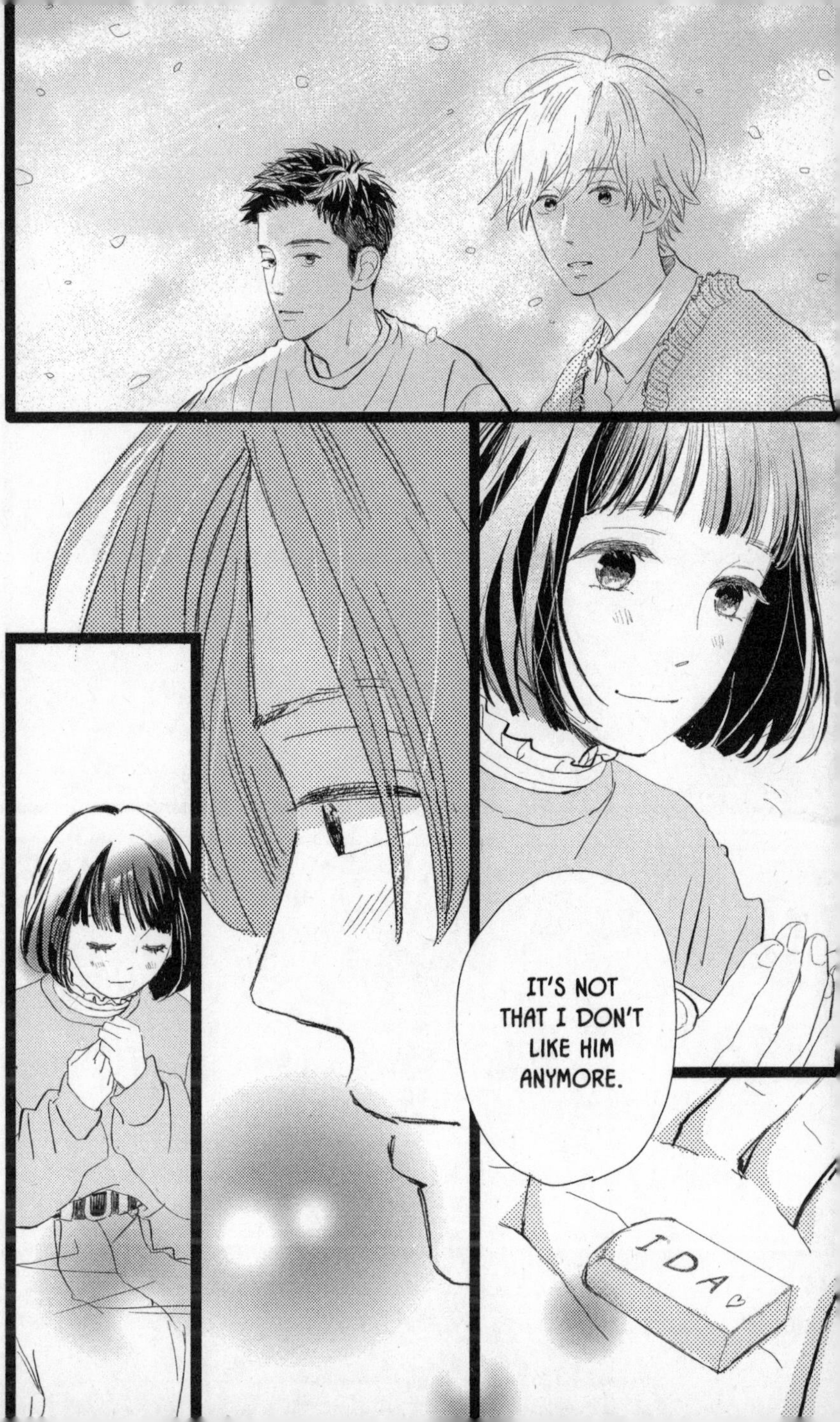
IT'S NOT THAT I DON'T LIKE HIM ANYMORE.
IDA

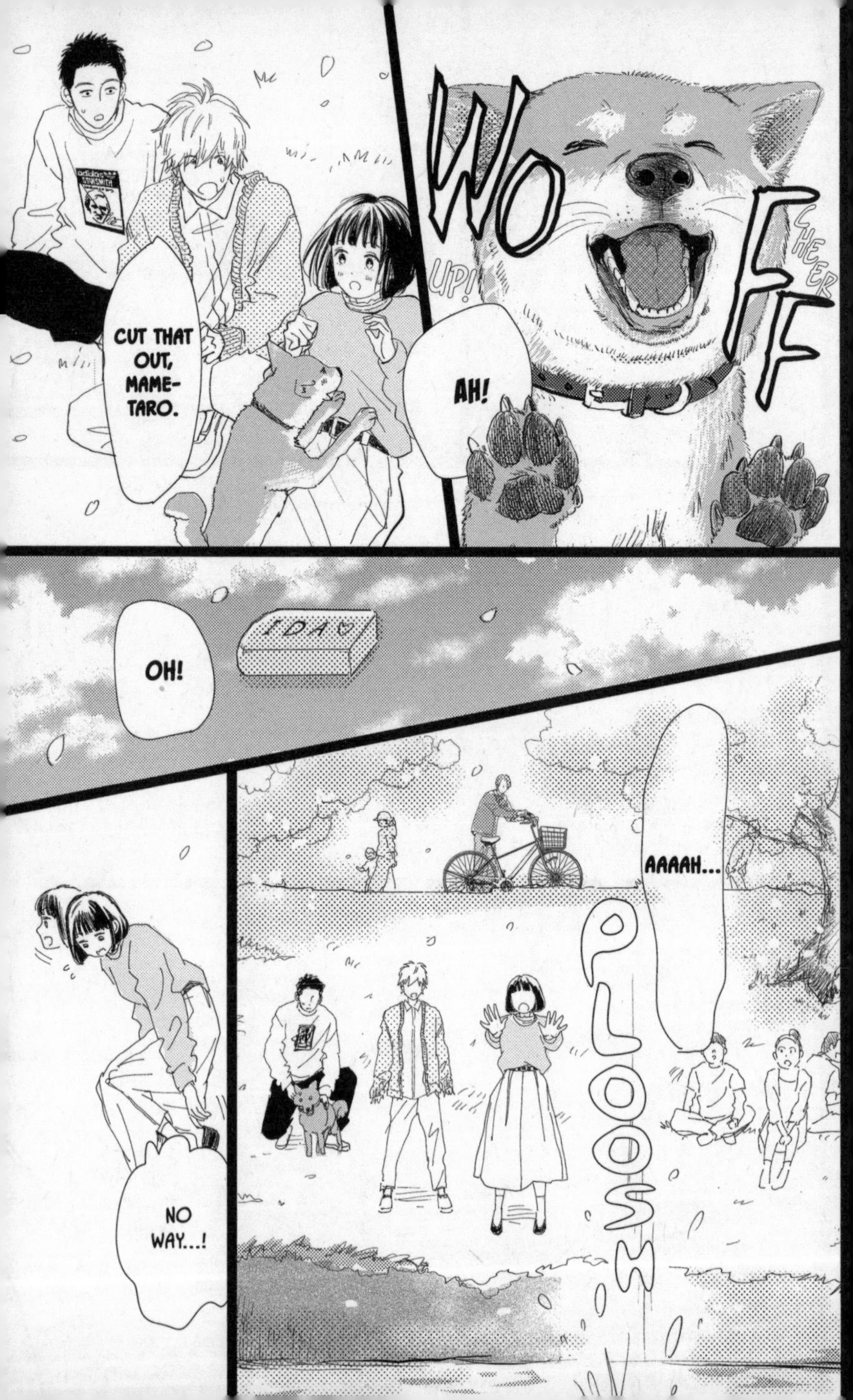
WOOFF
CHEER UP!
AH!
CUT THAT OUT, MAME-TARO.
OH!
IDA
AAAAH...
PLOOSH
NO WAY...!

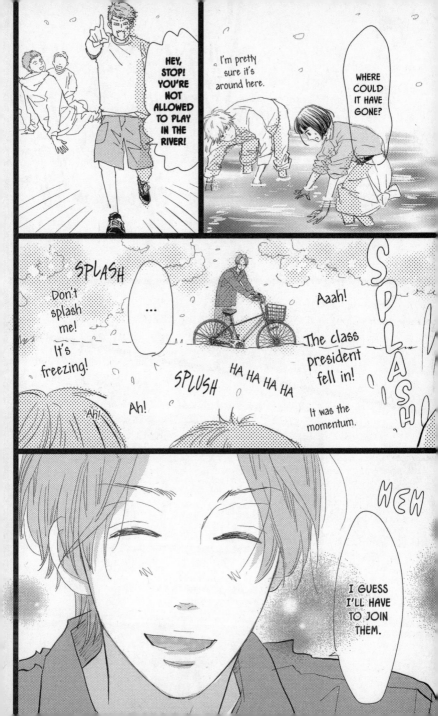

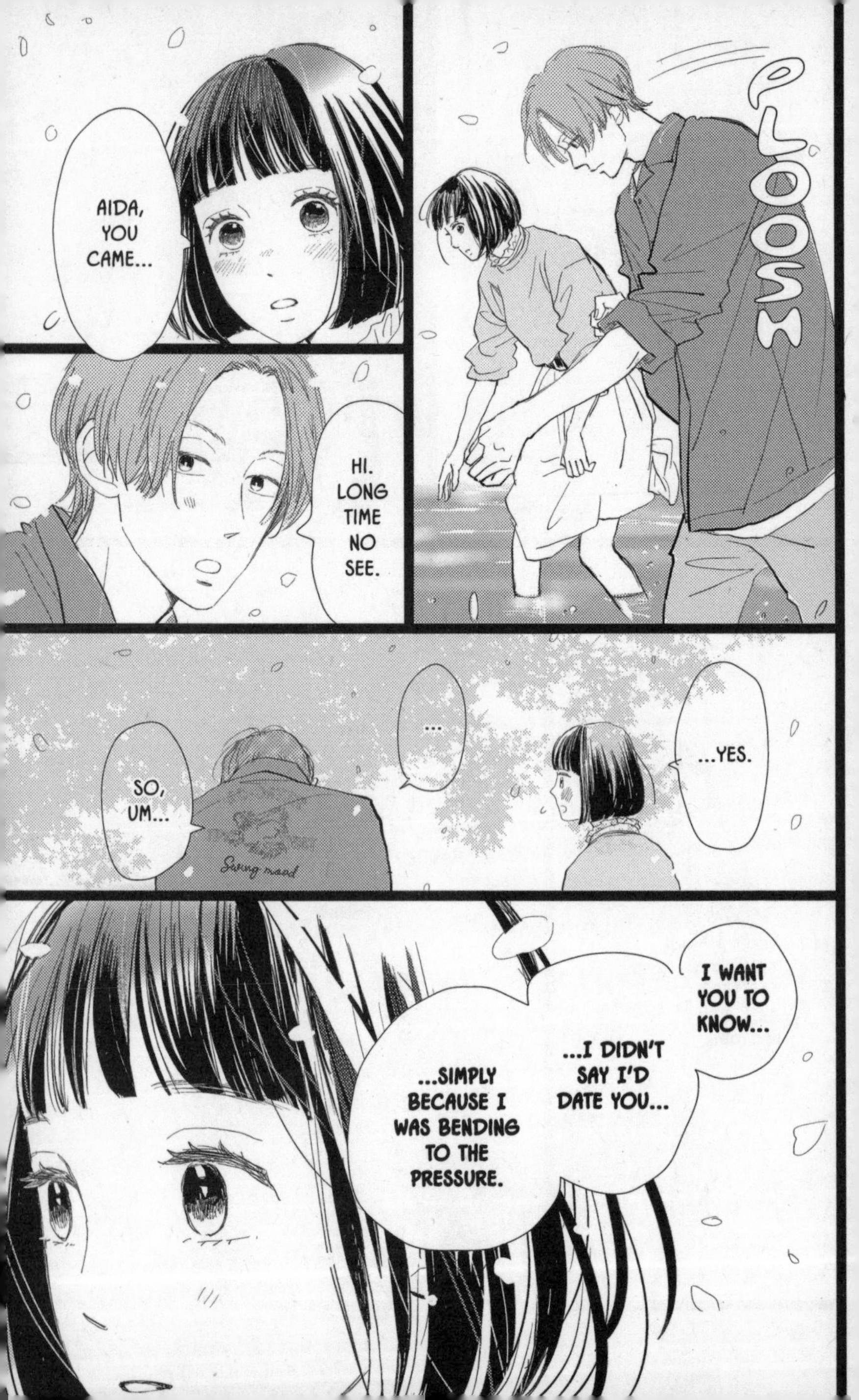
PLOOSH
AIDA, YOU CAME...
HI. LONG TIME NO SEE.
...YES.
...
SO, UM...
Swing mood
I WANT YOU TO KNOW...
...I DIDN'T SAY I'D DATE YOU...
...SIMPLY BECAUSE I WAS BENDING TO THE PRESSURE.

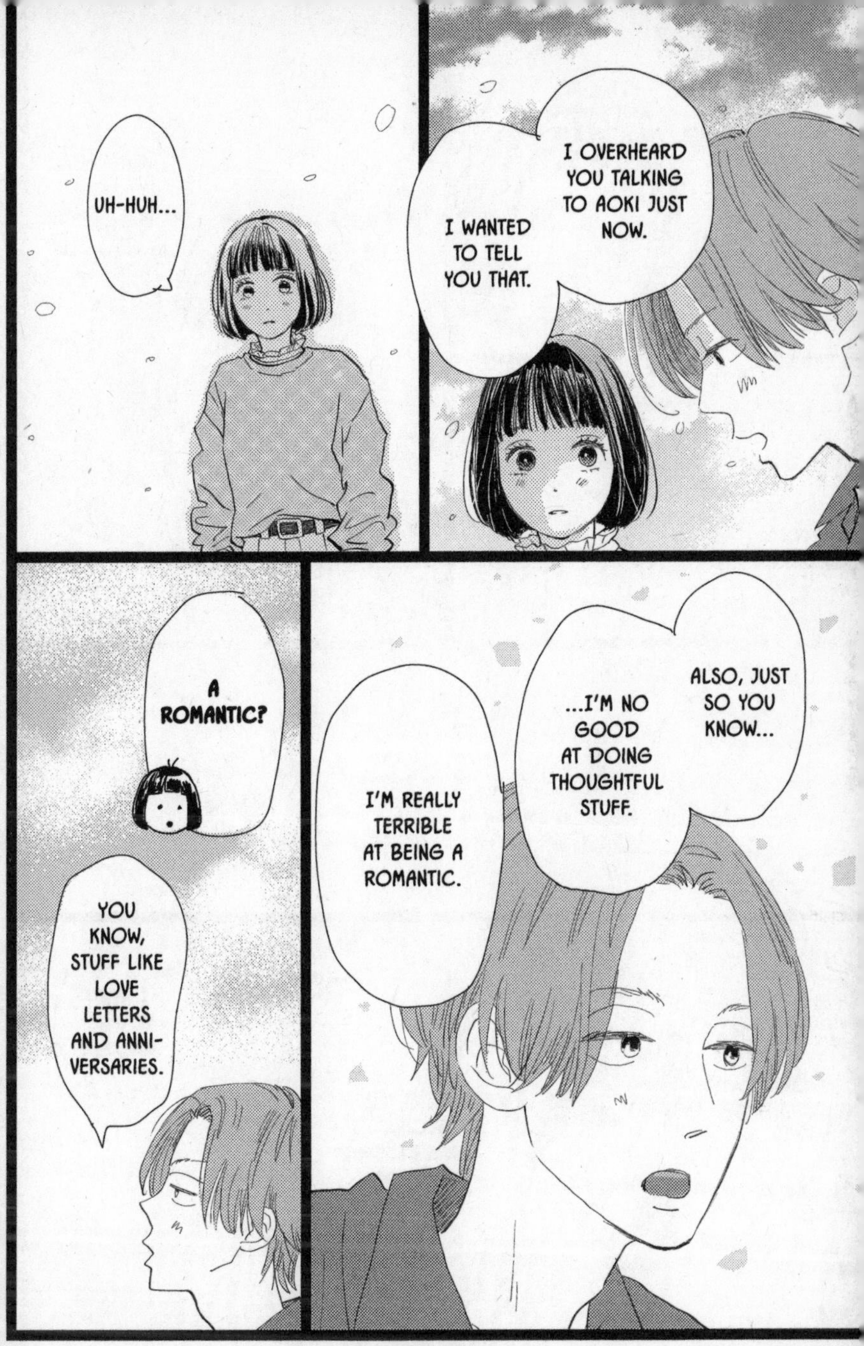
I OVERHEARD YOU TALKING TO AOKI JUST NOW.
I WANTED TO TELL YOU THAT.
UH-HUH...
ALSO, JUST SO YOU KNOW...
...I'M NO GOOD AT DOING THOUGHTFUL STUFF.
I'M REALLY TERRIBLE AT BEING A ROMANTIC.
A ROMANTIC?
YOU KNOW, STUFF LIKE LOVE LETTERS AND ANNI-VERSARIES.

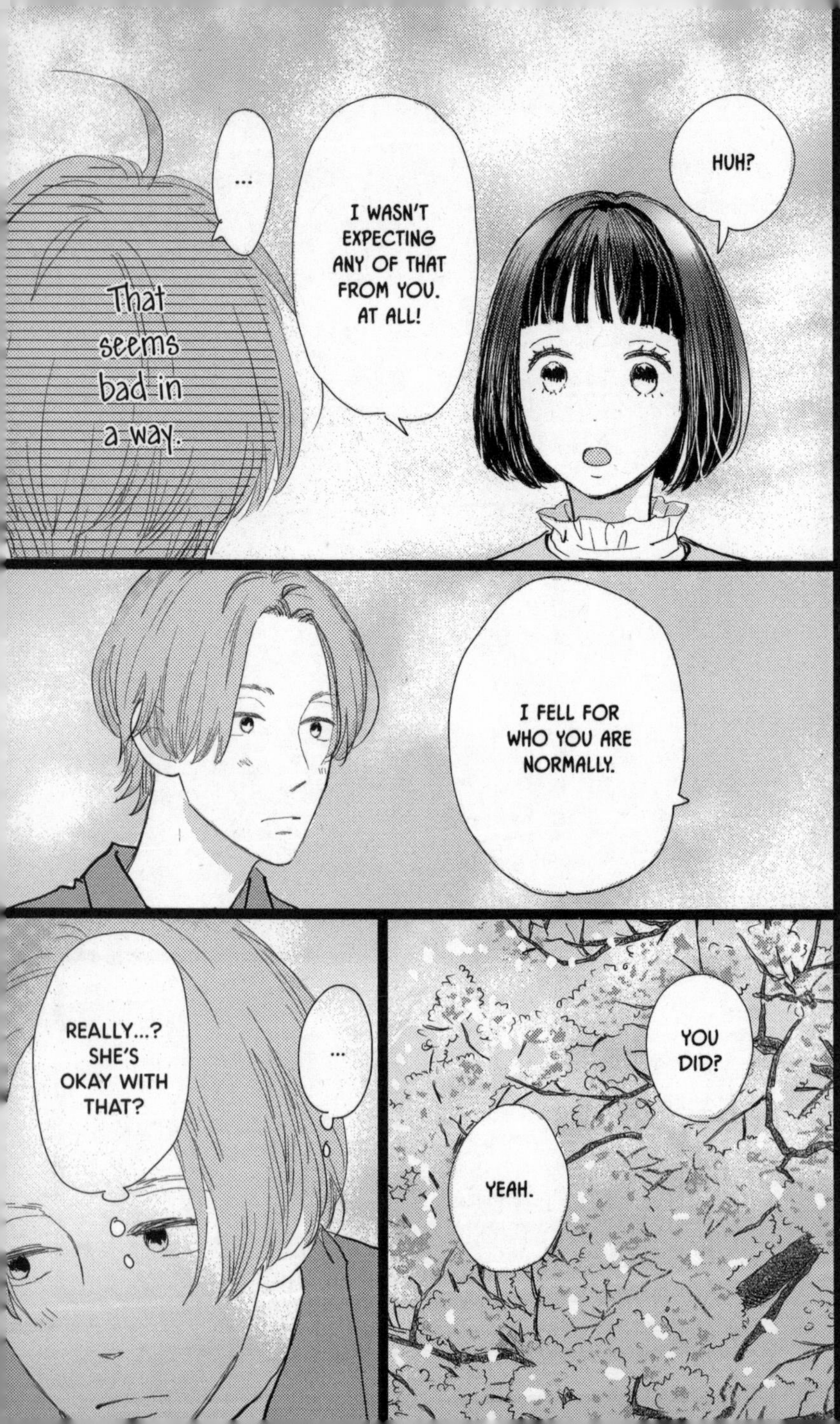
HUH?
I WASN'T EXPECTING ANY OF THAT FROM YOU. AT ALL!
...
That seems bad in a way.
I FELL FOR WHO YOU ARE NORMALLY.
YOU DID?
YEAH.
...
REALLY...? SHE'S OKAY WITH THAT?

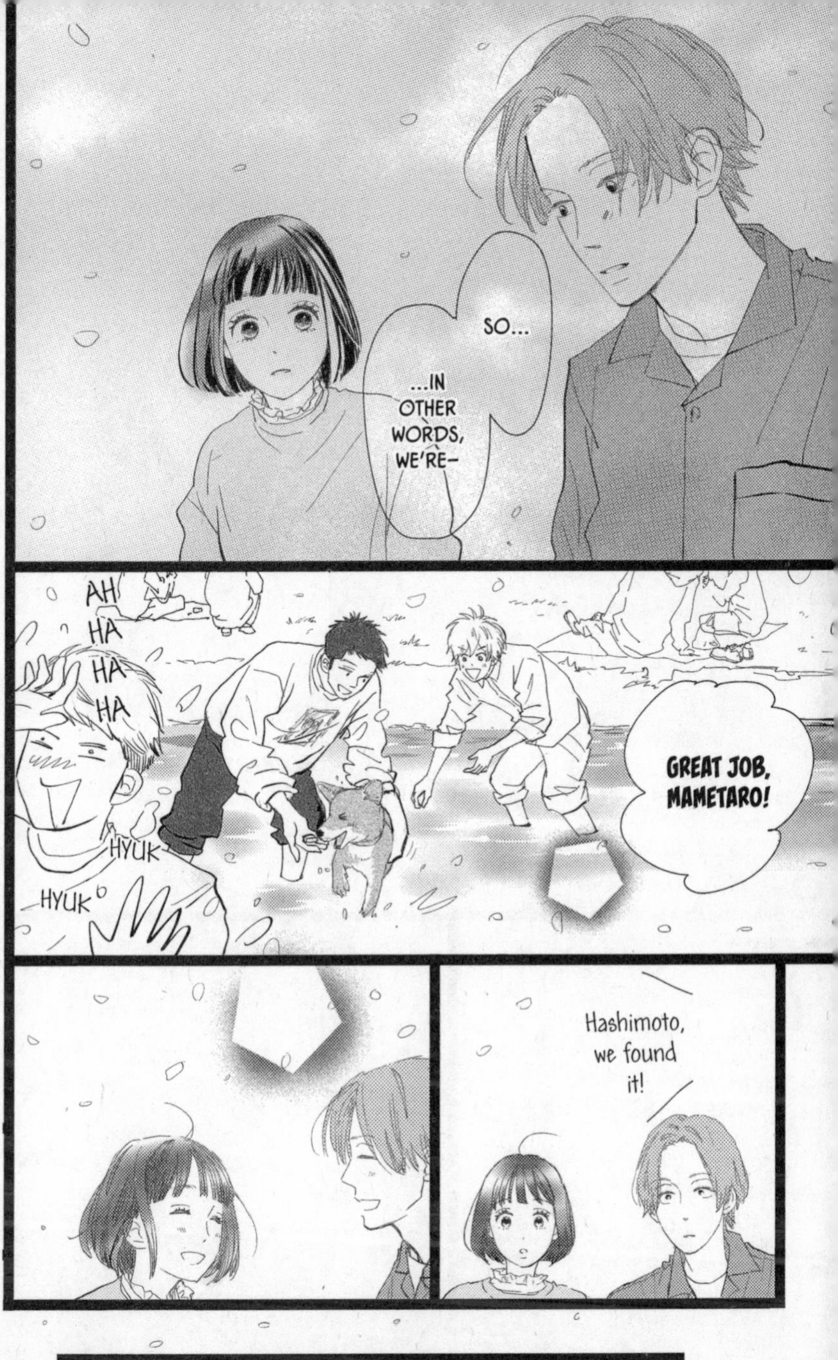
SO...
...IN OTHER WORDS, WE'RE–
GREAT JOB, MAMETARO!
AH HA HA HA
HYUK HYUK
Hashimoto, we found it!

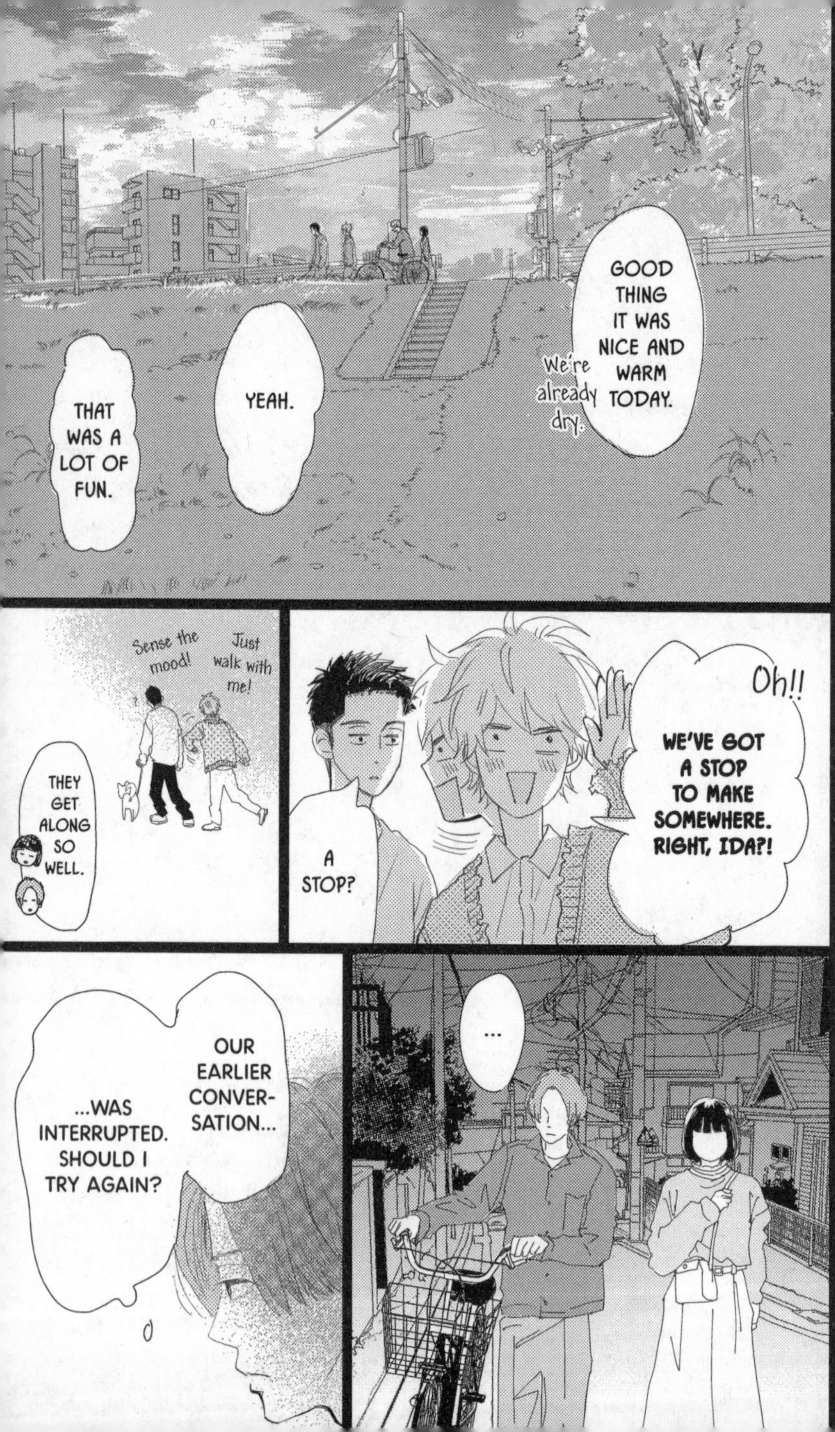
GOOD THING IT WAS NICE AND WARM TODAY.
We're already dry.
YEAH.
THAT WAS A LOT OF FUN.
Oh!!
WE'VE GOT A STOP TO MAKE SOMEWHERE. RIGHT, IDA?!
A STOP?
Just walk with me!
Sense the mood!
THEY GET ALONG SO WELL.
...
OUR EARLIER CONVERSATION...
...WAS INTERRUPTED. SHOULD I TRY AGAIN?

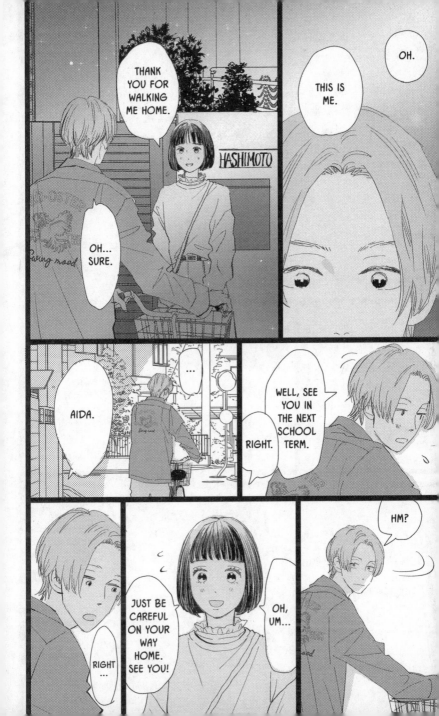

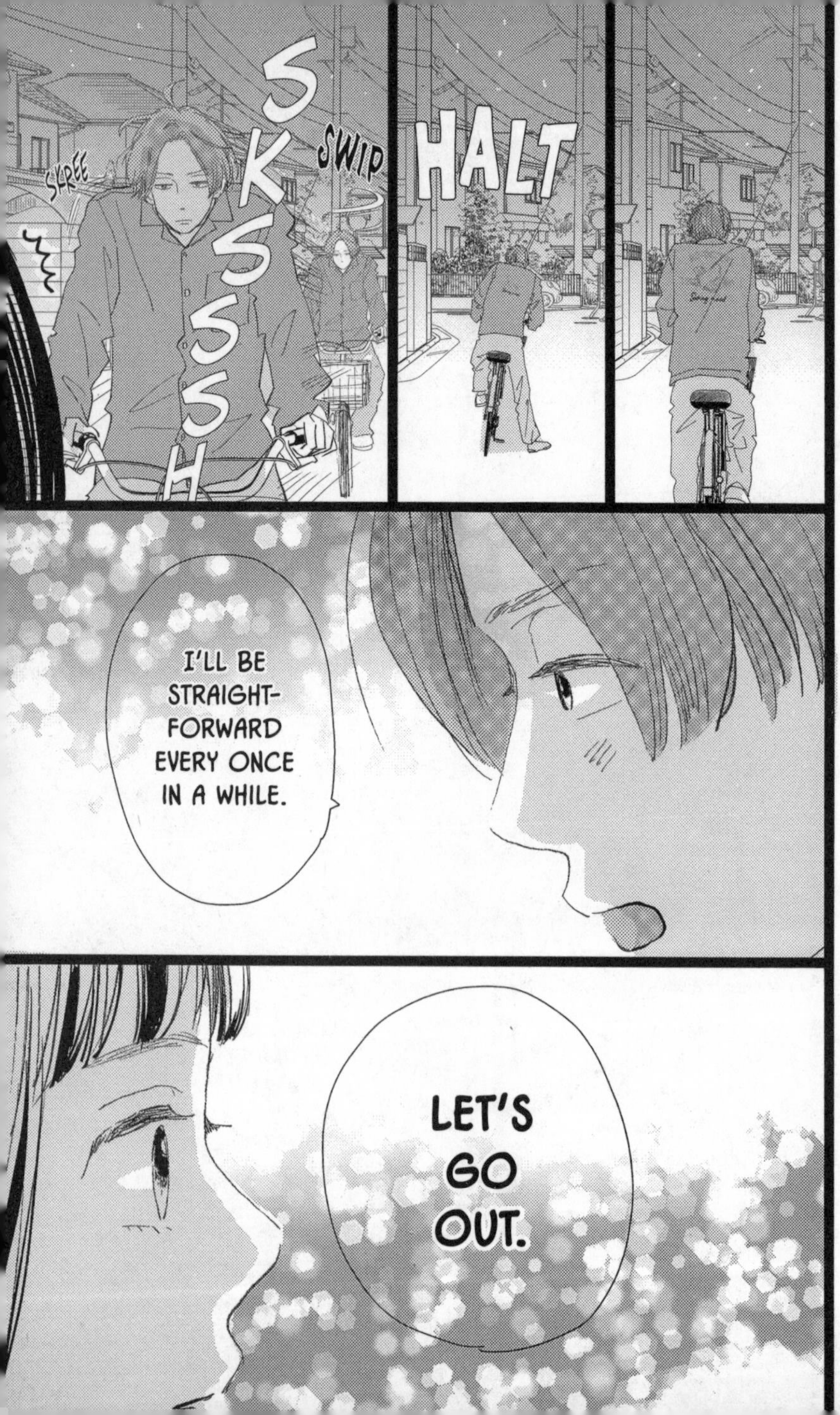
HALT
SWIP
SKSSSH
SKREE
I'LL BE STRAIGHT-FORWARD EVERY ONCE IN A WHILE.
LET'S GO OUT.

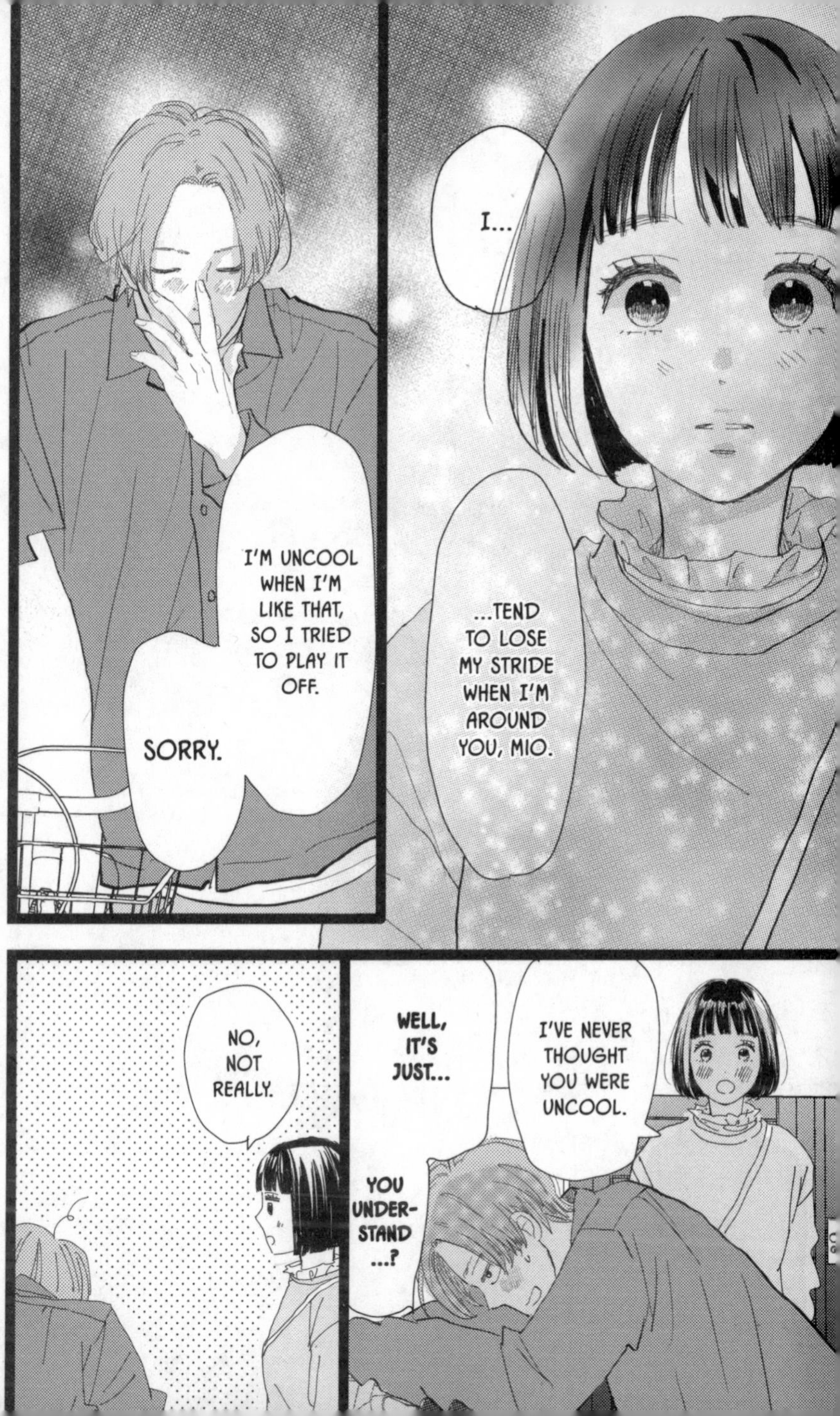
I...
...TEND TO LOSE MY STRIDE WHEN I'M AROUND YOU, MIO.
I'M UNCOOL WHEN I'M LIKE THAT, SO I TRIED TO PLAY IT OFF.
SORRY.
I'VE NEVER THOUGHT YOU WERE UNCOOL.
WELL, IT'S JUST...
YOU UNDER-STAND...?
NO, NOT REALLY.

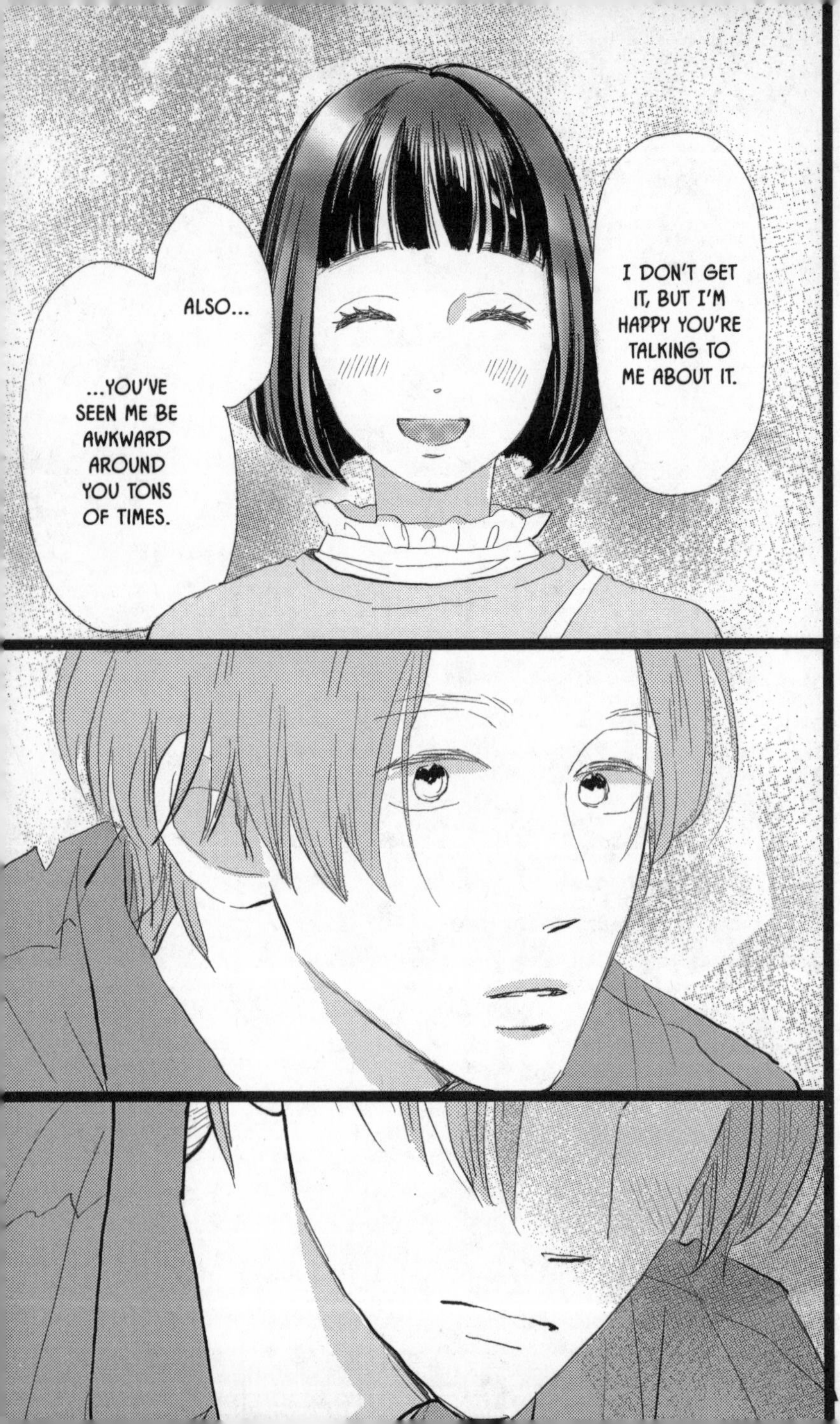
I DON'T GET IT, BUT I'M HAPPY YOU'RE TALKING TO ME ABOUT IT.
ALSO...
...YOU'VE SEEN ME BE AWKWARD AROUND YOU TONS OF TIMES.

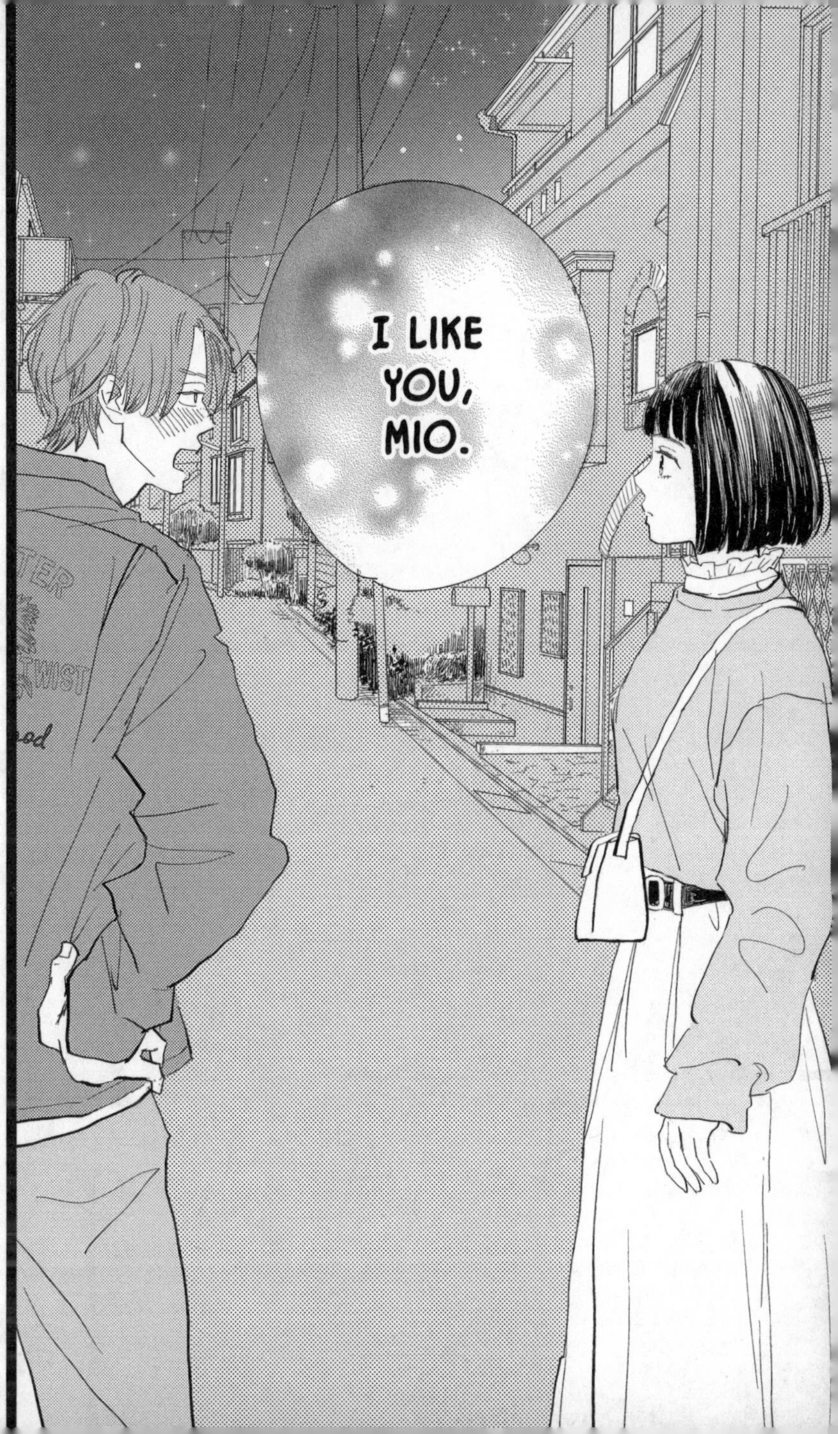
I LIKE YOU, MIO.

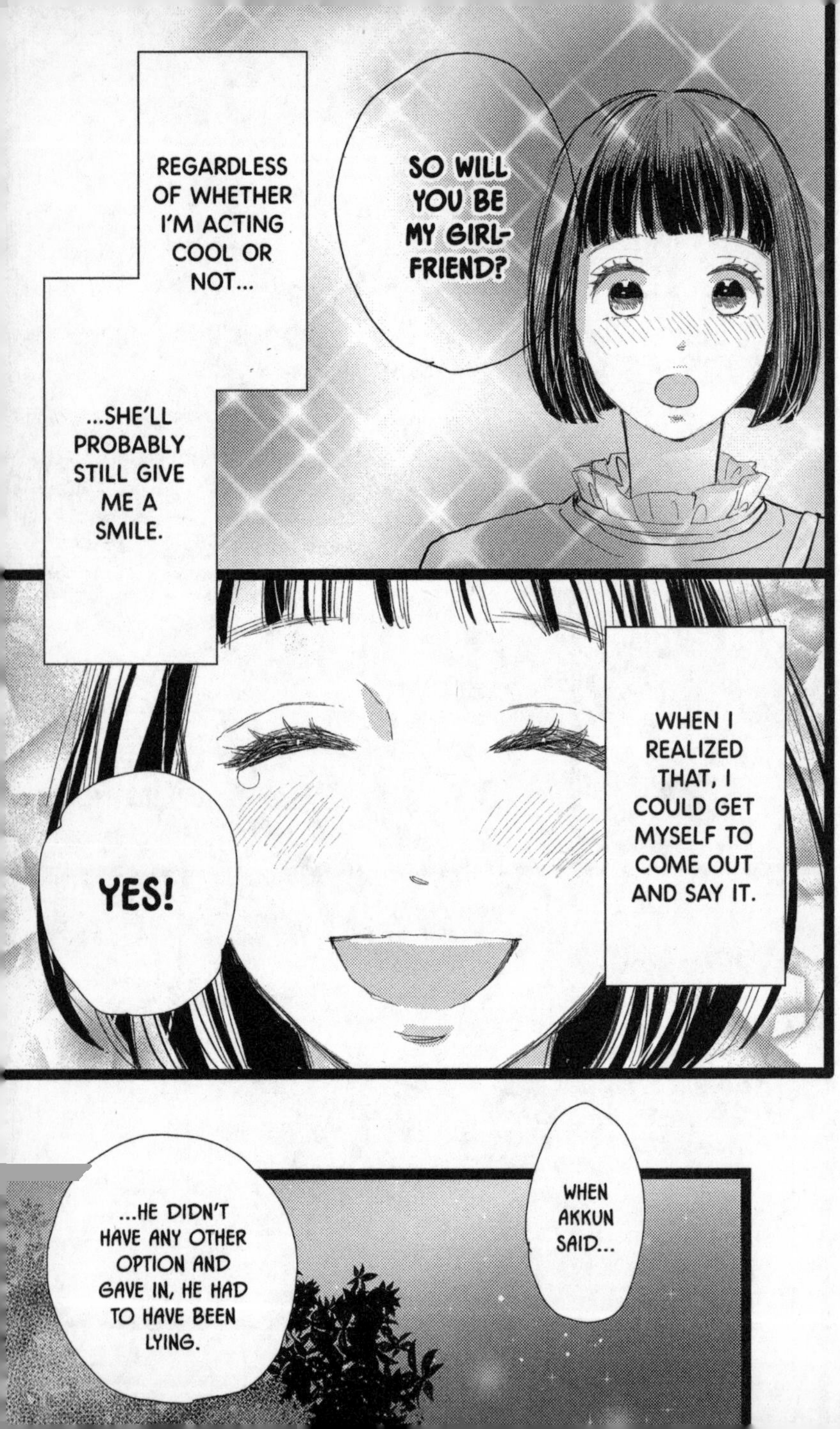
SO WILL YOU BE MY GIRL-FRIEND?
REGARDLESS OF WHETHER I'M ACTING COOL OR NOT...
...SHE'LL PROBABLY STILL GIVE ME A SMILE.
WHEN I REALIZED THAT, I COULD GET MYSELF TO COME OUT AND SAY IT.
YES!
WHEN AKKUN SAID...
...HE DIDN'T HAVE ANY OTHER OPTION AND GAVE IN, HE HAD TO HAVE BEEN LYING.

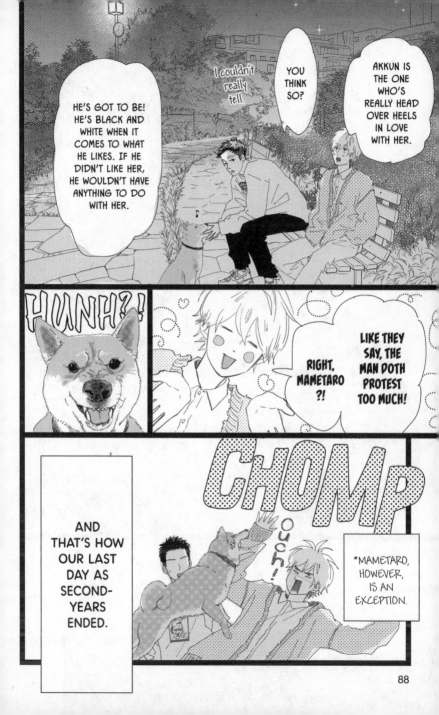

HE'S GOT TO BE! HE'S BLACK AND WHITE WHEN IT COMES TO WHAT HE LIKES. IF HE DIDN'T LIKE HER, HE WOULDN'T HAVE ANYTHING TO DO WITH HER.

I couldn't really tell.

YOU THINK SO?

AKKUN IS THE ONE WHO'S REALLY HEAD OVER HEELS IN LOVE WITH HER.

HUNH?!

RIGHT, MAMETARO?!

LIKE THEY SAY, THE MAN DOTH PROTEST TOO MUCH!

CHOMP

OUCH!

AND THAT'S HOW OUR LAST DAY AS SECOND-YEARS ENDED.

*MAMETARO, HOWEVER, IS AN EXCEPTION.

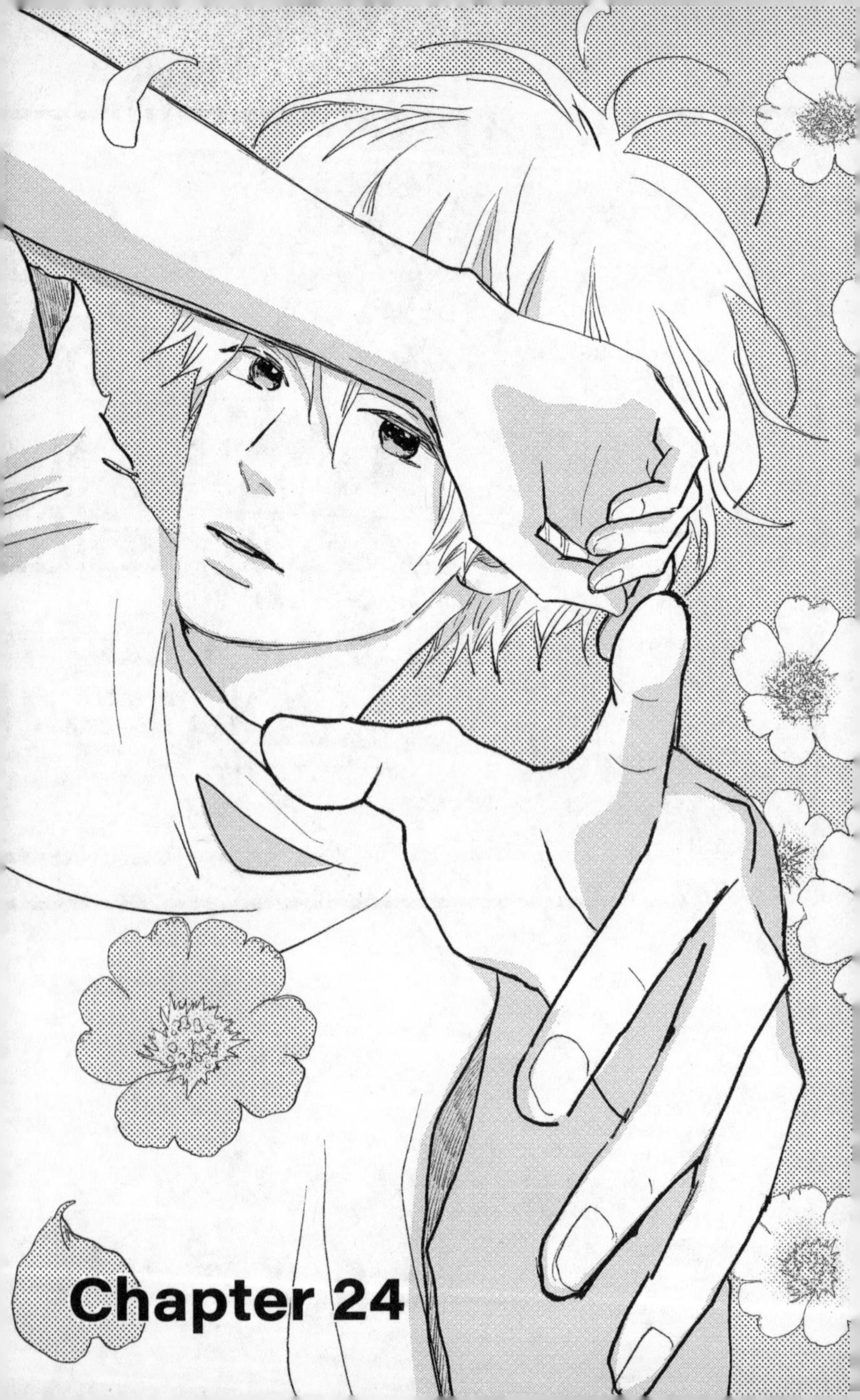

Chapter 24

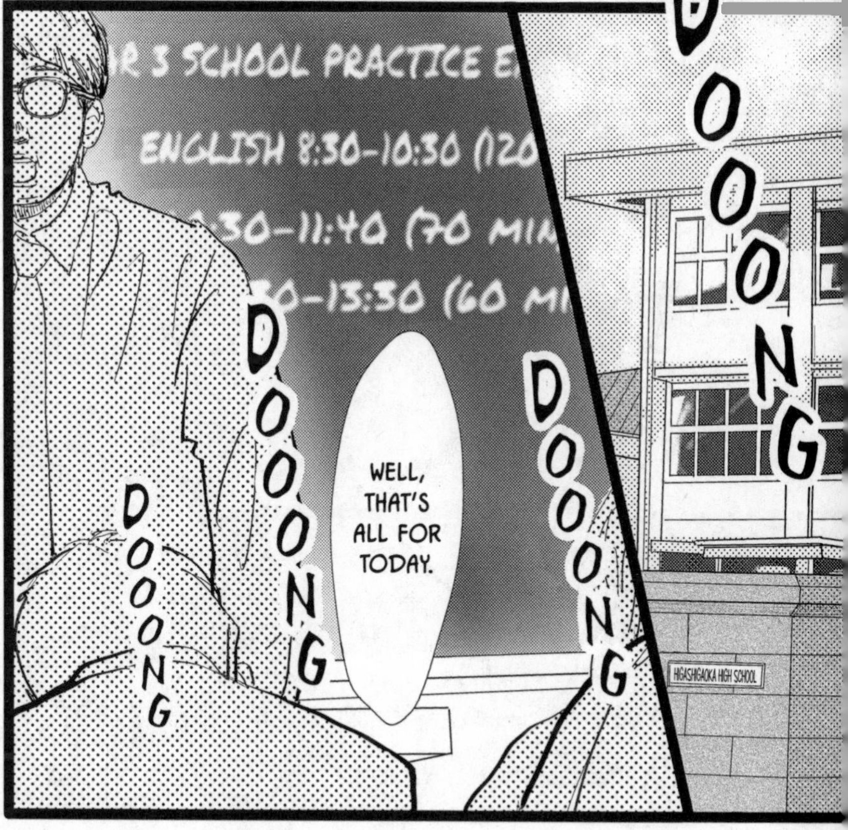
DOOOONG
HIGASHIGAOKA HIGH SCHOOL
ENGLISH 8:30-10:30 (120
DOOOONG
WELL, THAT'S ALL FOR TODAY.
DOOOONG
DOOOONG

My Love Mix-Up!

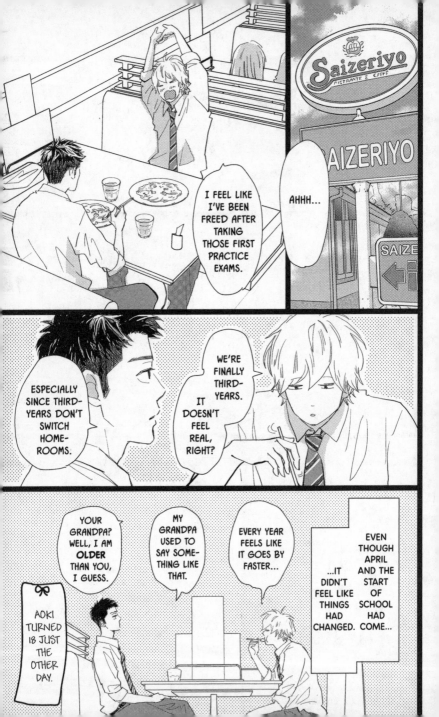

AHHH...

I FEEL LIKE I'VE BEEN FREED AFTER TAKING THOSE FIRST PRACTICE EXAMS.

WE'RE FINALLY THIRD-YEARS. IT DOESN'T FEEL REAL, RIGHT?

ESPECIALLY SINCE THIRD-YEARS DON'T SWITCH HOMEROOMS.

YOUR GRANDPA? WELL, I AM **OLDER** THAN YOU, I GUESS.

MY GRANDPA USED TO SAY SOMETHING LIKE THAT.

EVERY YEAR FEELS LIKE IT GOES BY FASTER...

EVEN THOUGH APRIL AND THE START OF SCHOOL HAD COME...

...IT DIDN'T FEEL LIKE THINGS HAD CHANGED.

AOKI TURNED 18 JUST THE OTHER DAY.

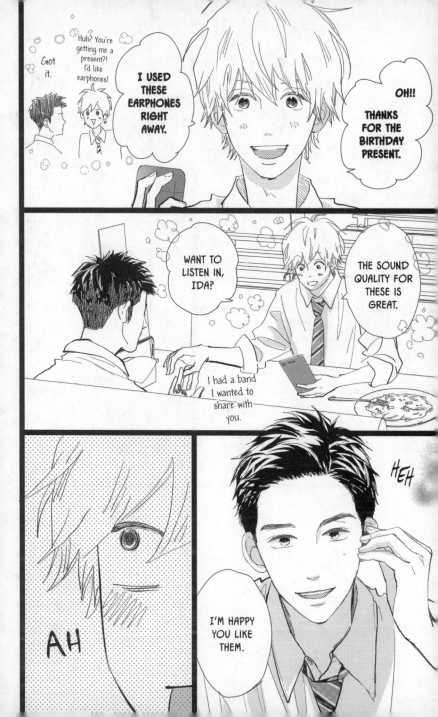

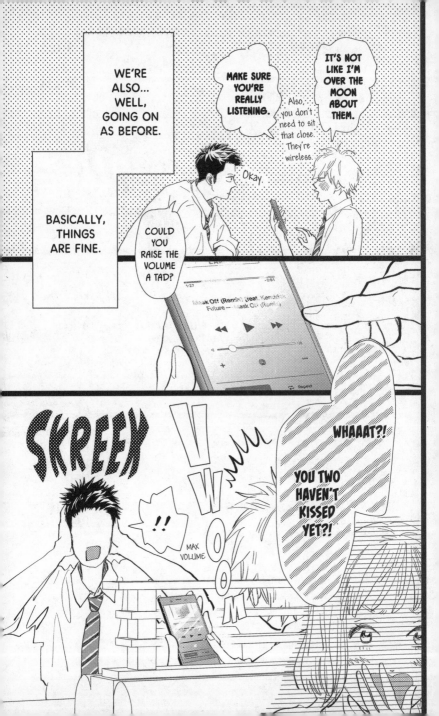

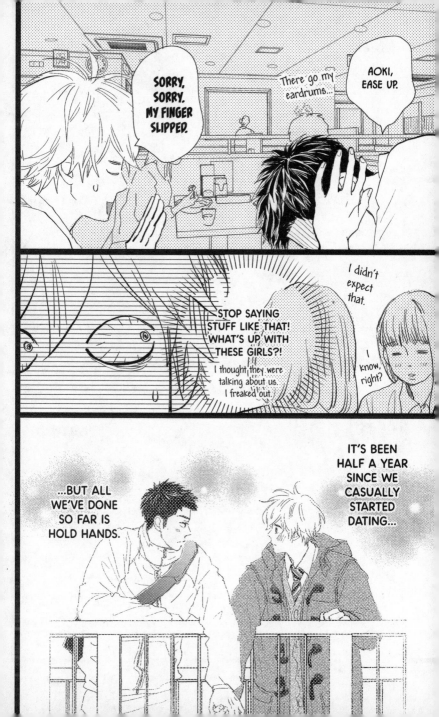

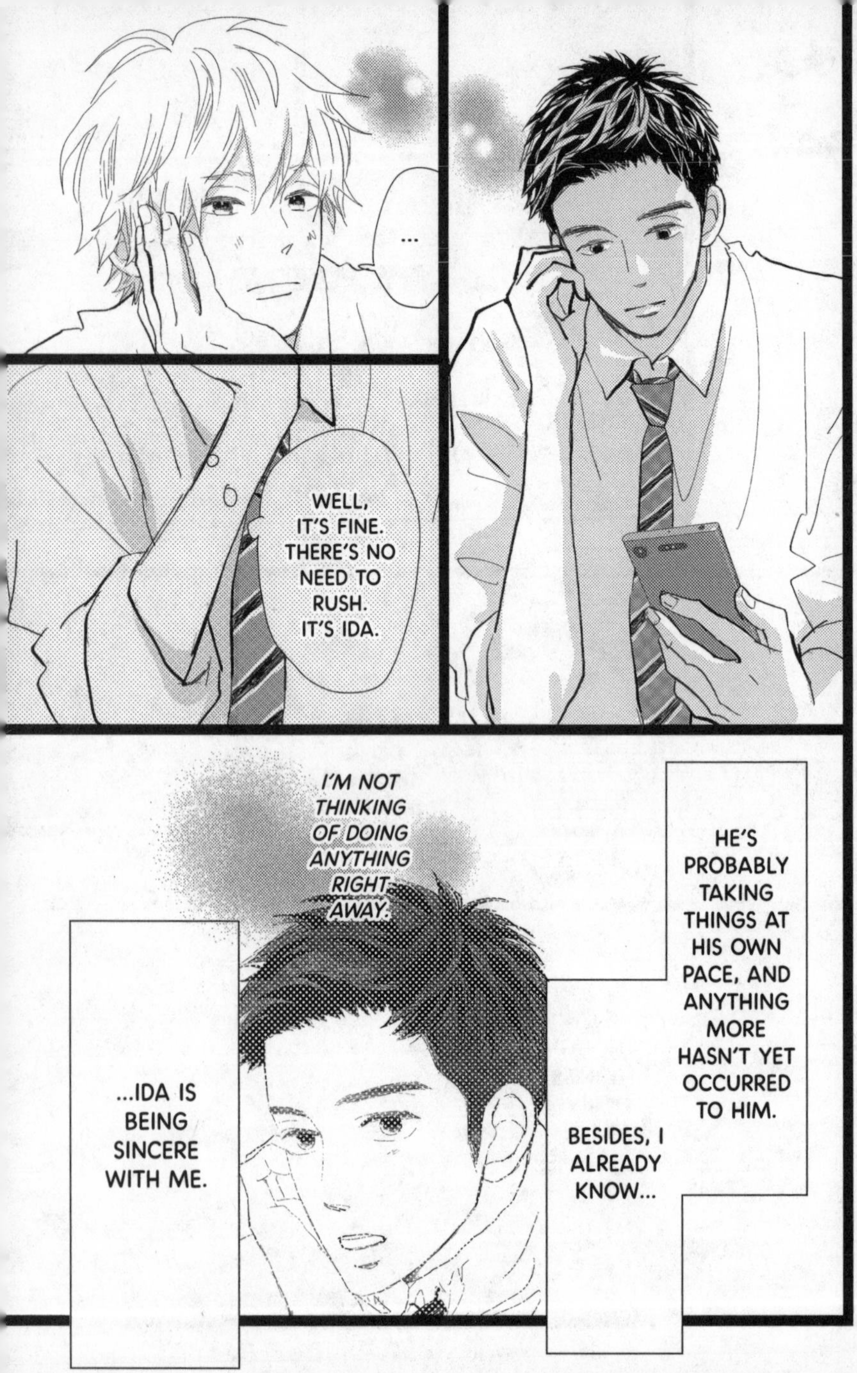
...
WELL, IT'S FINE. THERE'S NO NEED TO RUSH. IT'S IDA.
HE'S PROBABLY TAKING THINGS AT HIS OWN PACE, AND ANYTHING MORE HASN'T YET OCCURRED TO HIM.
I'M NOT THINKING OF DOING ANYTHING RIGHT AWAY.
BESIDES, I ALREADY KNOW...
...IDA IS BEING SINCERE WITH ME.

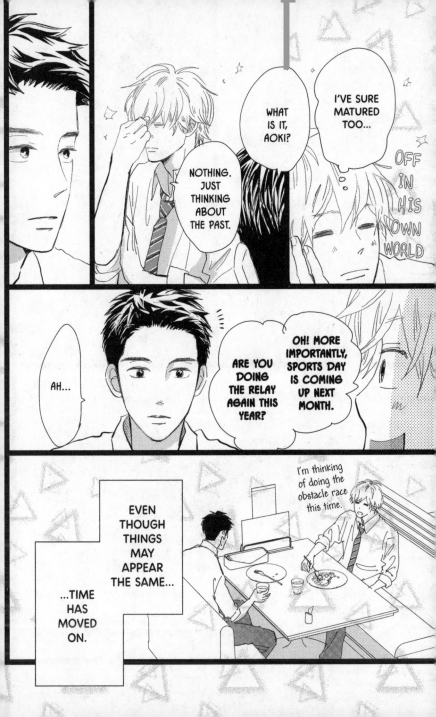

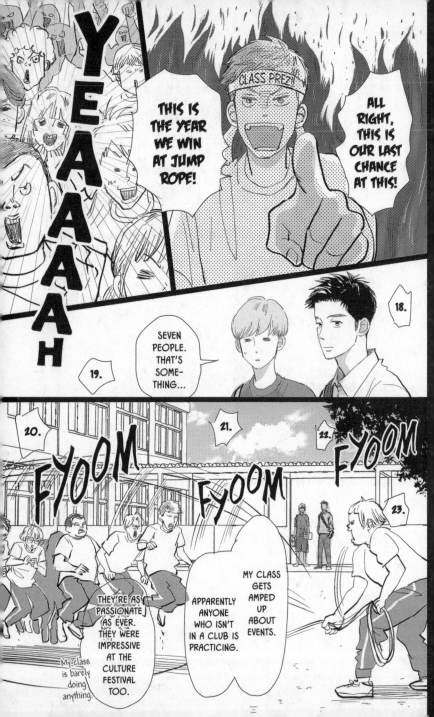

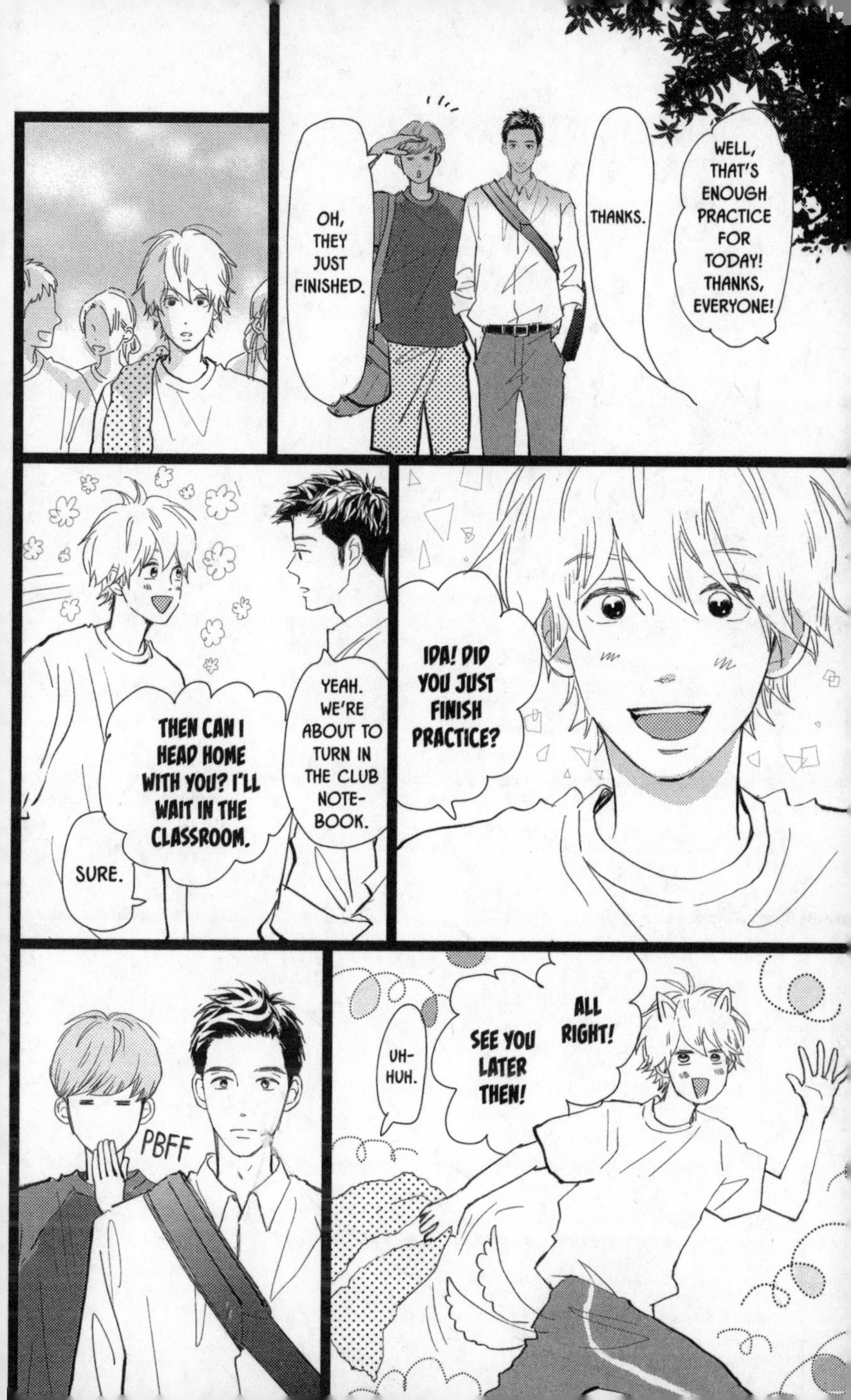
WELL, THAT'S ENOUGH PRACTICE FOR TODAY! THANKS, EVERYONE!
THANKS.
OH, THEY JUST FINISHED.
IDA! DID YOU JUST FINISH PRACTICE?
YEAH. WE'RE ABOUT TO TURN IN THE CLUB NOTEBOOK.
THEN CAN I HEAD HOME WITH YOU? I'LL WAIT IN THE CLASSROOM.
SURE.
ALL RIGHT!
SEE YOU LATER THEN!
UH-HUH.
PBFF

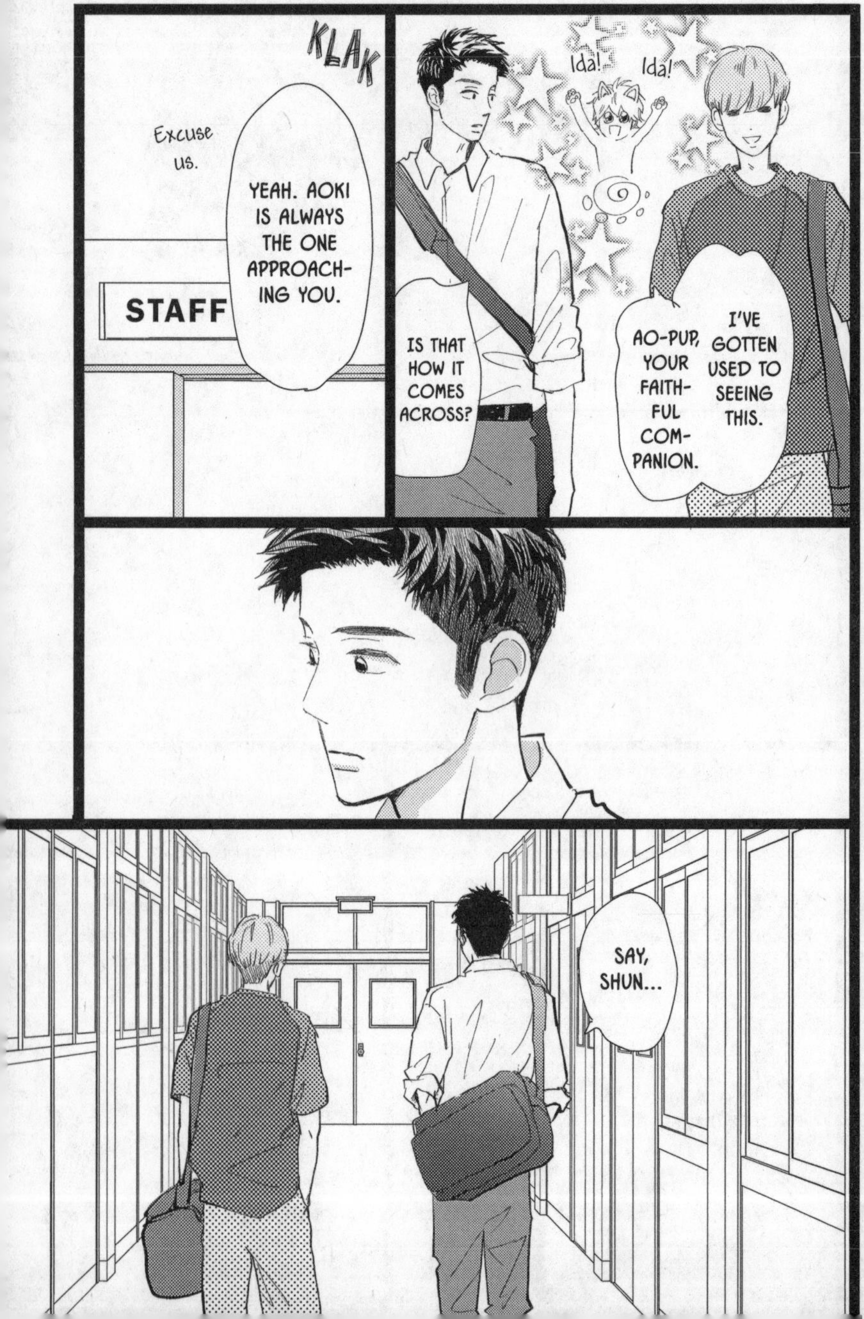
Ida!
Ida!
I'VE GOTTEN USED TO SEEING THIS.
AO-PUP, YOUR FAITHFUL COMPANION.
IS THAT HOW IT COMES ACROSS?
KLAK
YEAH. AOKI IS ALWAYS THE ONE APPROACHING YOU.
Excuse us.
STAFF
SAY, SHUN...

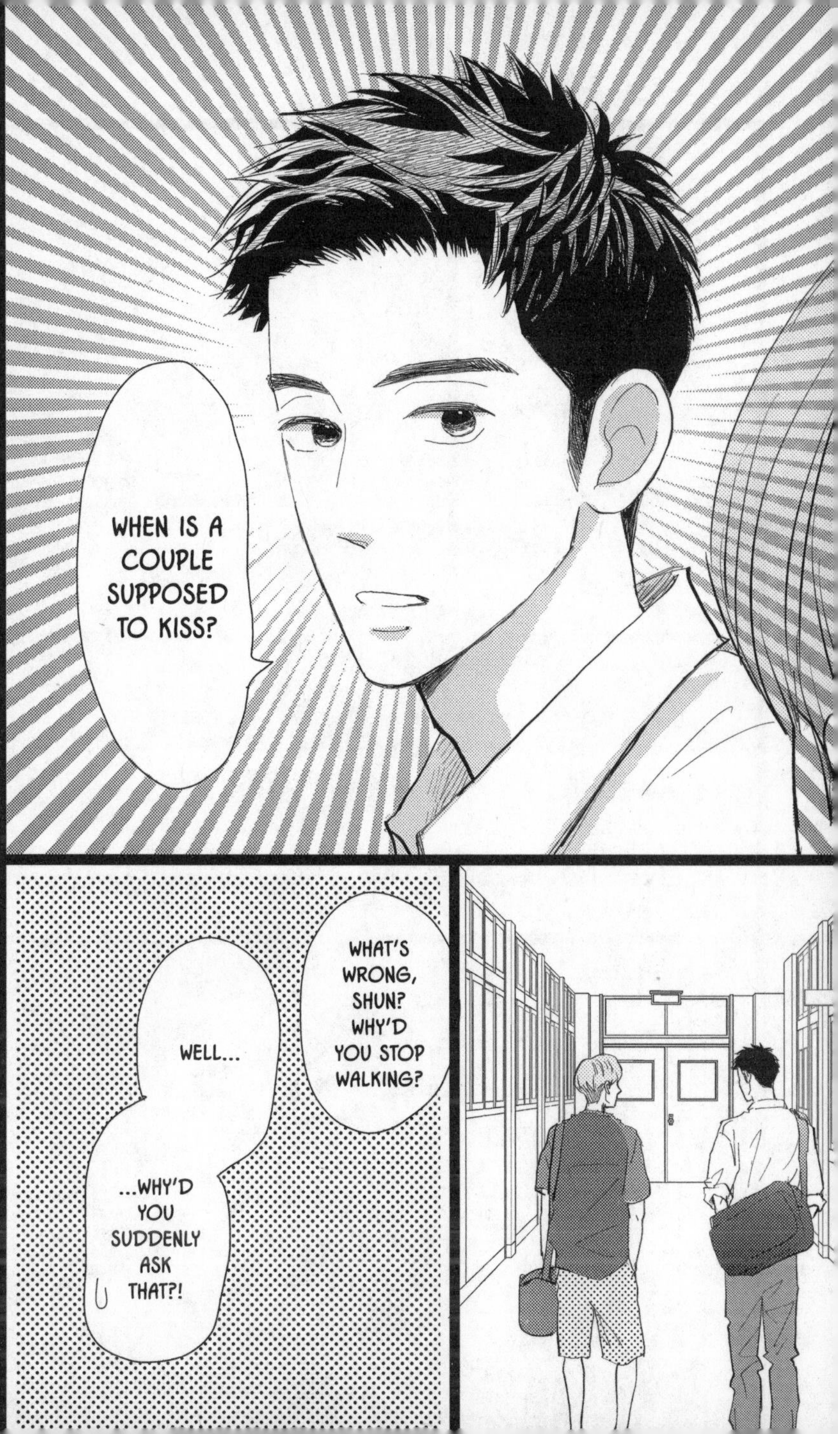
WHEN IS A COUPLE SUPPOSED TO KISS?
WHAT'S WRONG, SHUN? WHY'D YOU STOP WALKING?
WELL...
...WHY'D YOU SUDDENLY ASK THAT?!

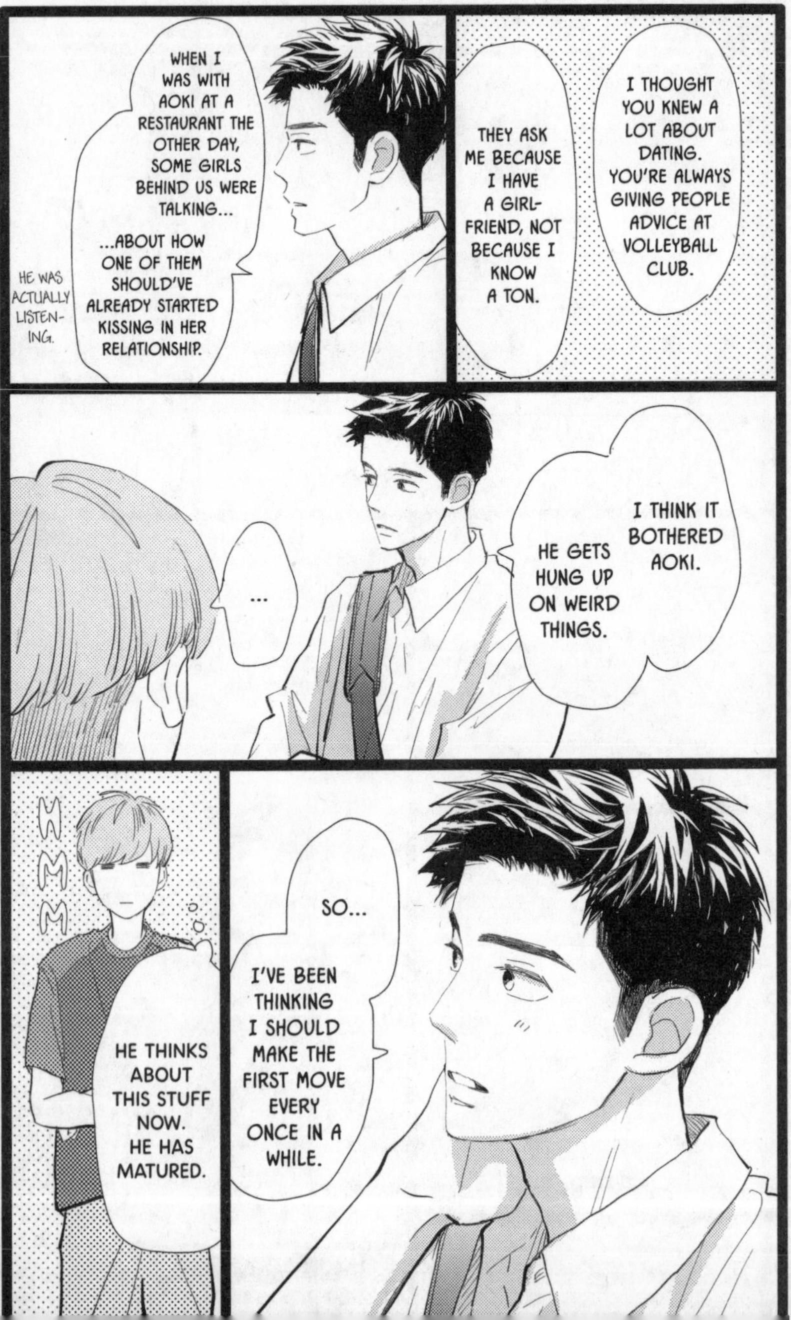
I THOUGHT YOU KNEW A LOT ABOUT DATING. YOU'RE ALWAYS GIVING PEOPLE ADVICE AT VOLLEYBALL CLUB.
THEY ASK ME BECAUSE I HAVE A GIRL-FRIEND, NOT BECAUSE I KNOW A TON.
WHEN I WAS WITH AOKI AT A RESTAURANT THE OTHER DAY, SOME GIRLS BEHIND US WERE TALKING...
...ABOUT HOW ONE OF THEM SHOULD'VE ALREADY STARTED KISSING IN HER RELATIONSHIP.
HE WAS ACTUALLY LISTEN-ING.
I THINK IT BOTHERED AOKI.
HE GETS HUNG UP ON WEIRD THINGS.
...
SO...
I'VE BEEN THINKING I SHOULD MAKE THE FIRST MOVE EVERY ONCE IN A WHILE.
HMMM
HE THINKS ABOUT THIS STUFF NOW. HE HAS MATURED.

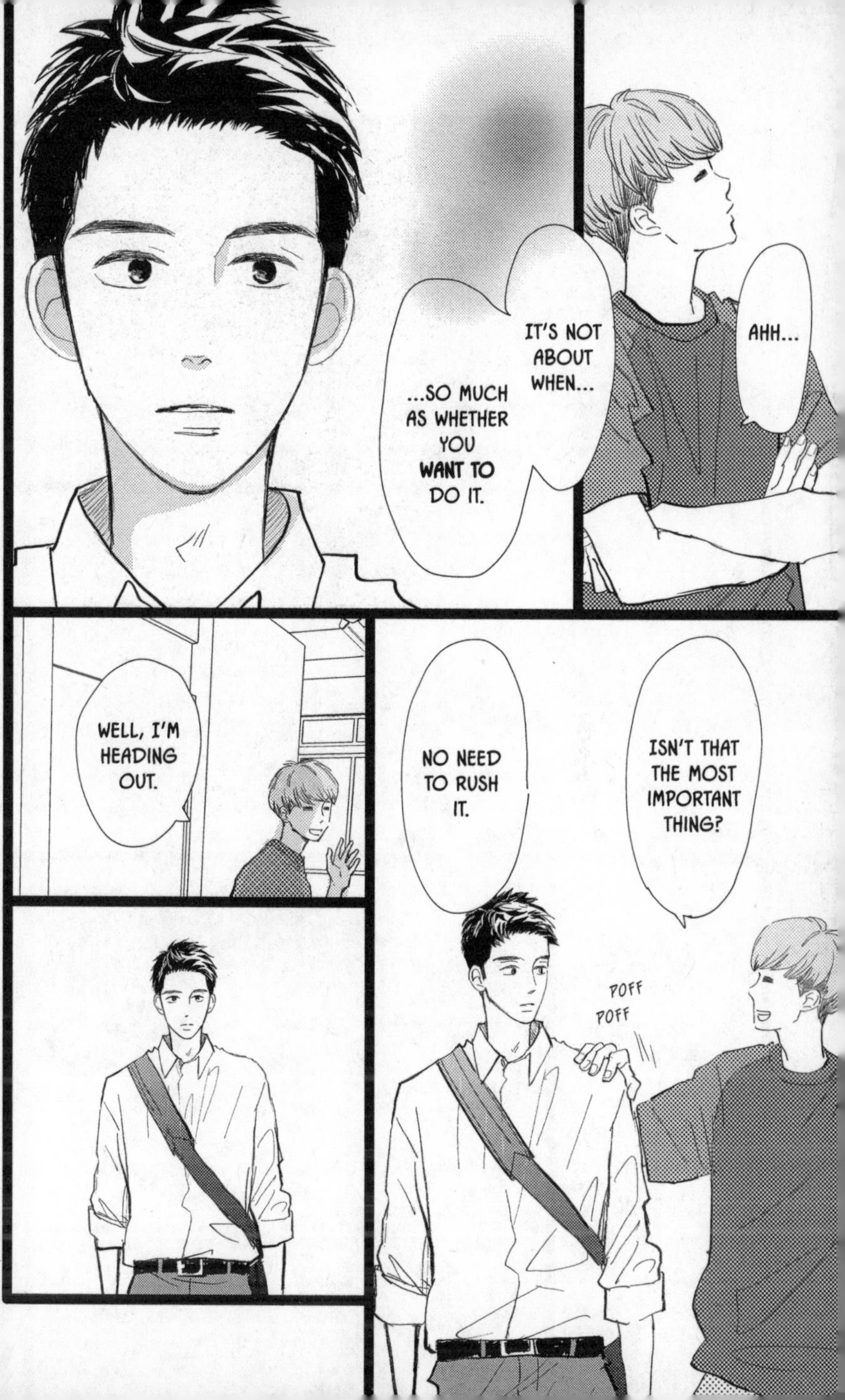
AHH...
IT'S NOT ABOUT WHEN...
...SO MUCH AS WHETHER YOU WANT TO DO IT.
ISN'T THAT THE MOST IMPORTANT THING?
NO NEED TO RUSH IT.
POFF POFF
WELL, I'M HEADING OUT.

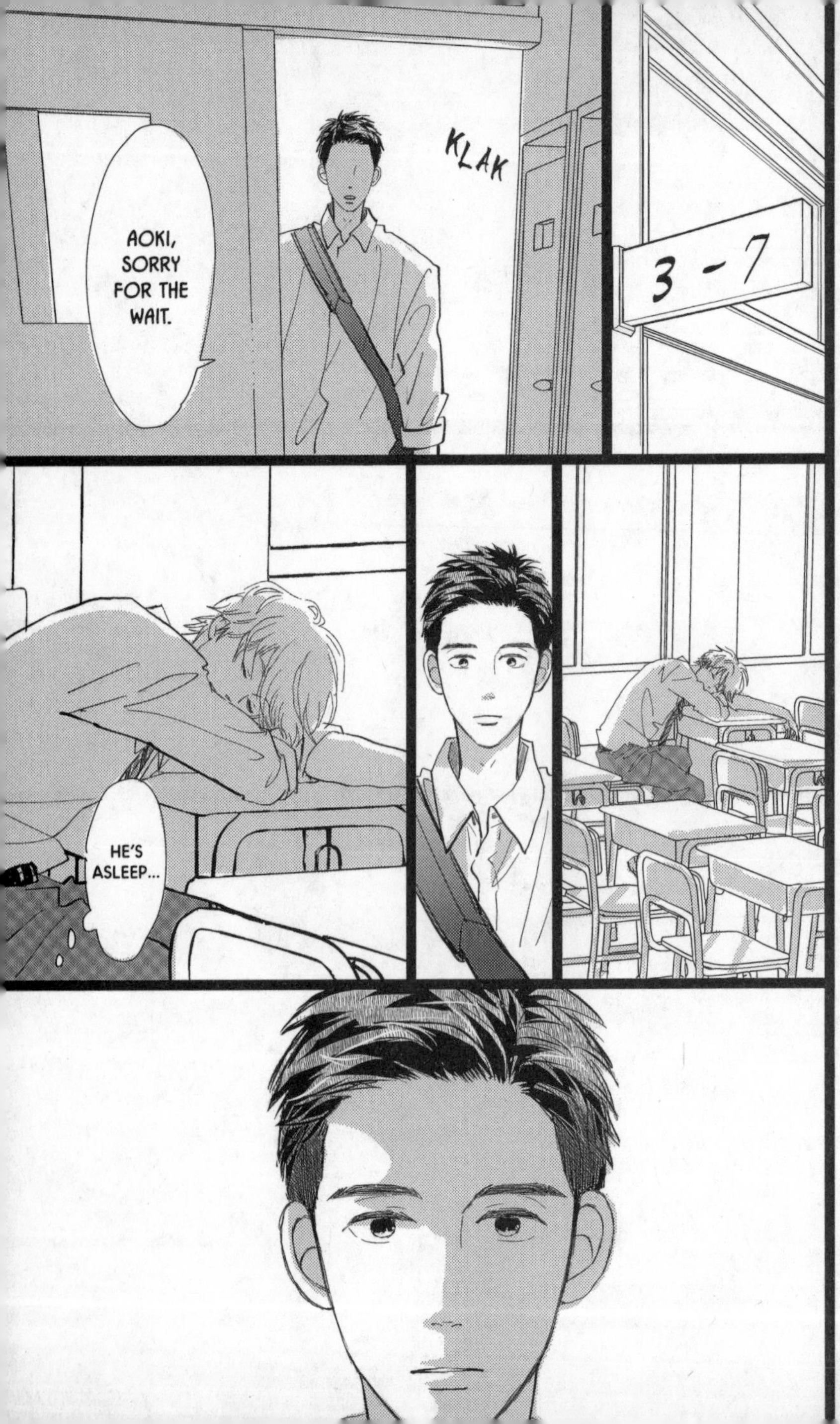
3-7
KLAK
AOKI, SORRY FOR THE WAIT.
HE'S ASLEEP...

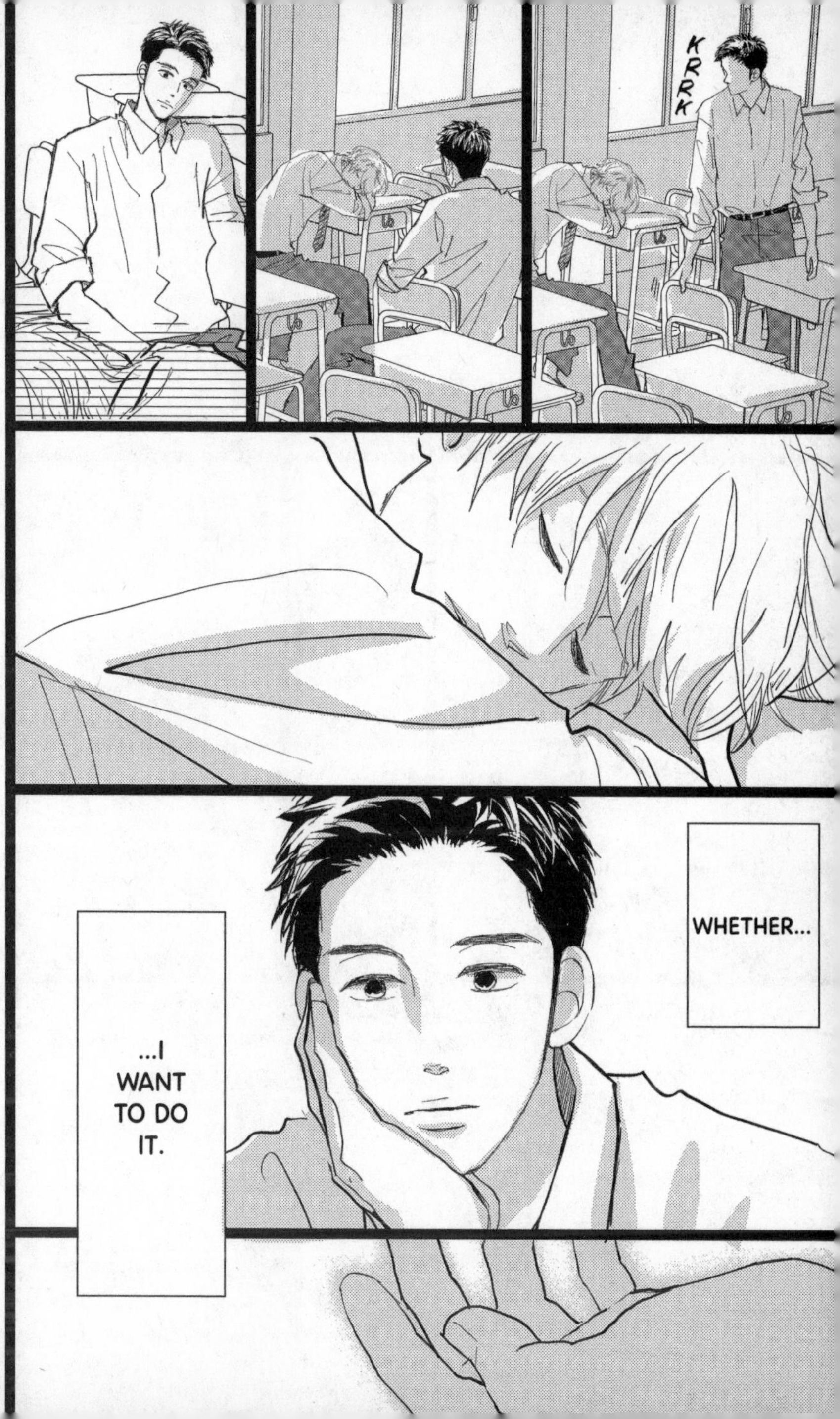
KRRK
WHETHER...
...I WANT TO DO IT.

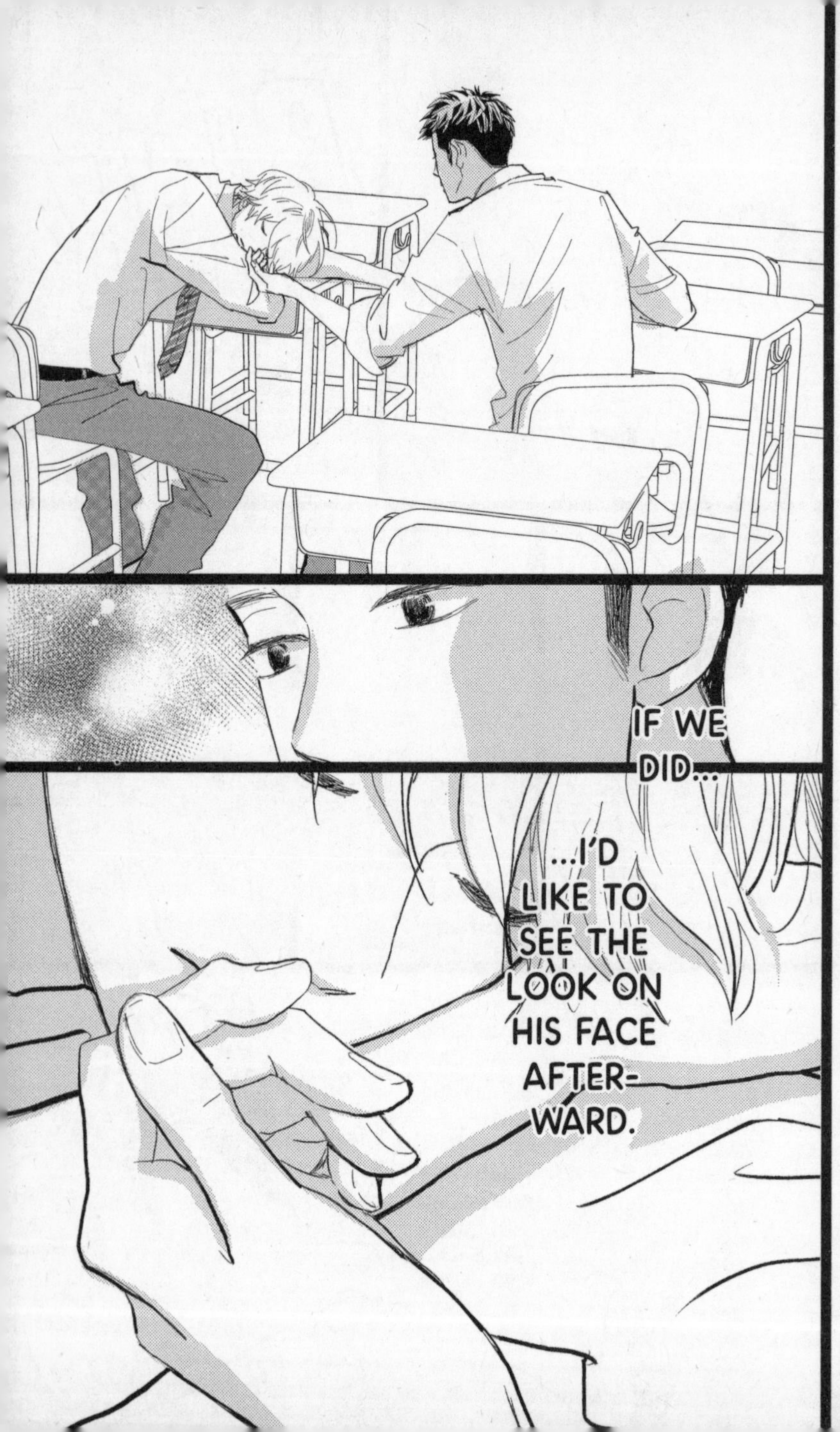
IF WE DID...
...I'D LIKE TO SEE THE LOOK ON HIS FACE AFTER-WARD.

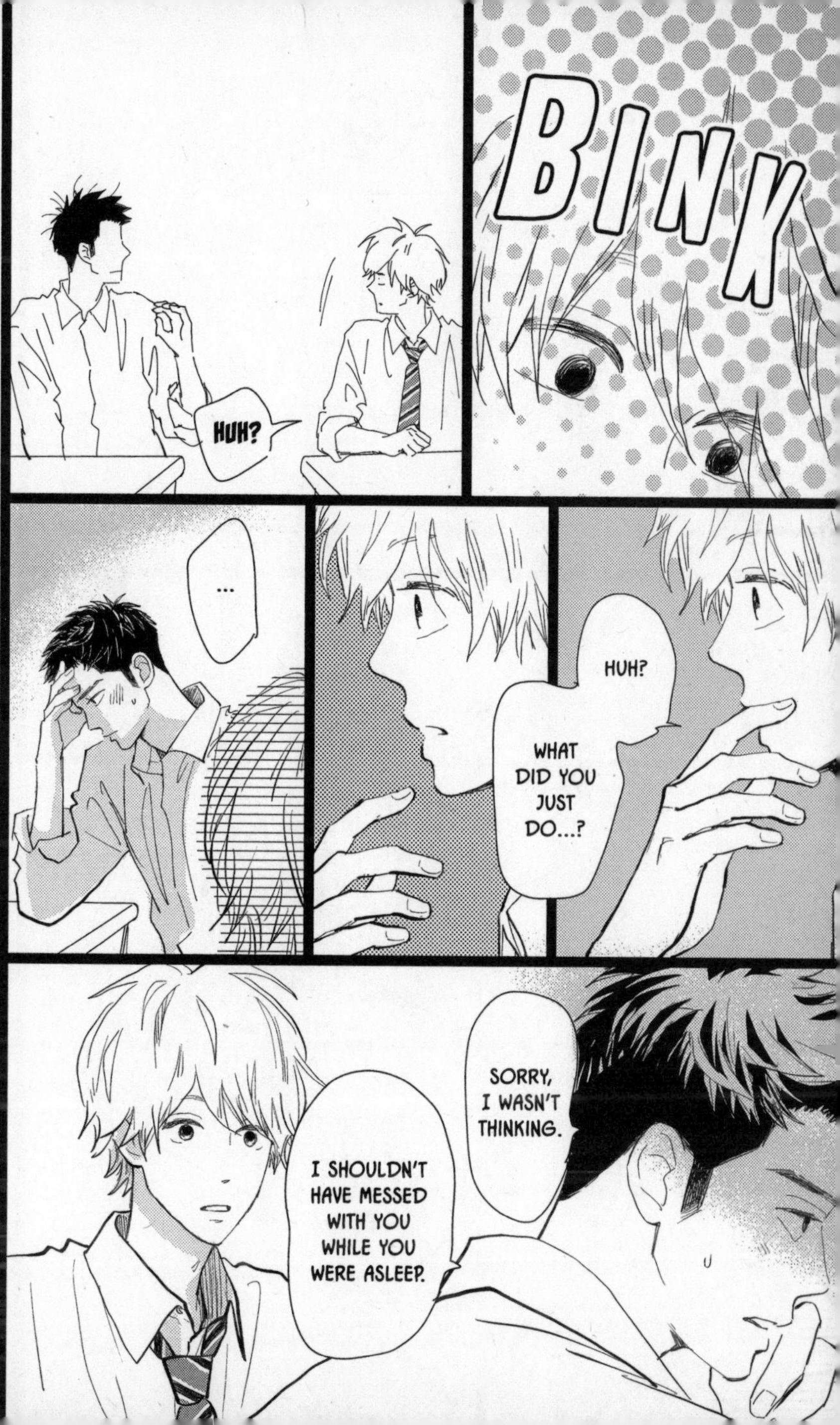
BINK
HUH?
HUH?
WHAT DID YOU JUST DO...?
...
SORRY, I WASN'T THINKING.
I SHOULDN'T HAVE MESSED WITH YOU WHILE YOU WERE ASLEEP.

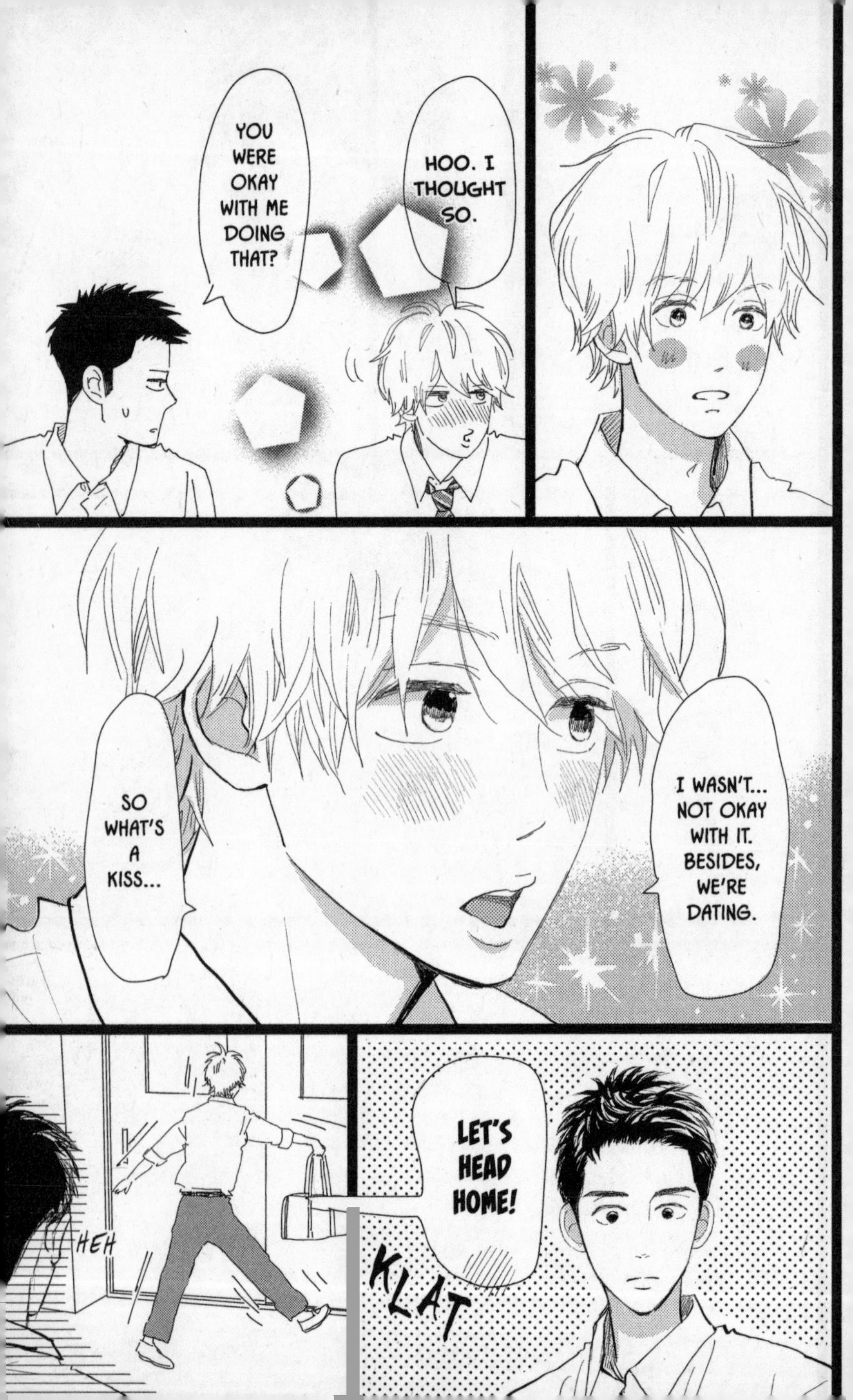
HOO. I THOUGHT SO.
YOU WERE OKAY WITH ME DOING THAT?
I WASN'T... NOT OKAY WITH IT. BESIDES, WE'RE DATING.
SO WHAT'S A KISS...
LET'S HEAD HOME!
KLAT
HEH

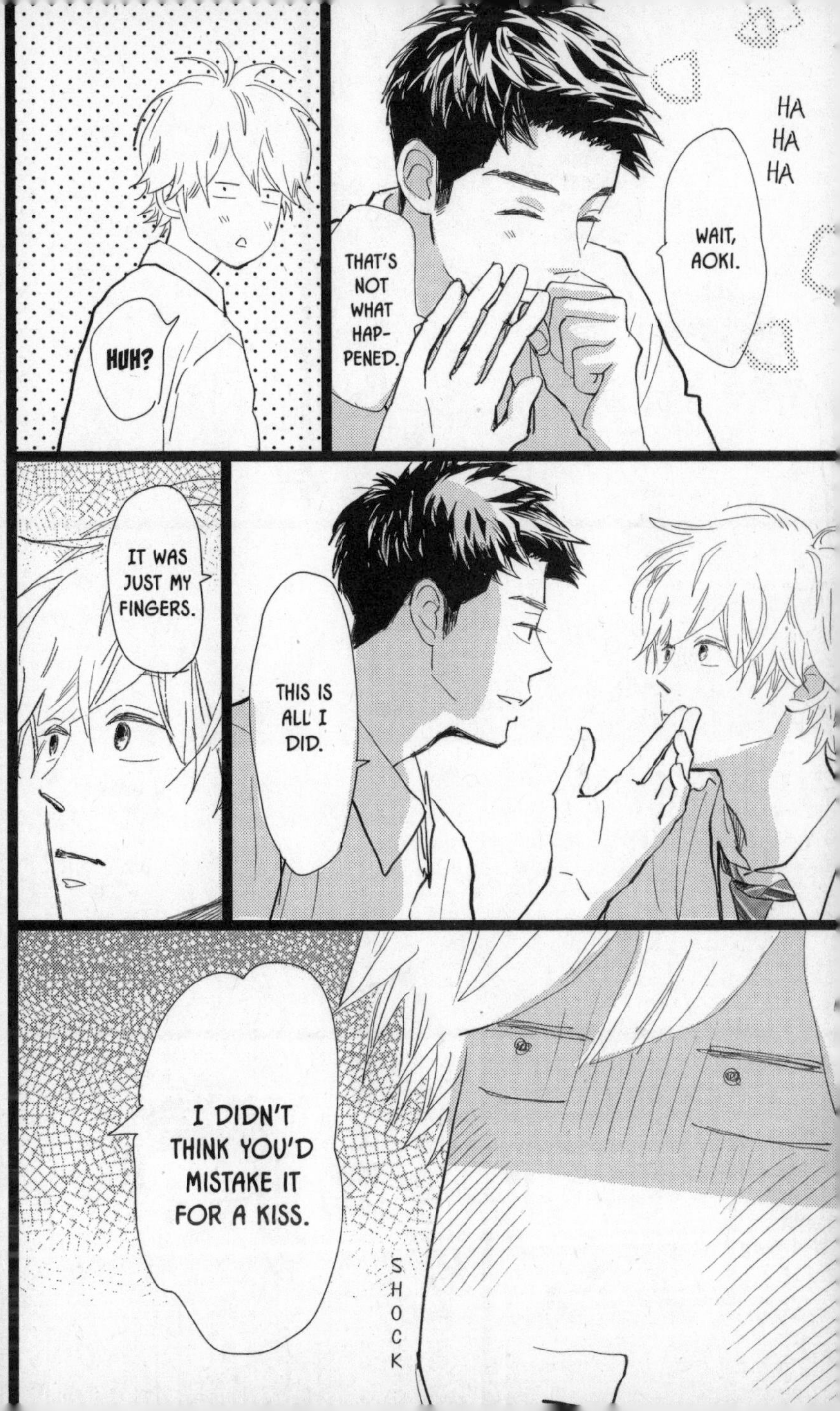
HA HA HA
WAIT, AOKI.
THAT'S NOT WHAT HAP-PENED.
HUH?
THIS IS ALL I DID.
IT WAS JUST MY FINGERS.
I DIDN'T THINK YOU'D MISTAKE IT FOR A KISS.
SHOCK

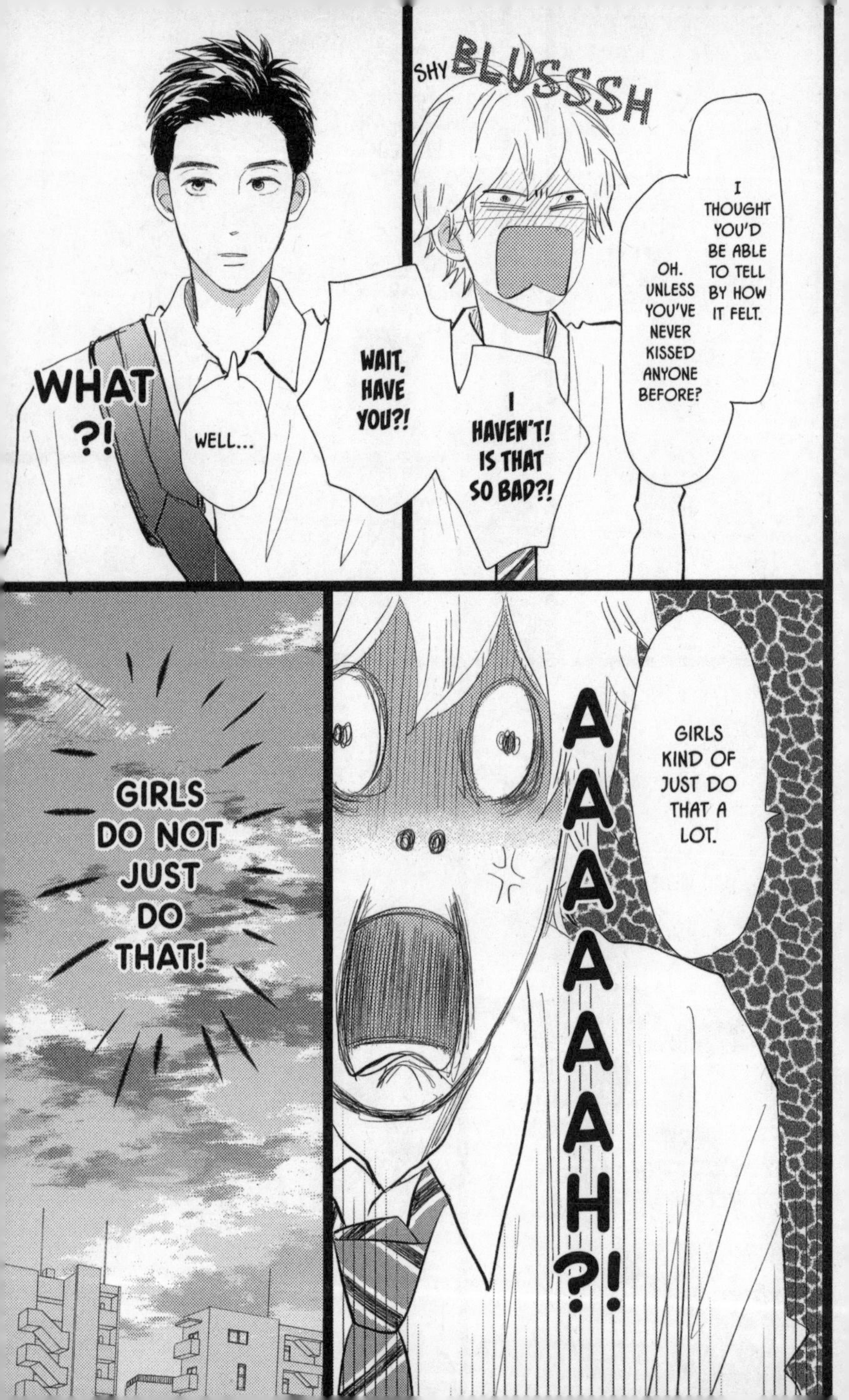
SHY BLUSSSH
I THOUGHT YOU'D BE ABLE TO TELL BY HOW IT FELT.
OH. UNLESS YOU'VE NEVER KISSED ANYONE BEFORE?
I HAVEN'T! IS THAT SO BAD?!
WAIT, HAVE YOU?!
WELL...
WHAT ?!
GIRLS KIND OF JUST DO THAT A LOT.
AAAAAAH?!
GIRLS DO NOT JUST DO THAT!

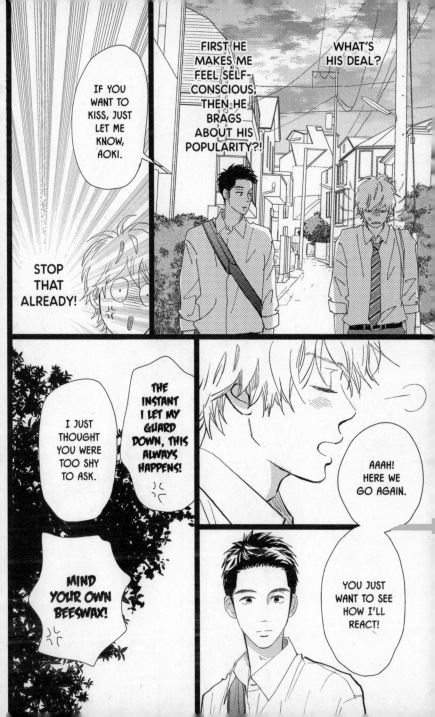

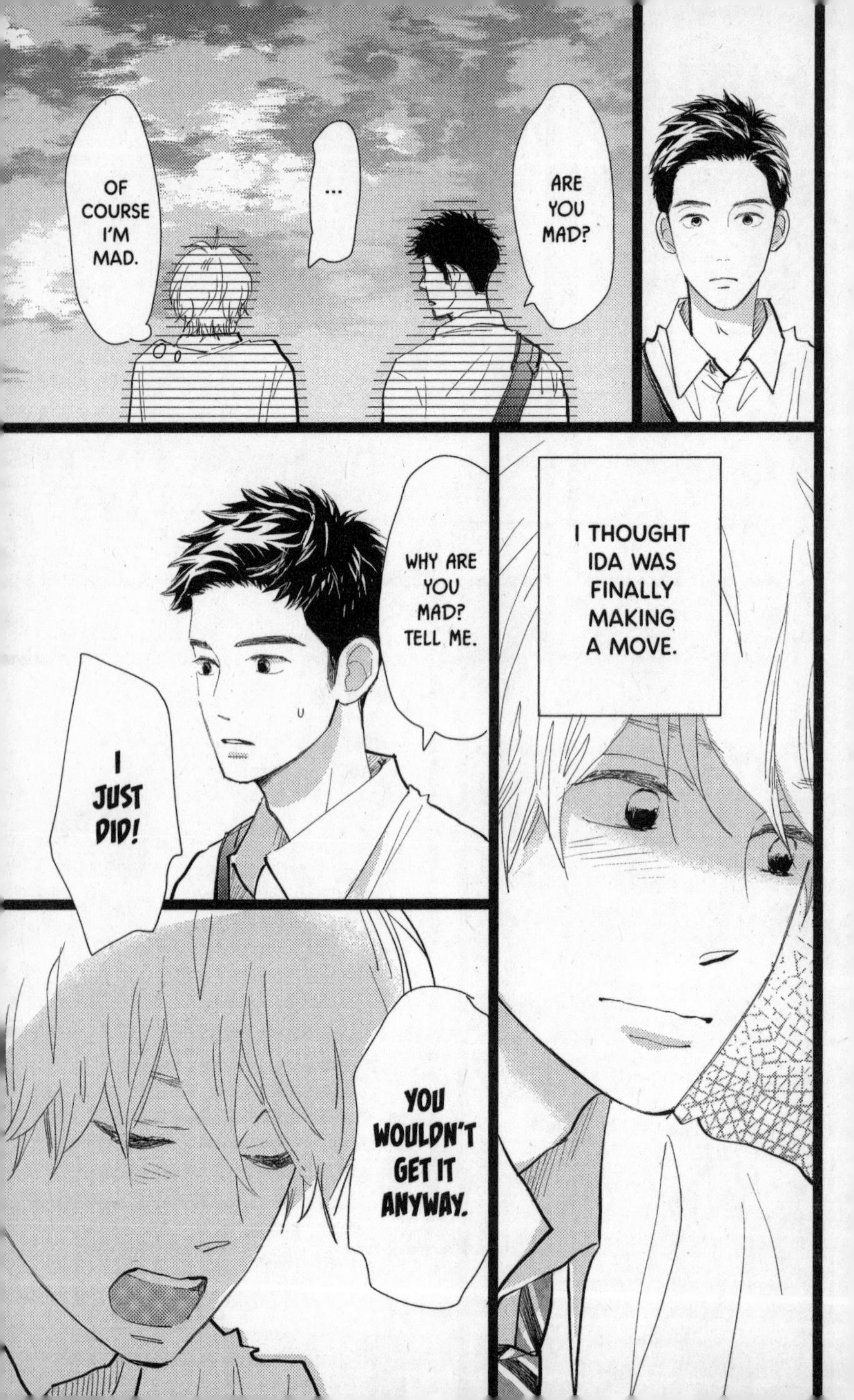
ARE YOU MAD?
...
OF COURSE I'M MAD.
I THOUGHT IDA WAS FINALLY MAKING A MOVE.
WHY ARE YOU MAD? TELL ME.
I JUST DID!
YOU WOULDN'T GET IT ANYWAY.

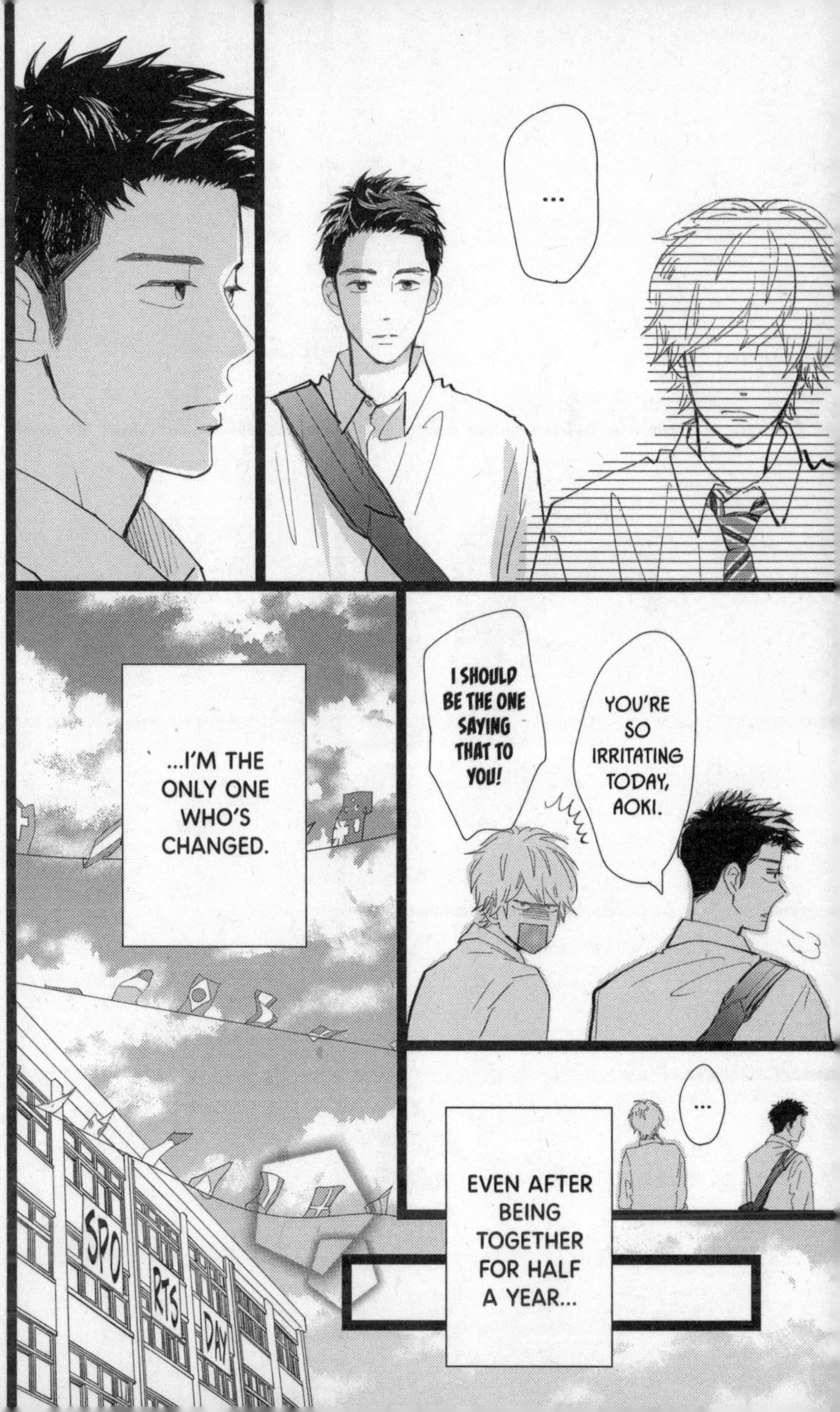
...
YOU'RE SO IRRITATING TODAY, AOKI.
I SHOULD BE THE ONE SAYING THAT TO YOU!
...
EVEN AFTER BEING TOGETHER FOR HALF A YEAR...
...I'M THE ONLY ONE WHO'S CHANGED.
SPORTS DAY

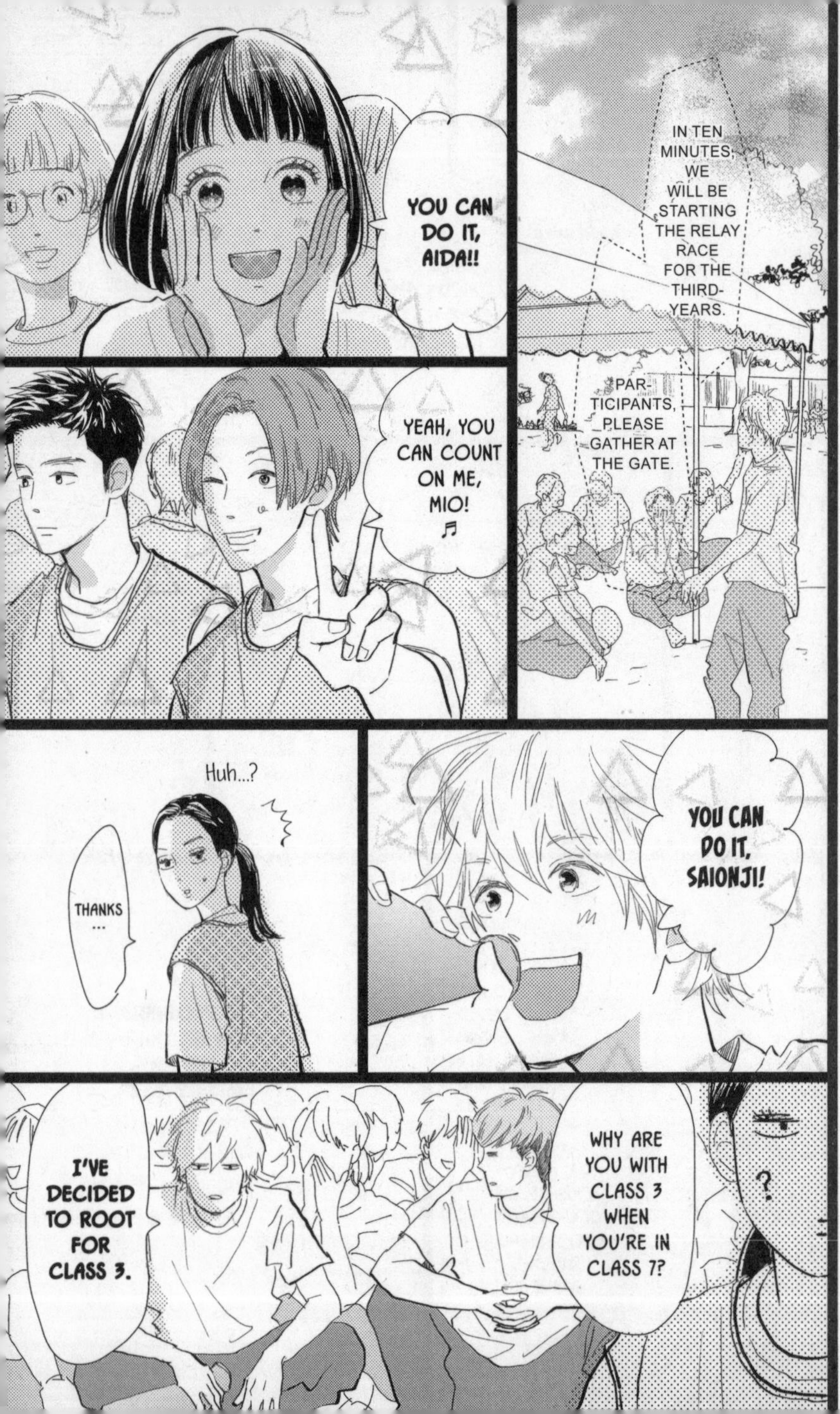
IN TEN MINUTES, WE WILL BE STARTING THE RELAY RACE FOR THE THIRD-YEARS.
PARTICIPANTS, PLEASE GATHER AT THE GATE.
YOU CAN DO IT, AIDA!!
YEAH, YOU CAN COUNT ON ME, MIO! ♬
YOU CAN DO IT, SAIONJI!
Huh...?
THANKS...
WHY ARE YOU WITH CLASS 3 WHEN YOU'RE IN CLASS 7?
I'VE DECIDED TO ROOT FOR CLASS 3.

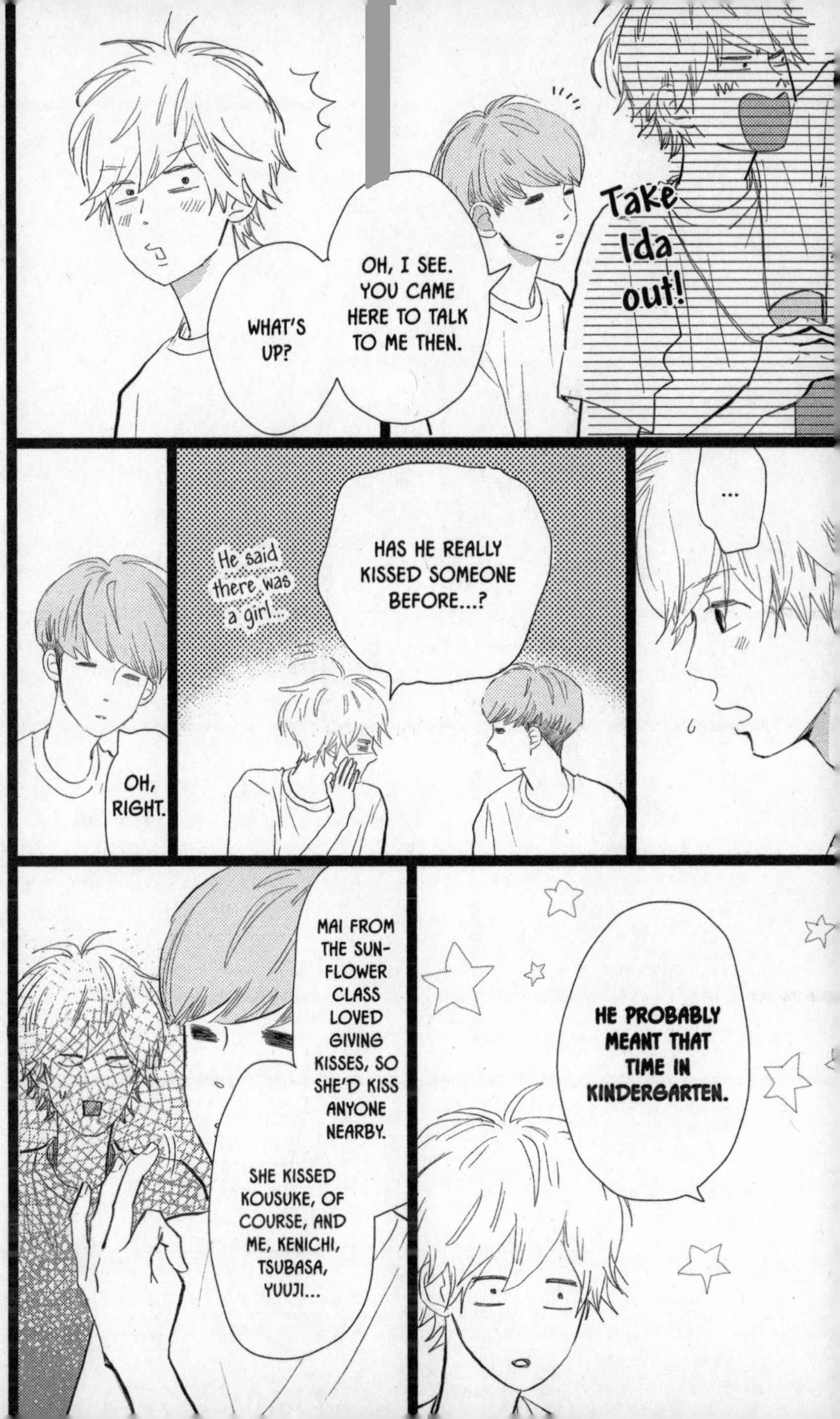
Take Ida out!
OH, I SEE. YOU CAME HERE TO TALK TO ME THEN.
WHAT'S UP?
...
HAS HE REALLY KISSED SOMEONE BEFORE...?
He said there was a girl...
OH, RIGHT.
HE PROBABLY MEANT THAT TIME IN KINDERGARTEN.
MAI FROM THE SUN-FLOWER CLASS LOVED GIVING KISSES, SO SHE'D KISS ANYONE NEARBY.
SHE KISSED KOUSUKE, OF COURSE, AND ME, KENICHI, TSUBASA, YUUJI...

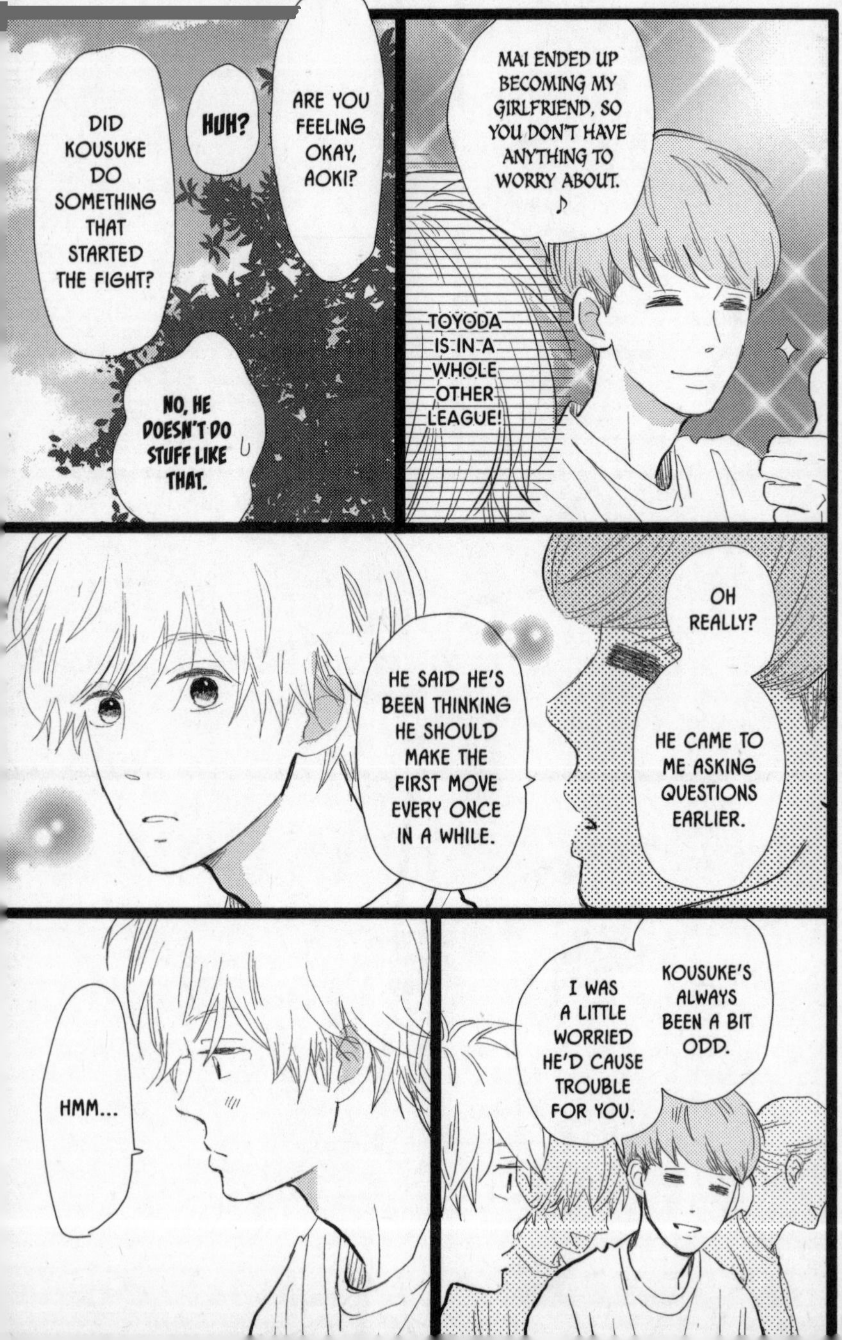
MAI ENDED UP BECOMING MY GIRLFRIEND, SO YOU DON'T HAVE ANYTHING TO WORRY ABOUT. ♪
TOYODA IS IN A WHOLE OTHER LEAGUE!
ARE YOU FEELING OKAY, AOKI?
HUH?
DID KOUSUKE DO SOMETHING THAT STARTED THE FIGHT?
NO, HE DOESN'T DO STUFF LIKE THAT.
OH REALLY?
HE CAME TO ME ASKING QUESTIONS EARLIER.
HE SAID HE'S BEEN THINKING HE SHOULD MAKE THE FIRST MOVE EVERY ONCE IN A WHILE.
KOUSUKE'S ALWAYS BEEN A BIT ODD.
I WAS A LITTLE WORRIED HE'D CAUSE TROUBLE FOR YOU.
HMM...

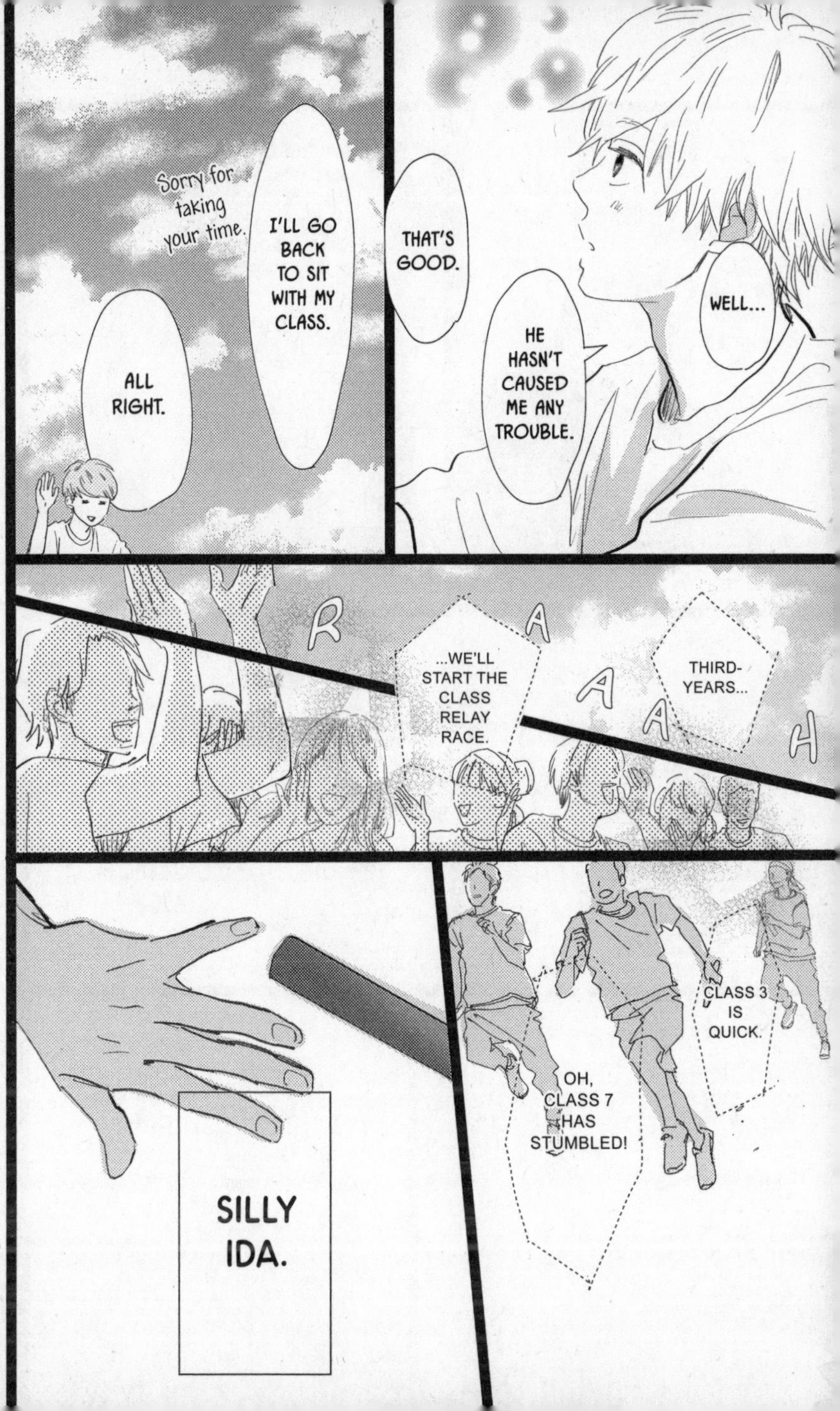
WELL...
HE HASN'T CAUSED ME ANY TROUBLE.
THAT'S GOOD.
I'LL GO BACK TO SIT WITH MY CLASS.
Sorry for taking your time.
ALL RIGHT.
THIRD-YEARS...
...WE'LL START THE CLASS RELAY RACE.
RAAAH
CLASS 3 IS QUICK.
OH, CLASS 7 HAS STUMBLED!
SILLY IDA.

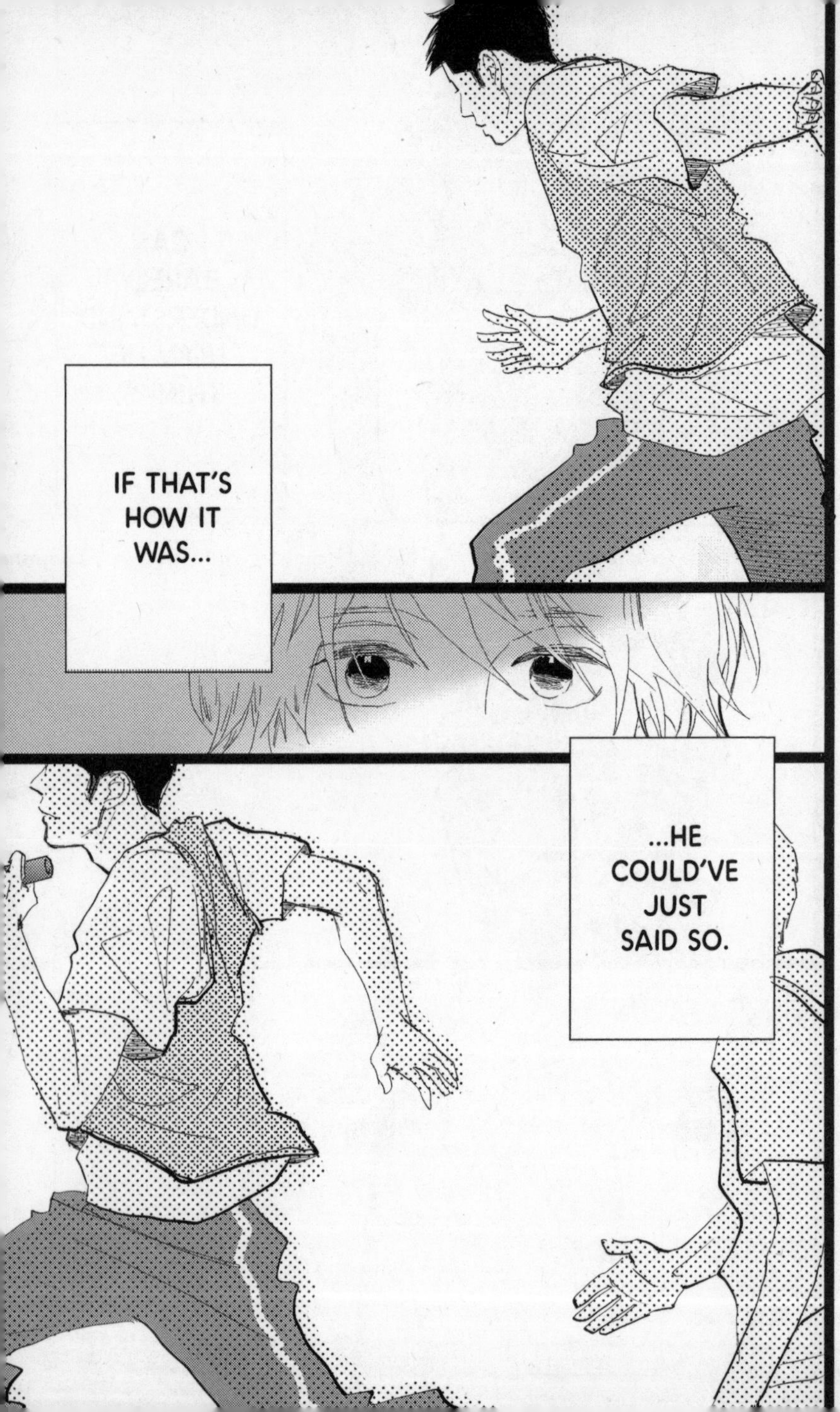
IF THAT'S HOW IT WAS...
...HE COULD'VE JUST SAID SO.

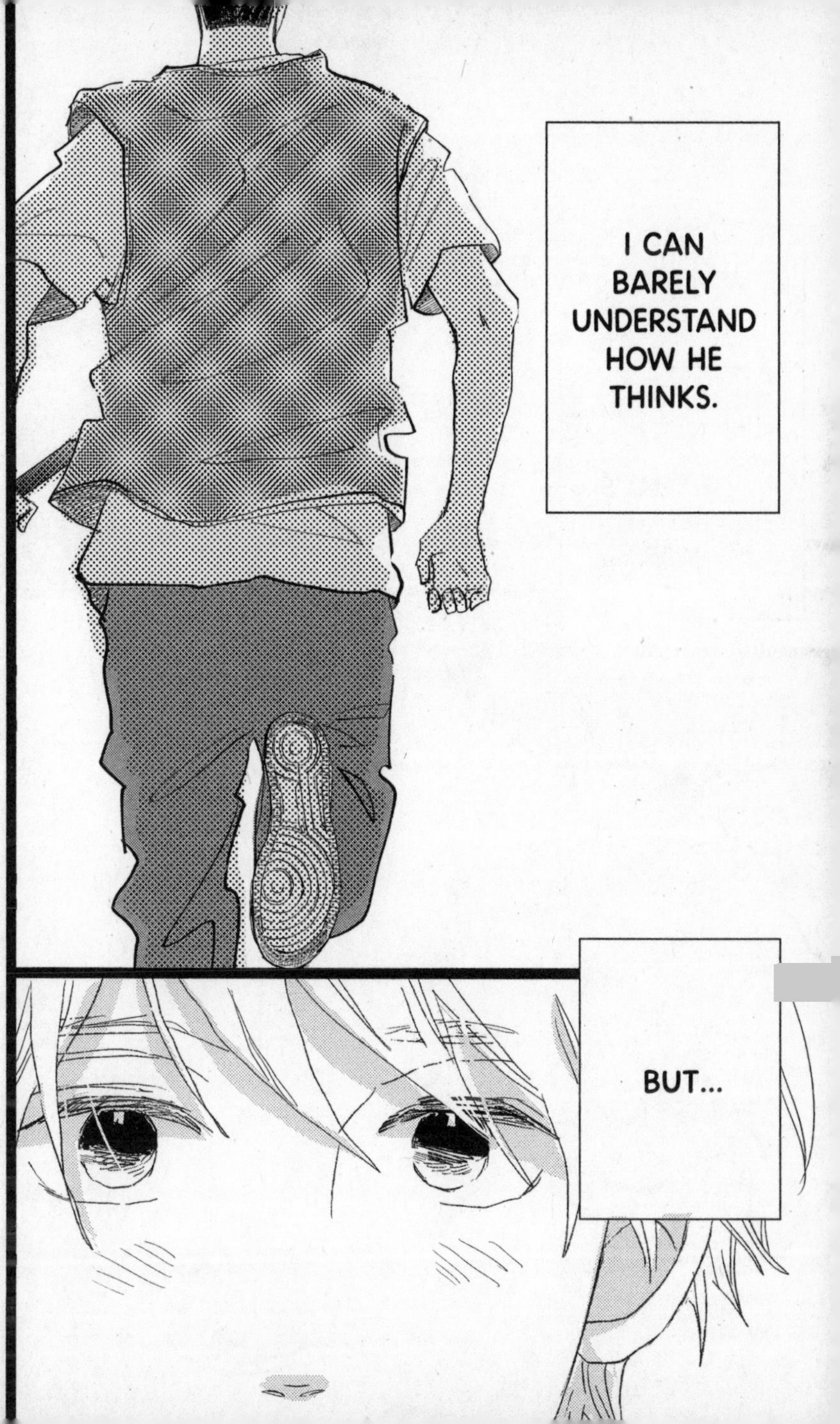
I CAN BARELY UNDERSTAND HOW HE THINKS.
BUT...

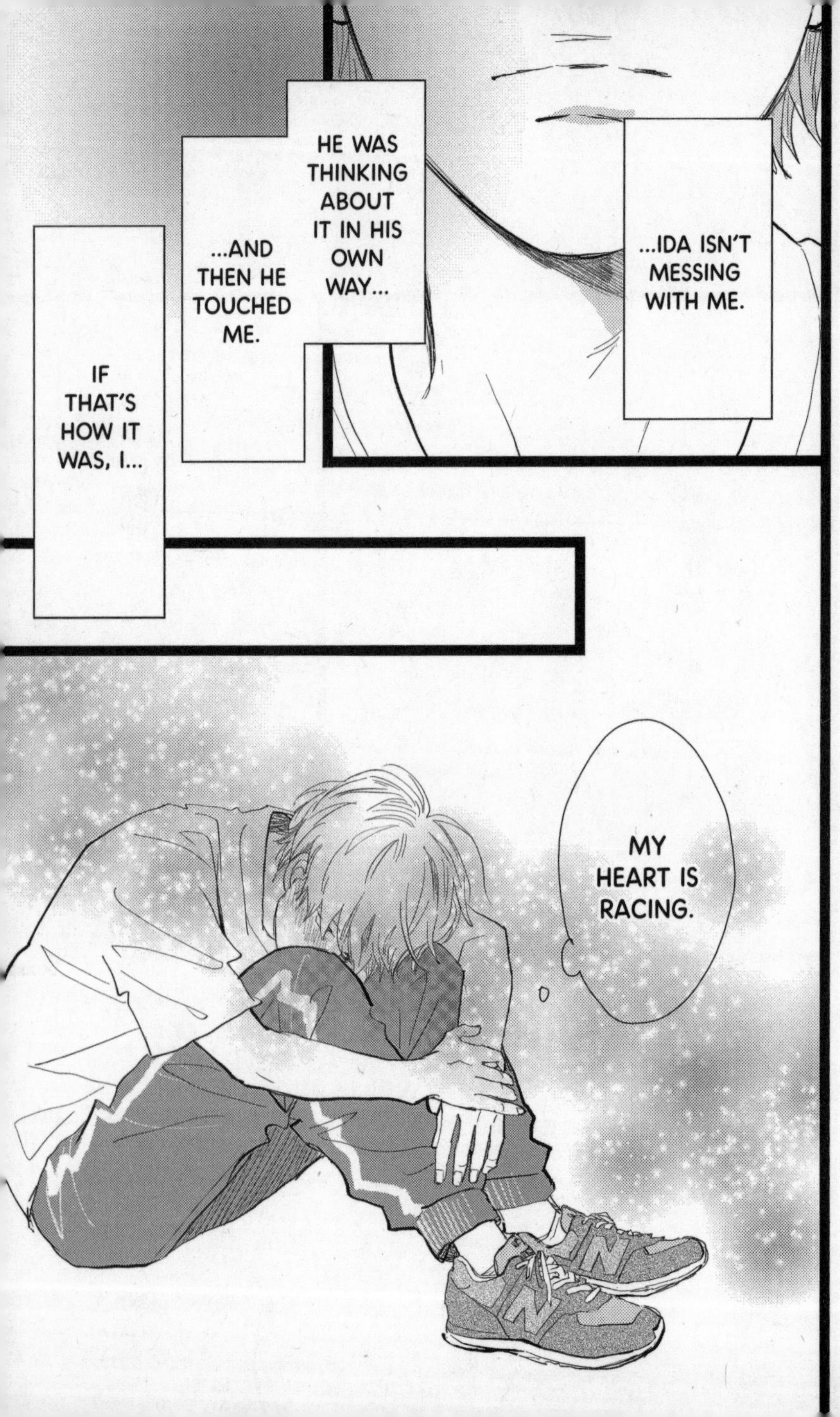
...IDA ISN'T MESSING WITH ME.
HE WAS THINKING ABOUT IT IN HIS OWN WAY...
...AND THEN HE TOUCHED ME.
IF THAT'S HOW IT WAS, I...
MY HEART IS RACING.

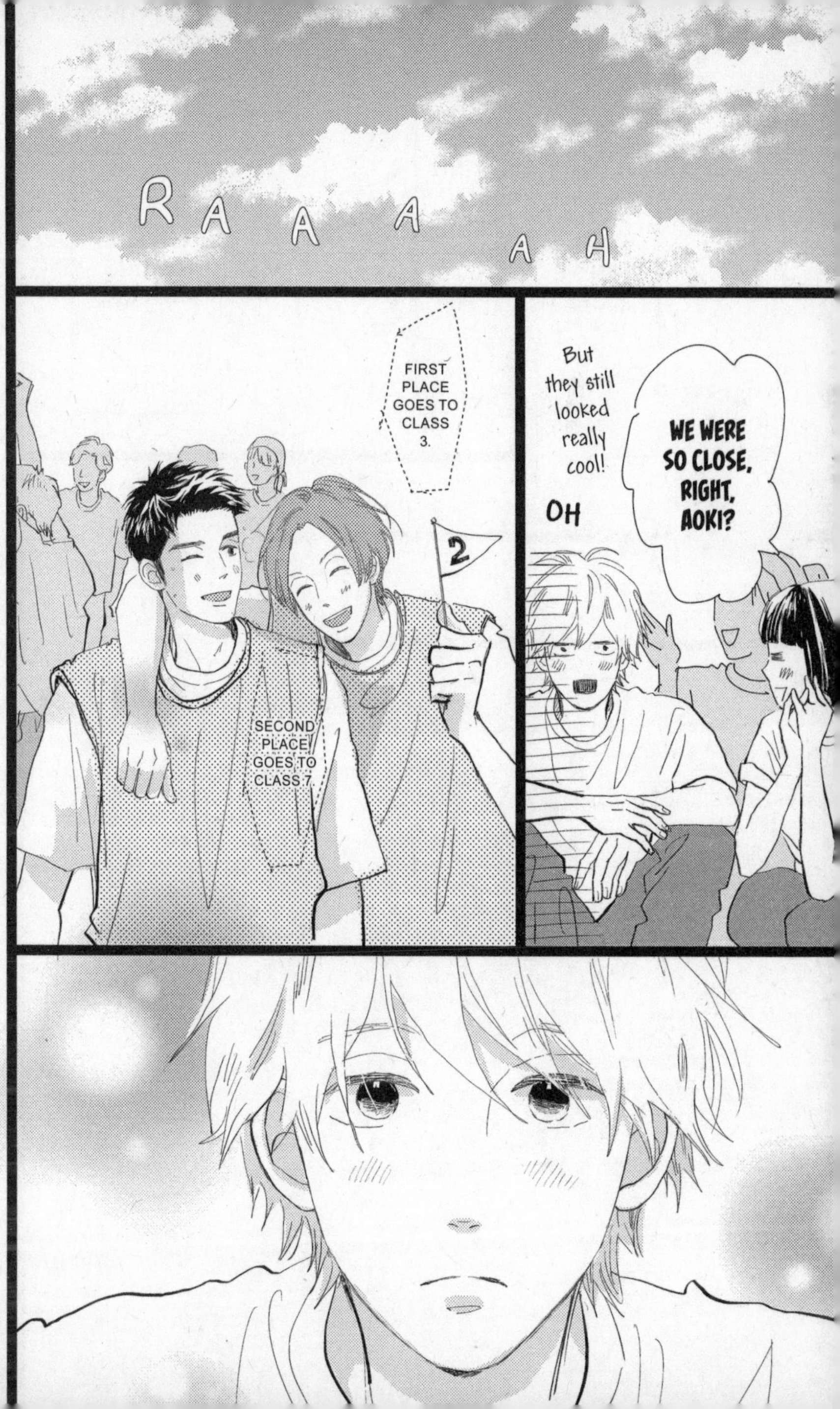
RAAAAH
WE WERE SO CLOSE, RIGHT, AOKI?
But they still looked really cool!
OH
FIRST PLACE GOES TO CLASS 3.
SECOND PLACE GOES TO CLASS 7.

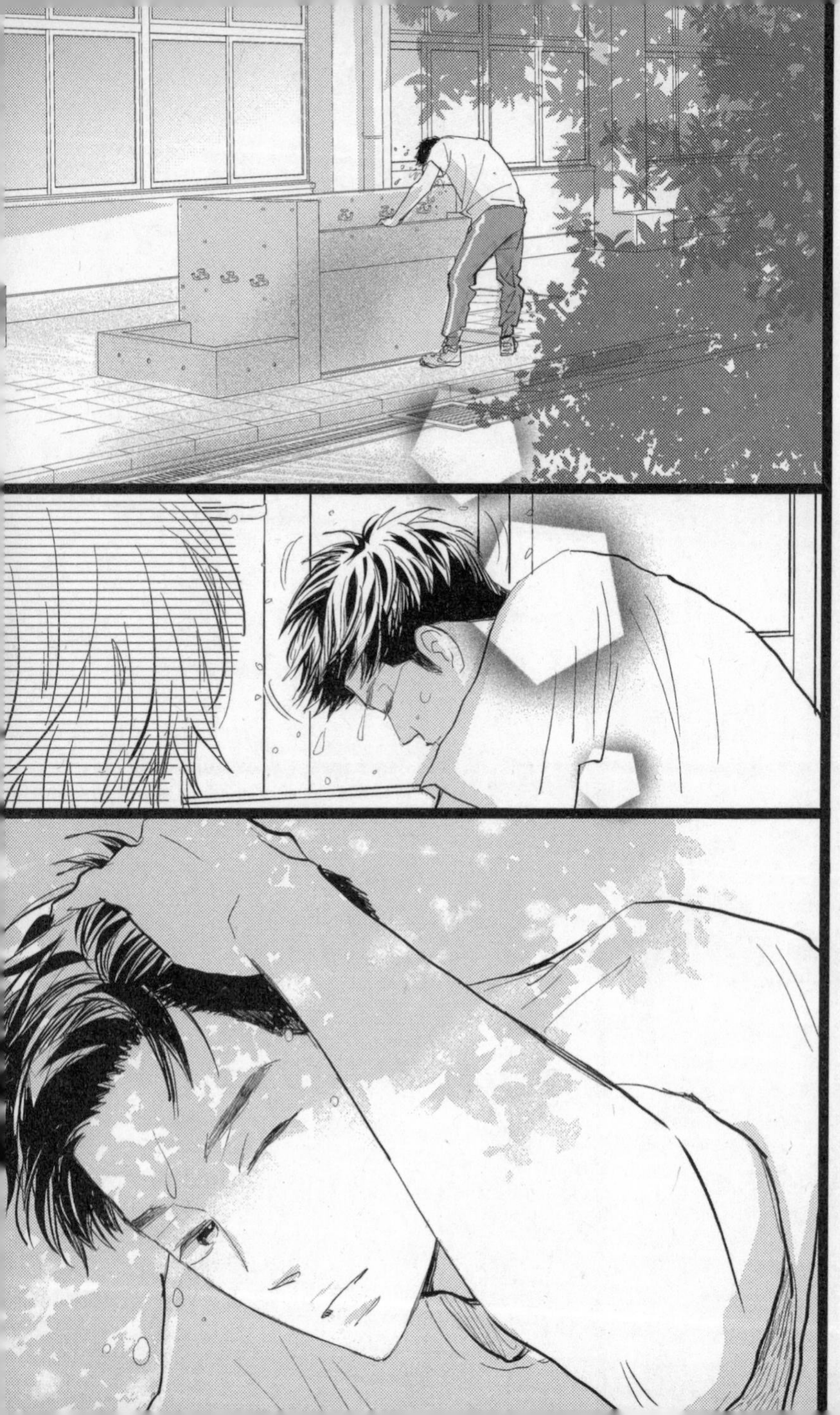

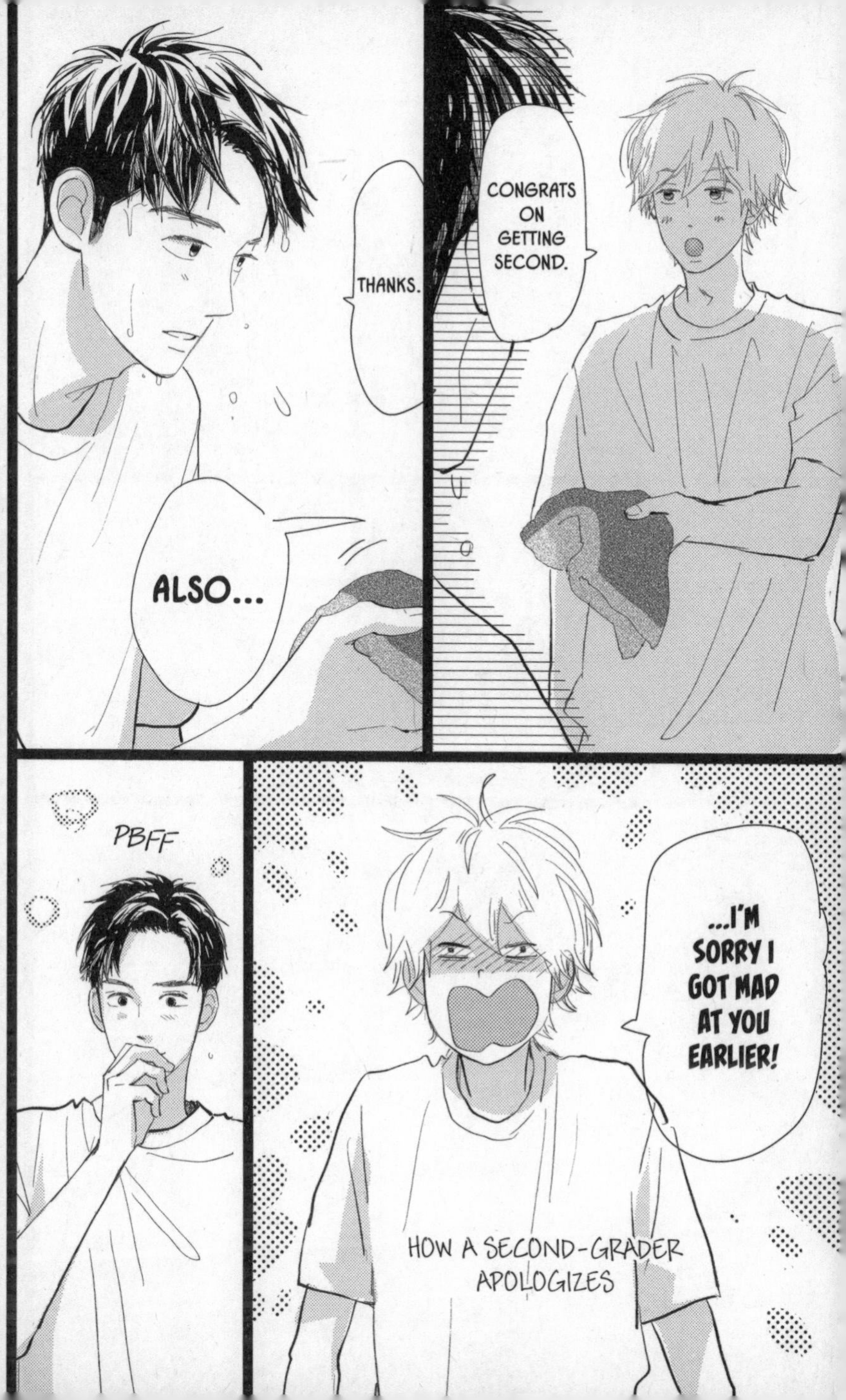
CONGRATS ON GETTING SECOND.
THANKS.
ALSO...
...I'M SORRY I GOT MAD AT YOU EARLIER!
HOW A SECOND-GRADER APOLOGIZES
PBFF

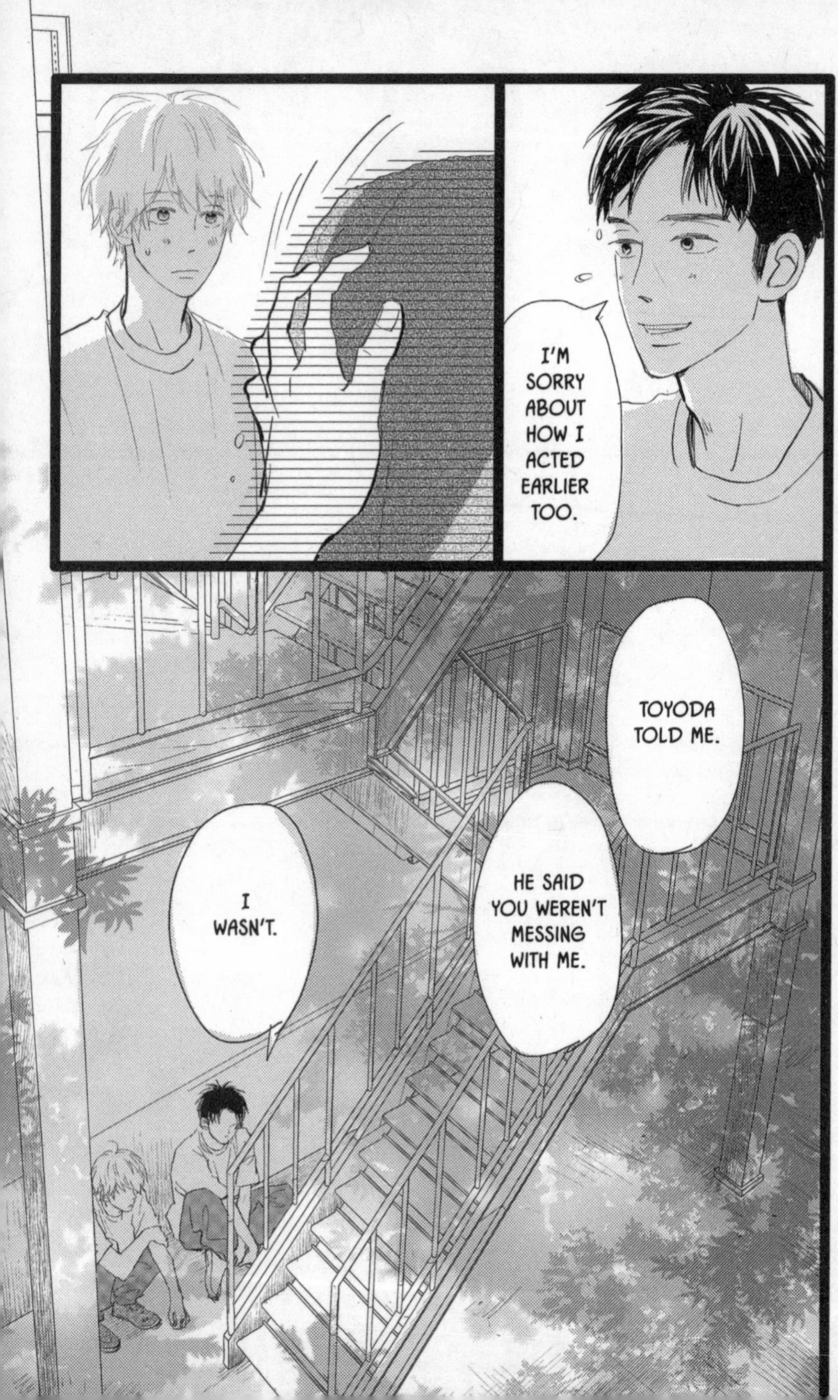
I'M SORRY ABOUT HOW I ACTED EARLIER TOO.
TOYODA TOLD ME.
HE SAID YOU WEREN'T MESSING WITH ME.
I WASN'T.

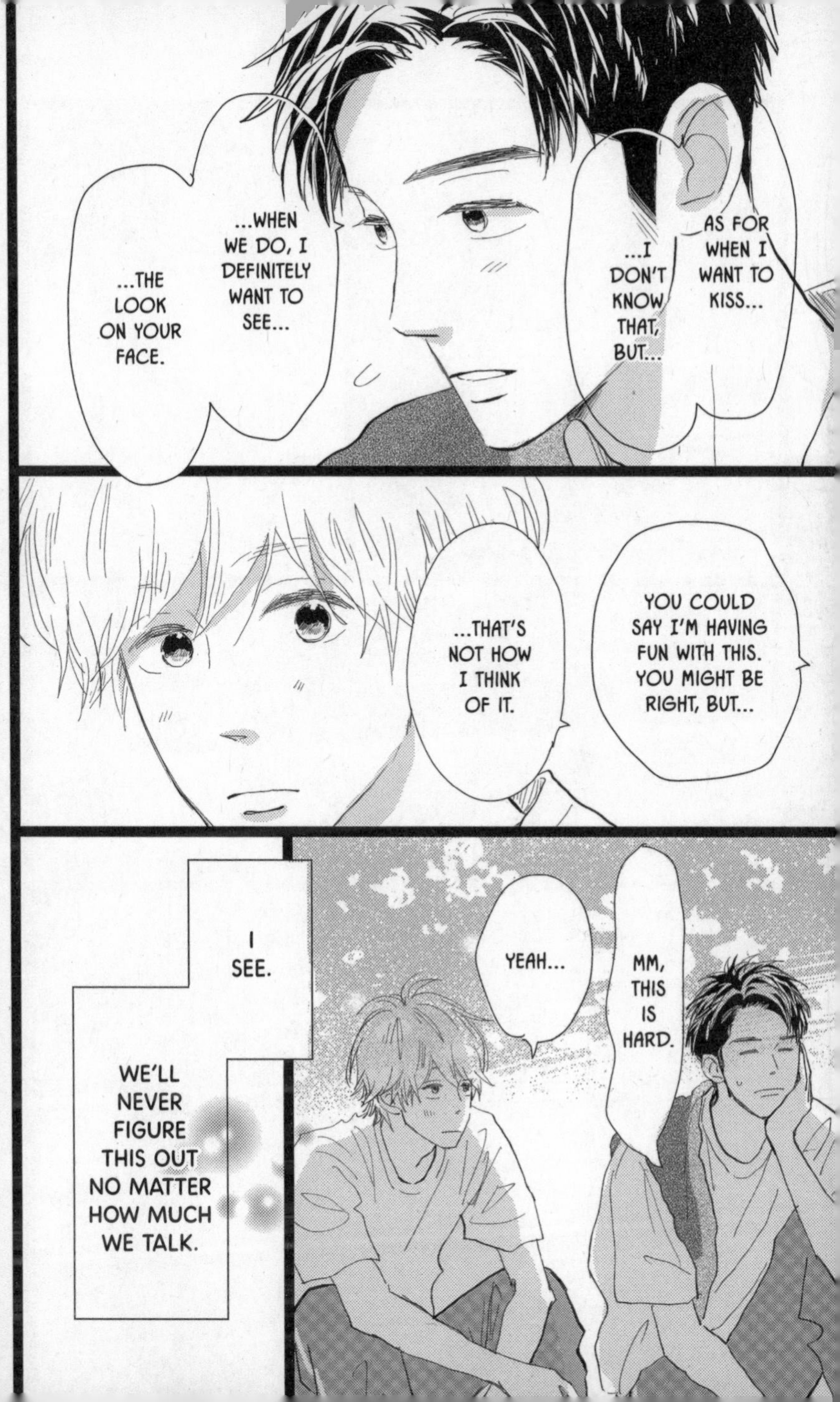
AS FOR WHEN I WANT TO KISS...
...I DON'T KNOW THAT, BUT...
...WHEN WE DO, I DEFINITELY WANT TO SEE...
...THE LOOK ON YOUR FACE.
YOU COULD SAY I'M HAVING FUN WITH THIS. YOU MIGHT BE RIGHT, BUT...
...THAT'S NOT HOW I THINK OF IT.
MM, THIS IS HARD.
YEAH...
I SEE.
WE'LL NEVER FIGURE THIS OUT NO MATTER HOW MUCH WE TALK.

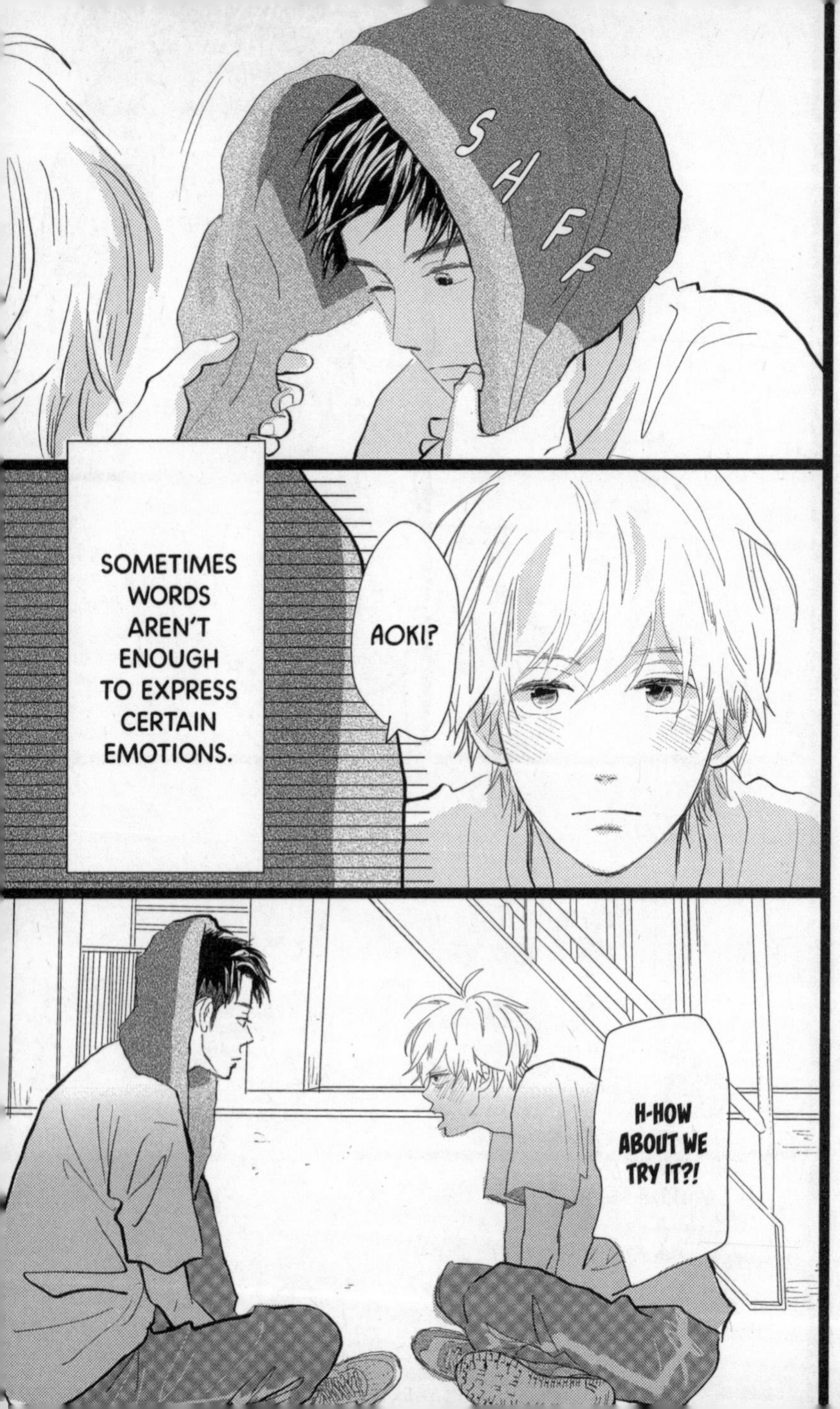
SHFF
AOKI?
SOMETIMES WORDS AREN'T ENOUGH TO EXPRESS CERTAIN EMOTIONS.
H-HOW ABOUT WE TRY IT?!

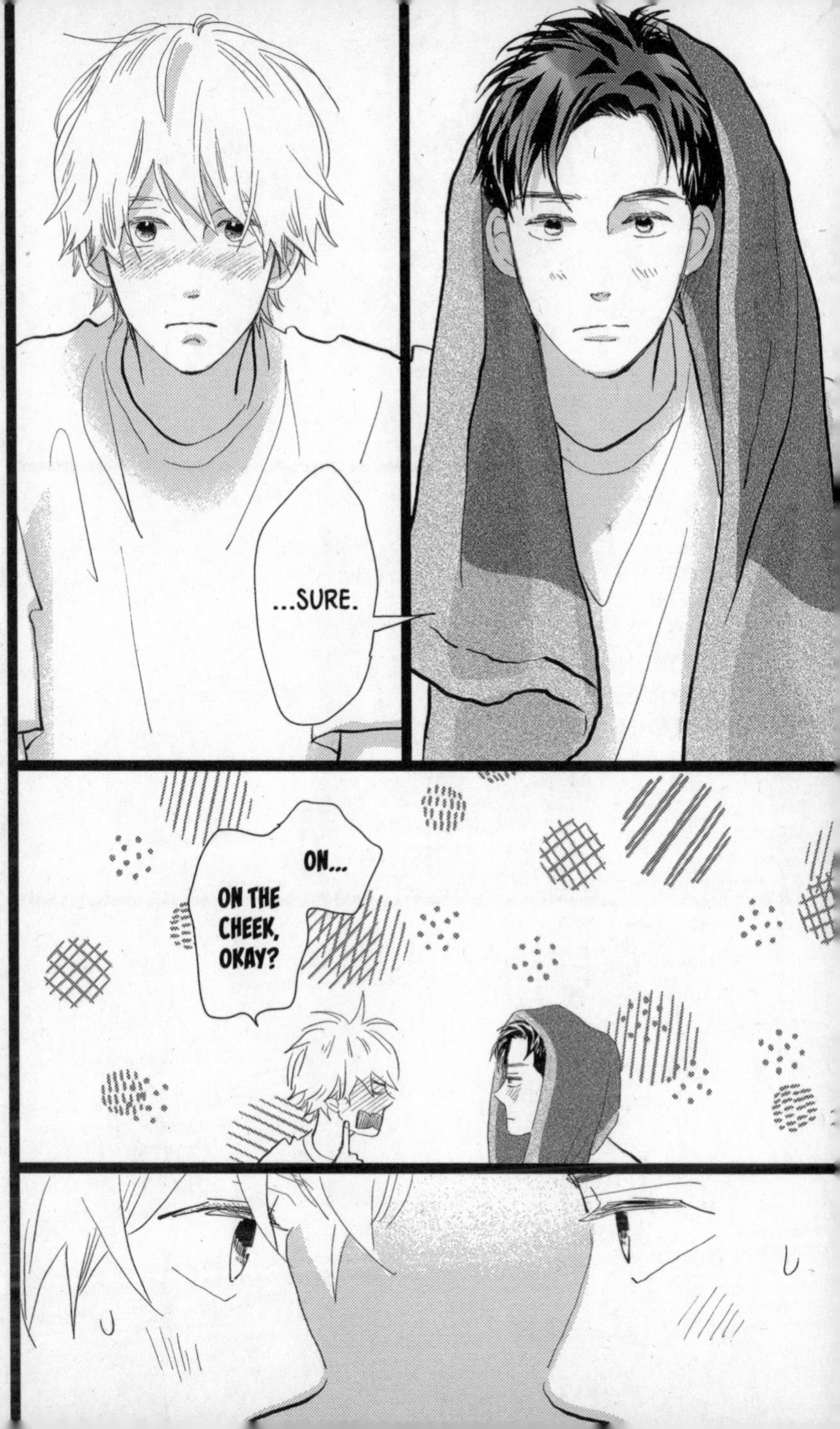
...SURE.
ON... ON THE CHEEK, OKAY?

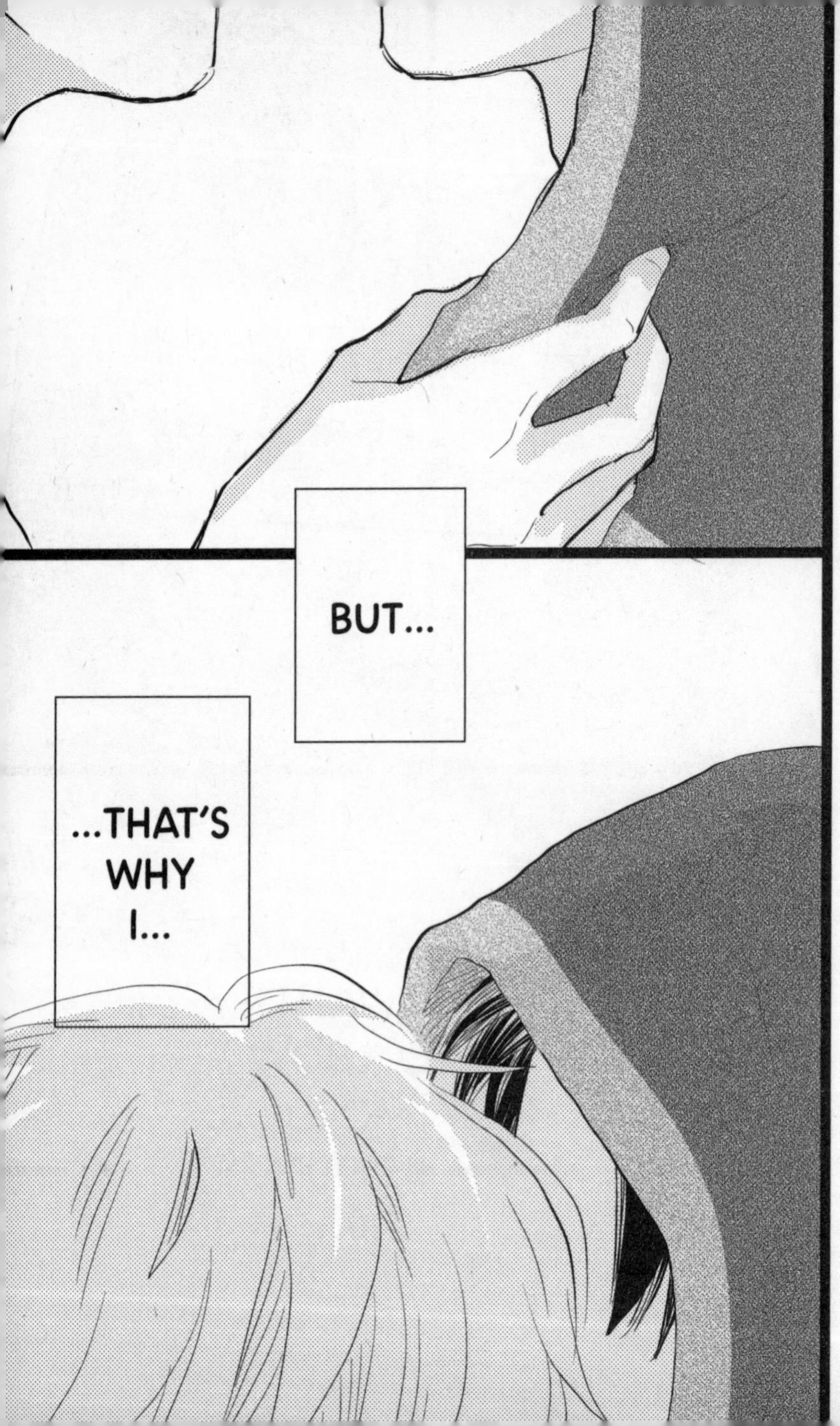
BUT...
...THAT'S WHY I...

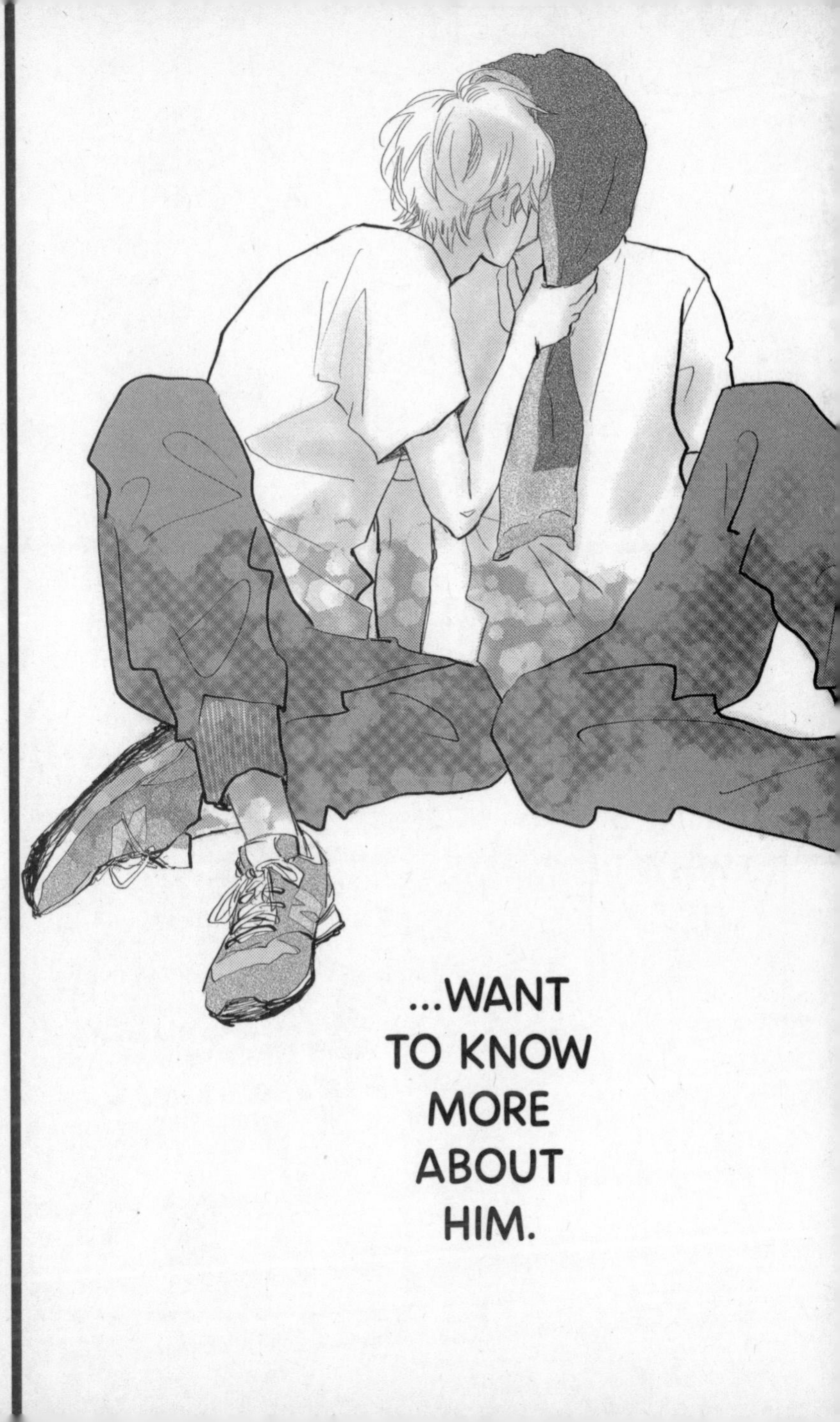
...WANT TO KNOW MORE ABOUT HIM.

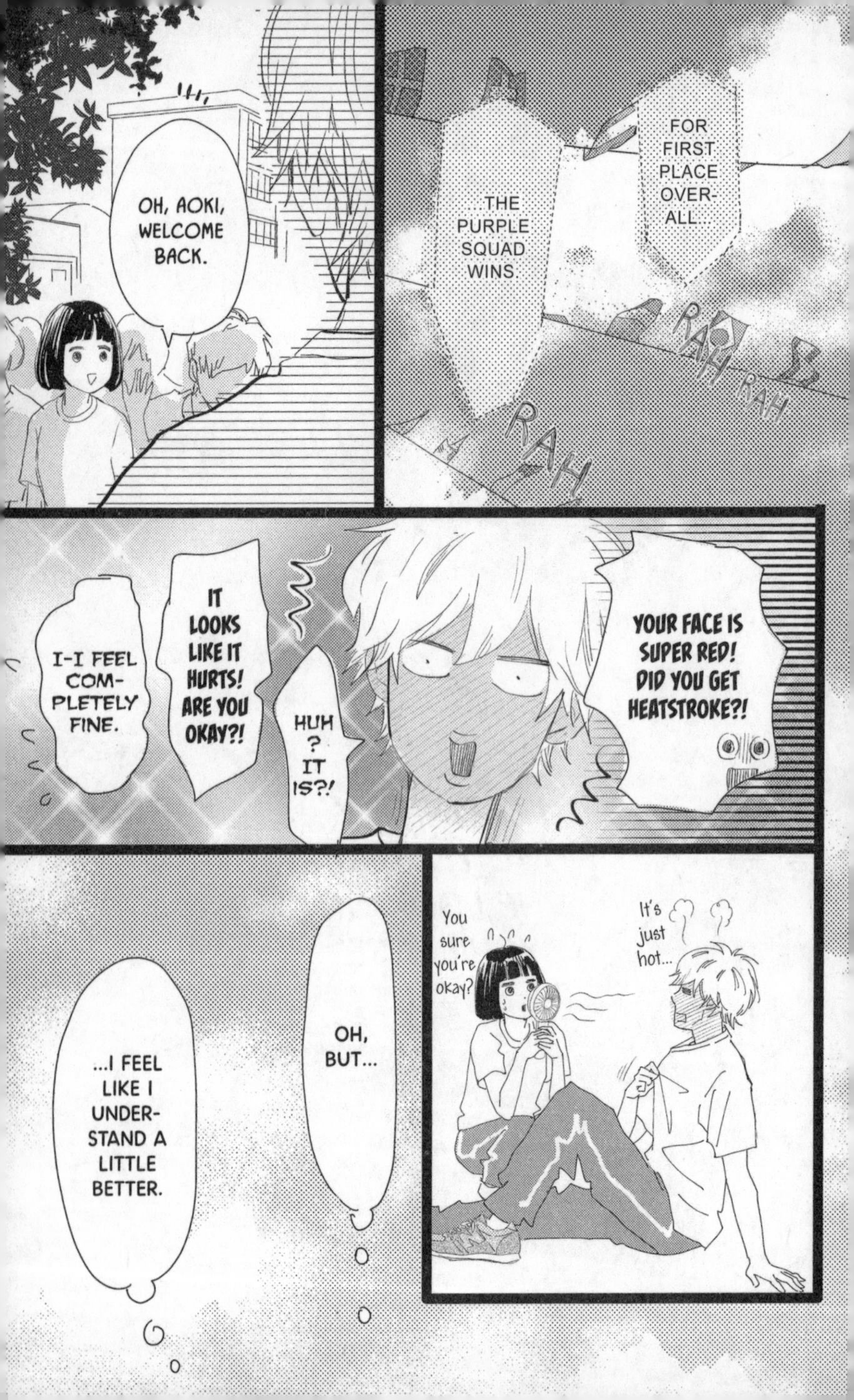
FOR FIRST PLACE OVER-ALL...
...THE PURPLE SQUAD WINS.
RAH RAH
RAH
OH, AOKI, WELCOME BACK.
YOUR FACE IS SUPER RED! DID YOU GET HEATSTROKE?!
HUH? IT IS?!
IT LOOKS LIKE IT HURTS! ARE YOU OKAY?!
I-I FEEL COM-PLETELY FINE.
It's just hot...
You sure you're okay?
OH, BUT...
...I FEEL LIKE I UNDER-STAND A LITTLE BETTER.

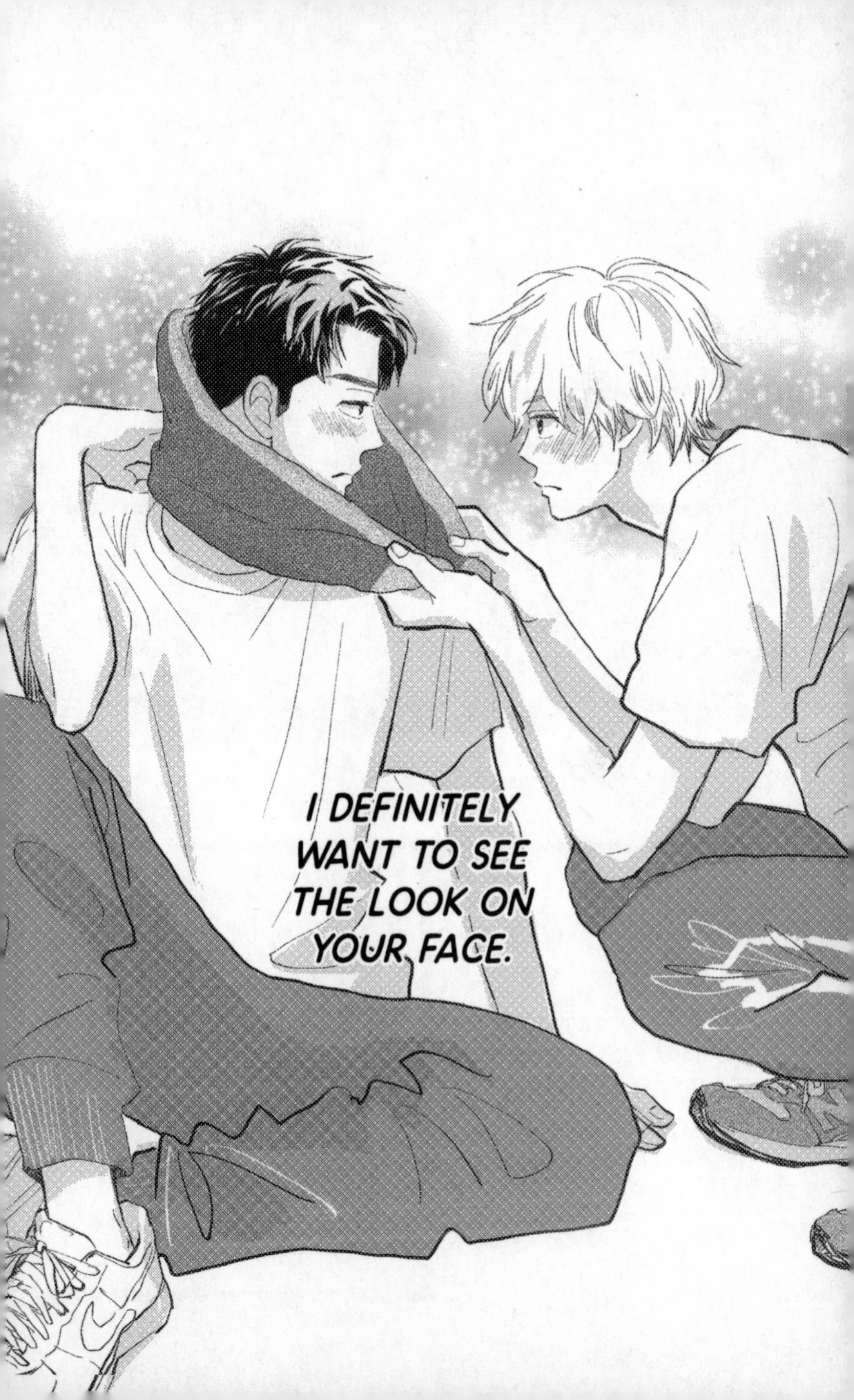
I DEFINITELY WANT TO SEE THE LOOK ON YOUR FACE.

Chapter 25

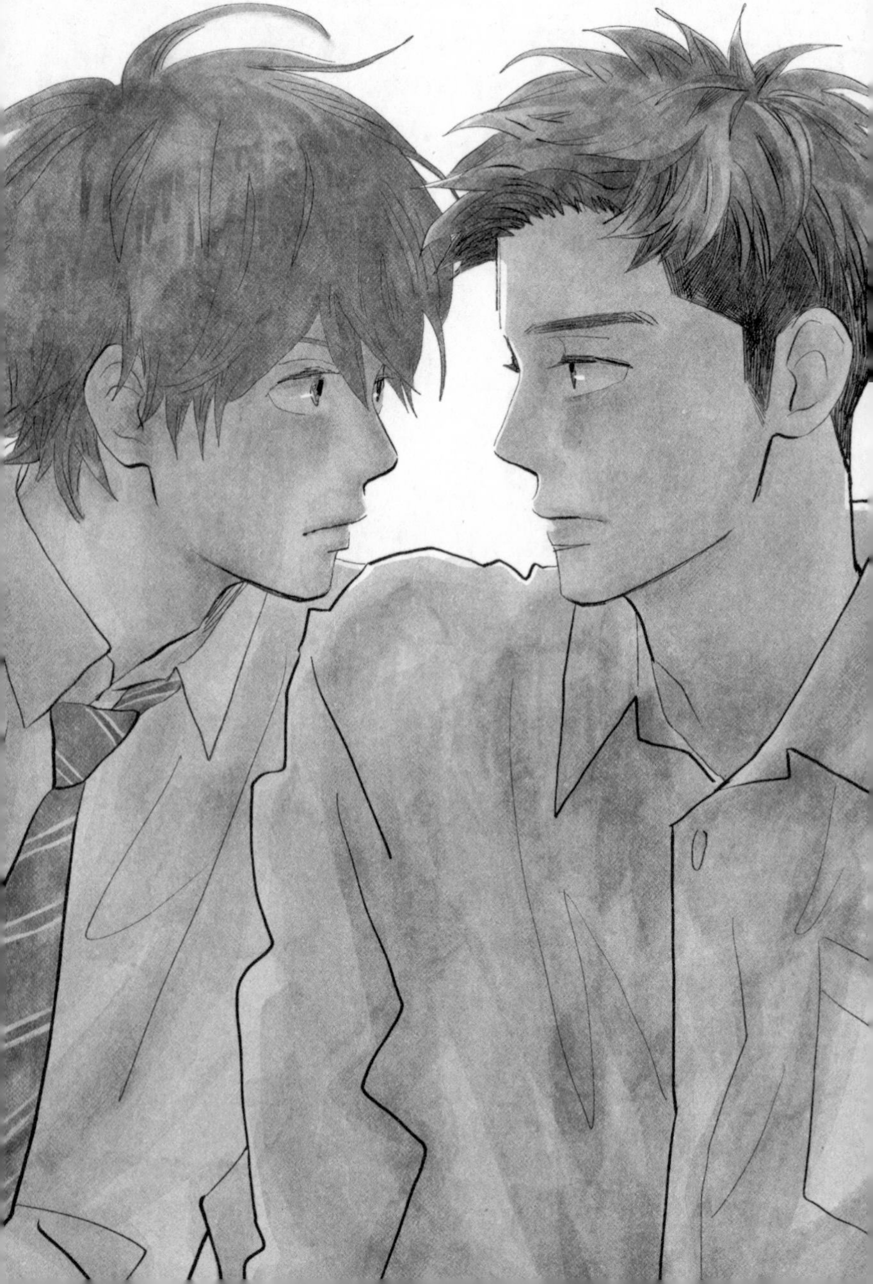

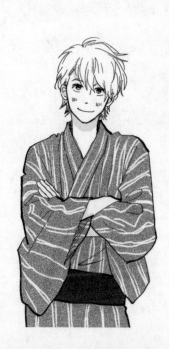

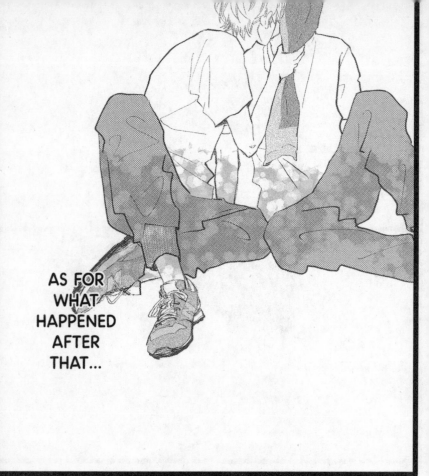

AS FOR
WHAT
HAPPENED
AFTER
THAT...

My Love
Mix-Up!

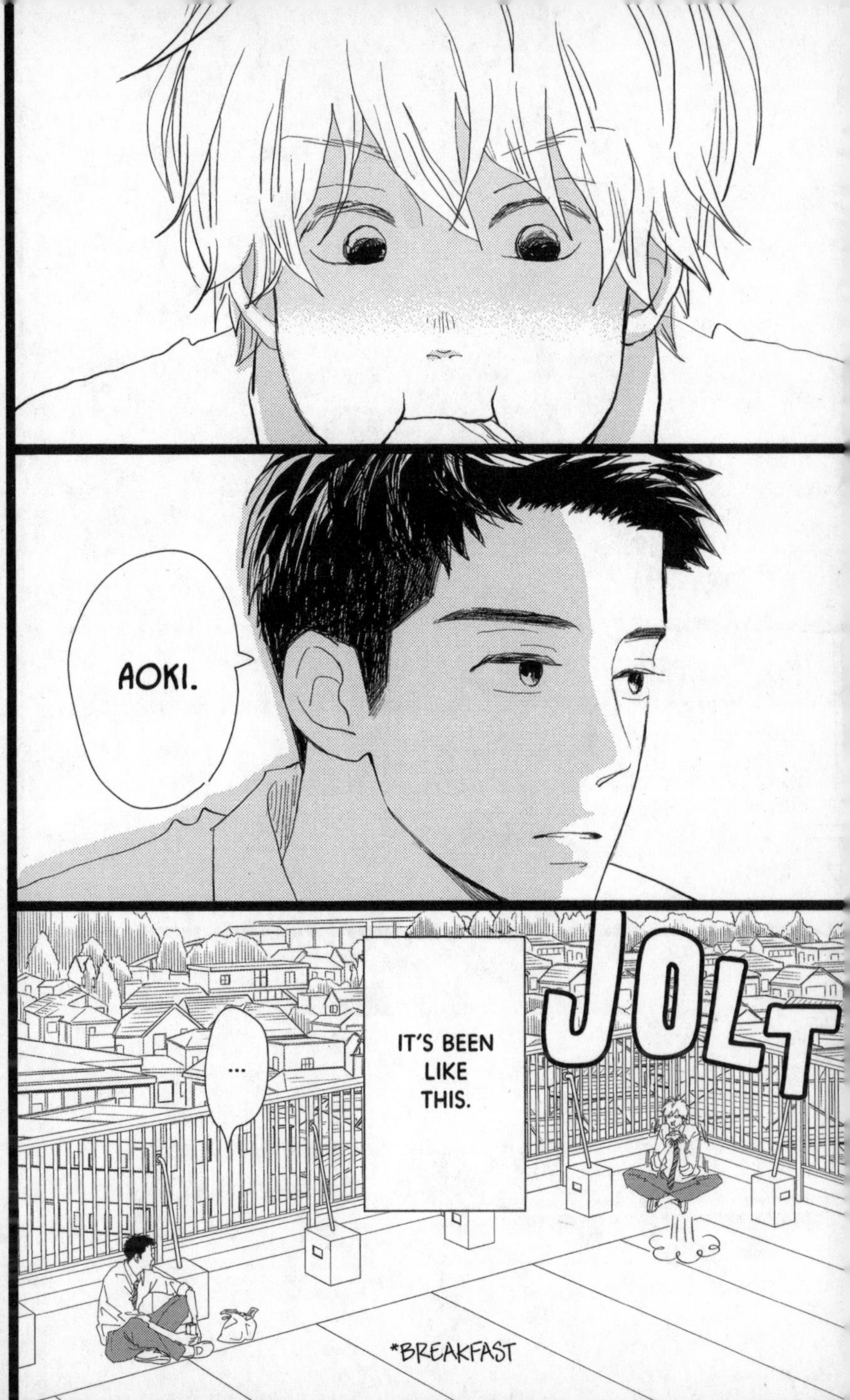
AOKI.
JOLT
IT'S BEEN LIKE THIS.
...
*BREAKFAST

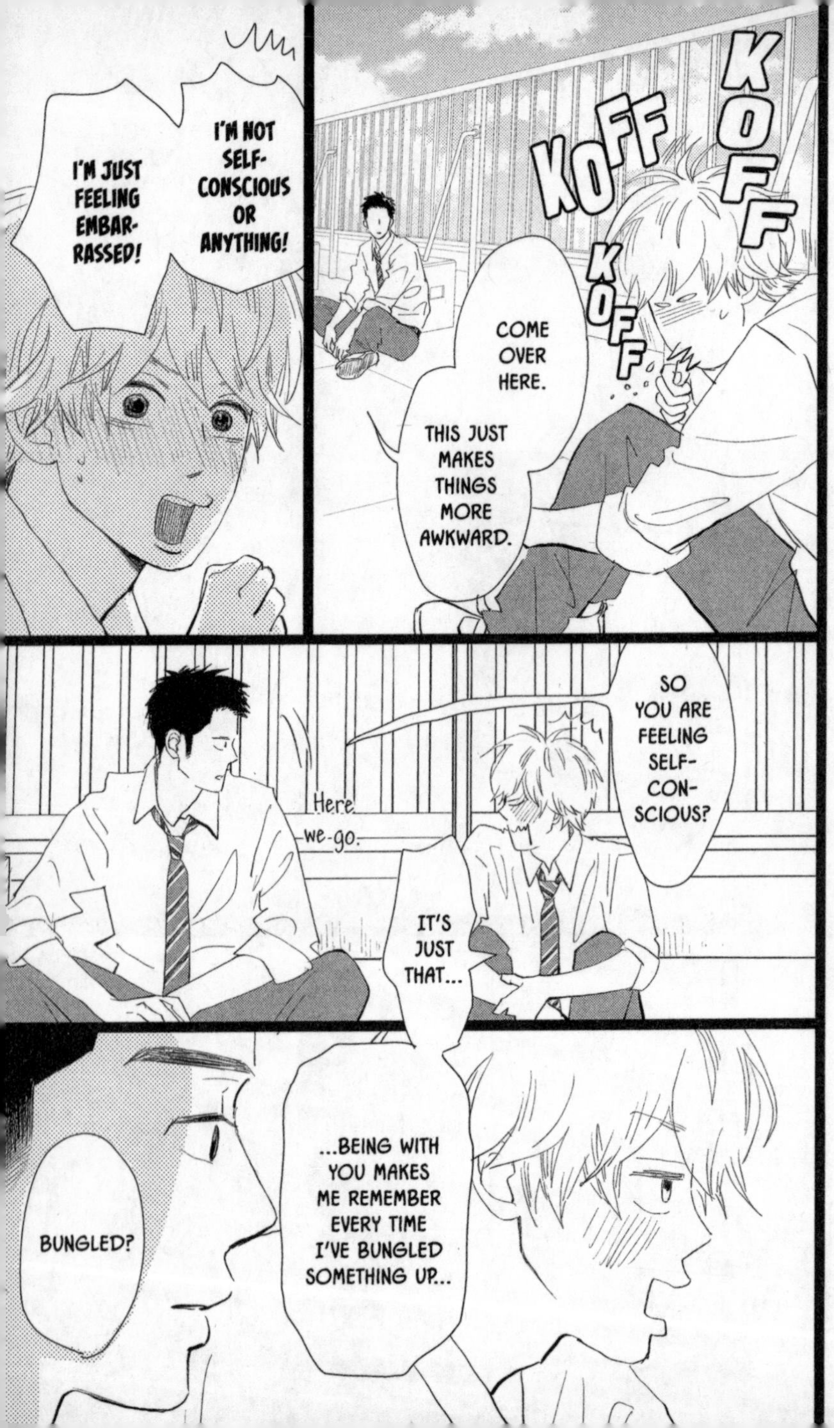
KOFF
KOFF
KOFF
KOFF
COME OVER HERE.
THIS JUST MAKES THINGS MORE AWKWARD.
I'M NOT SELF-CONSCIOUS OR ANYTHING!
I'M JUST FEELING EMBARRASSED!
SO YOU ARE FEELING SELF-CONSCIOUS?
Here we go.
IT'S JUST THAT...
...BEING WITH YOU MAKES ME REMEMBER EVERY TIME I'VE BUNGLED SOMETHING UP...
BUNGLED?

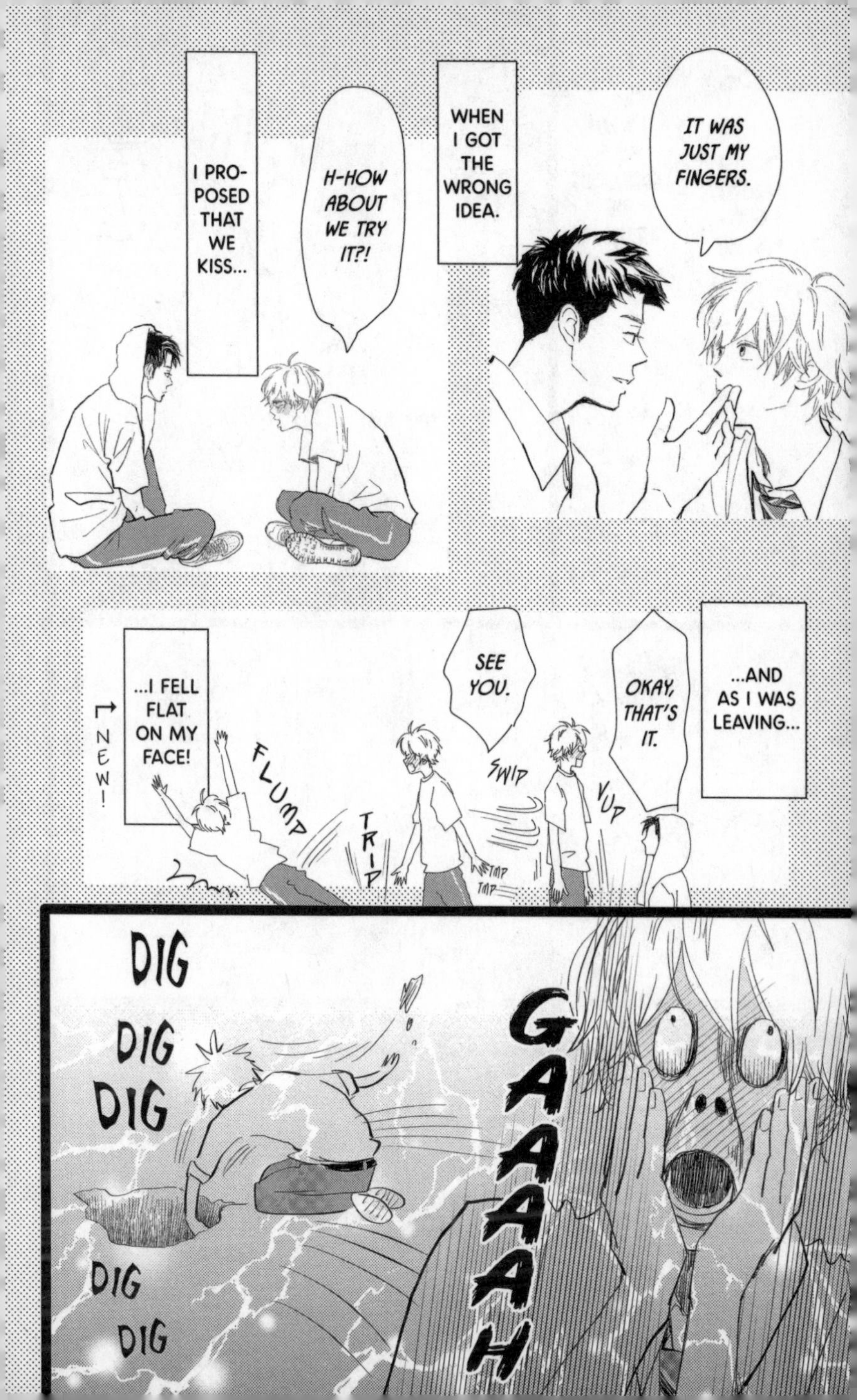
IT WAS JUST MY FINGERS.
WHEN I GOT THE WRONG IDEA.
H-HOW ABOUT WE TRY IT?!
I PROPOSED THAT WE KISS...
...AND AS I WAS LEAVING...
OKAY, THAT'S IT.
VUP
SEE YOU.
SWIP
TMP TMP
TRIP
FLUMP
...I FELL FLAT ON MY FACE!
NEW!
GAAAAAH
DIG
DIG
DIG
DIG
DIG

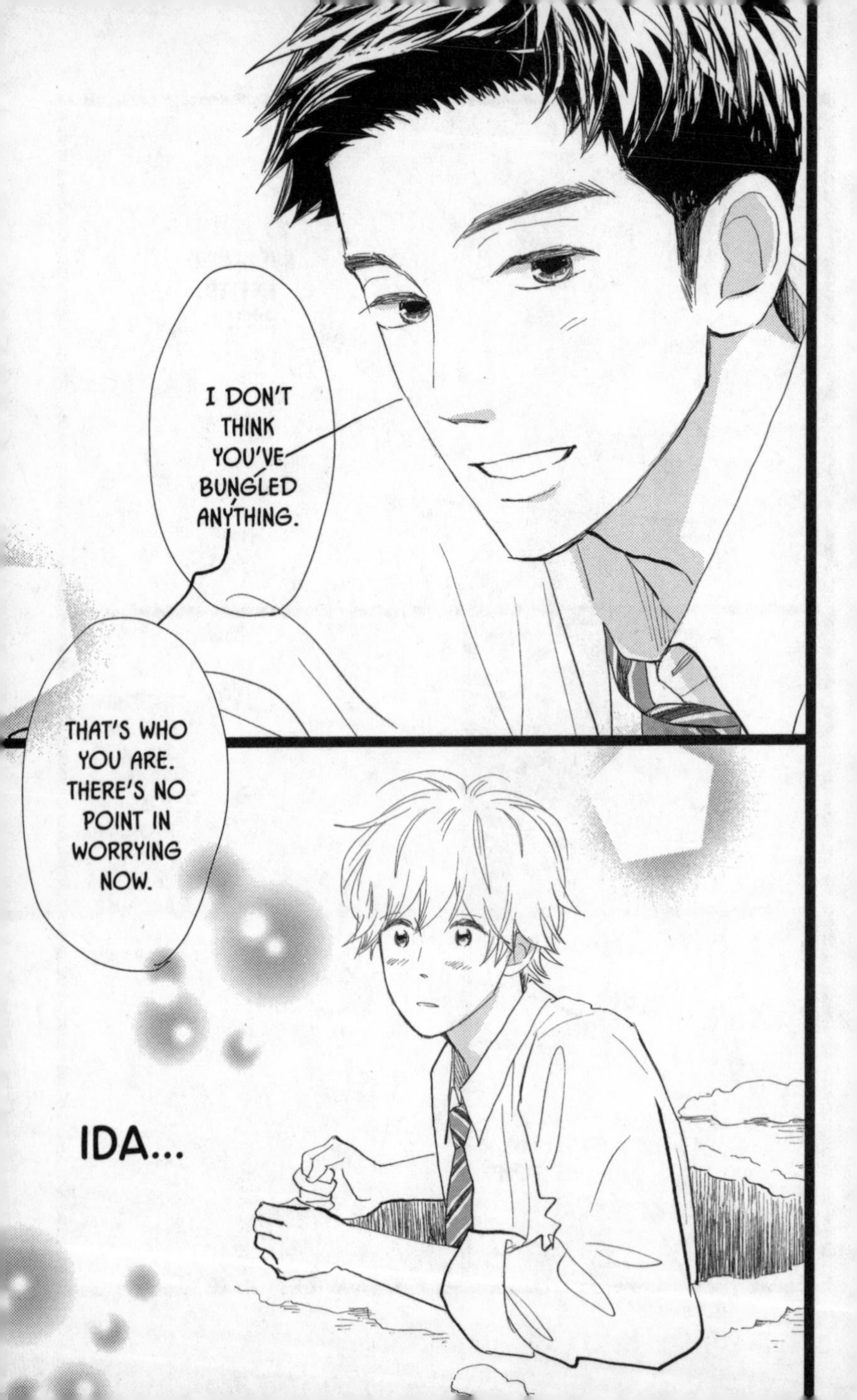
I DON'T THINK YOU'VE BUNGLED ANYTHING.
THAT'S WHO YOU ARE. THERE'S NO POINT IN WORRYING NOW.
IDA...

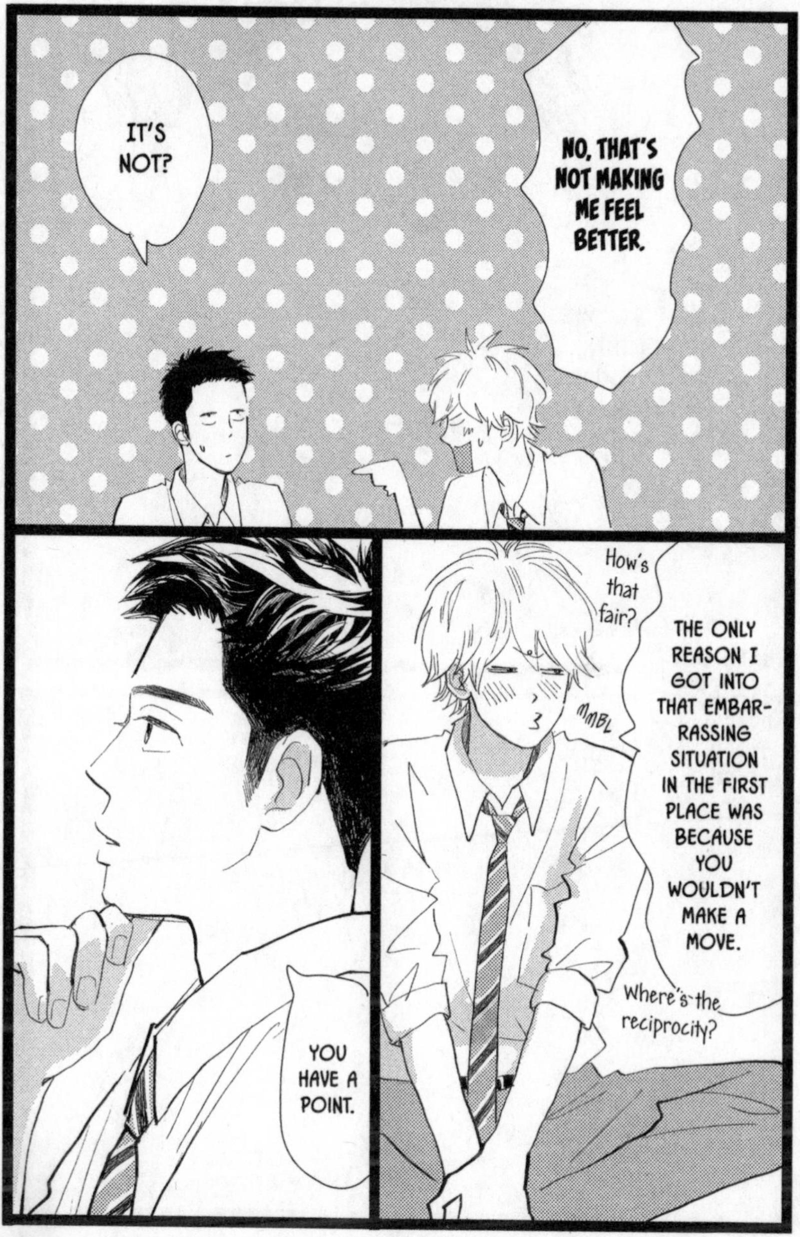
NO, THAT'S NOT MAKING ME FEEL BETTER.
IT'S NOT?
How's that fair?
THE ONLY REASON I GOT INTO THAT EMBAR-RASSING SITUATION IN THE FIRST PLACE WAS BECAUSE YOU WOULDN'T MAKE A MOVE.
MMBL
Where's the reciprocity?
YOU HAVE A POINT.

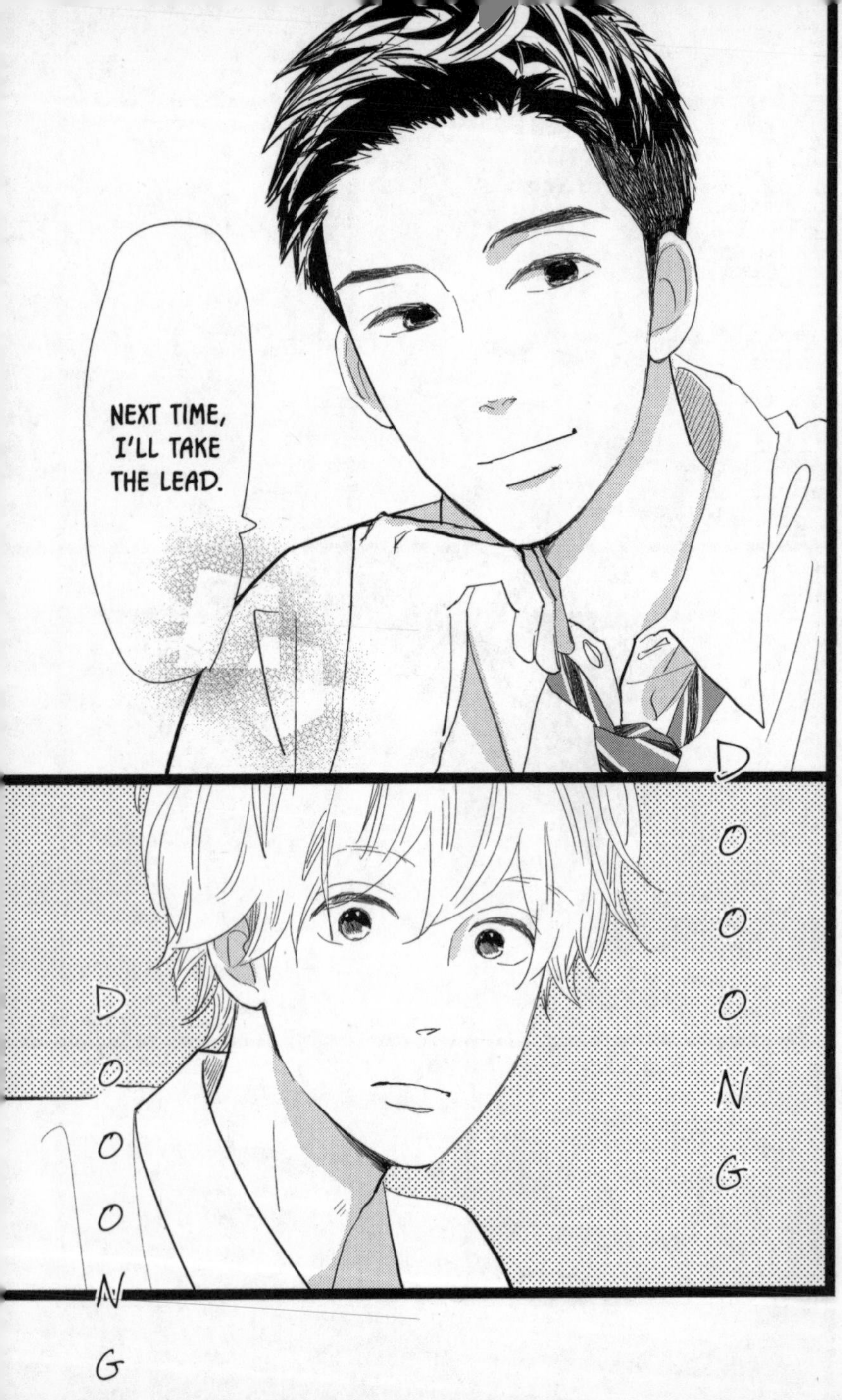
NEXT TIME, I'LL TAKE THE LEAD.
DOOOONG
DOOOONG

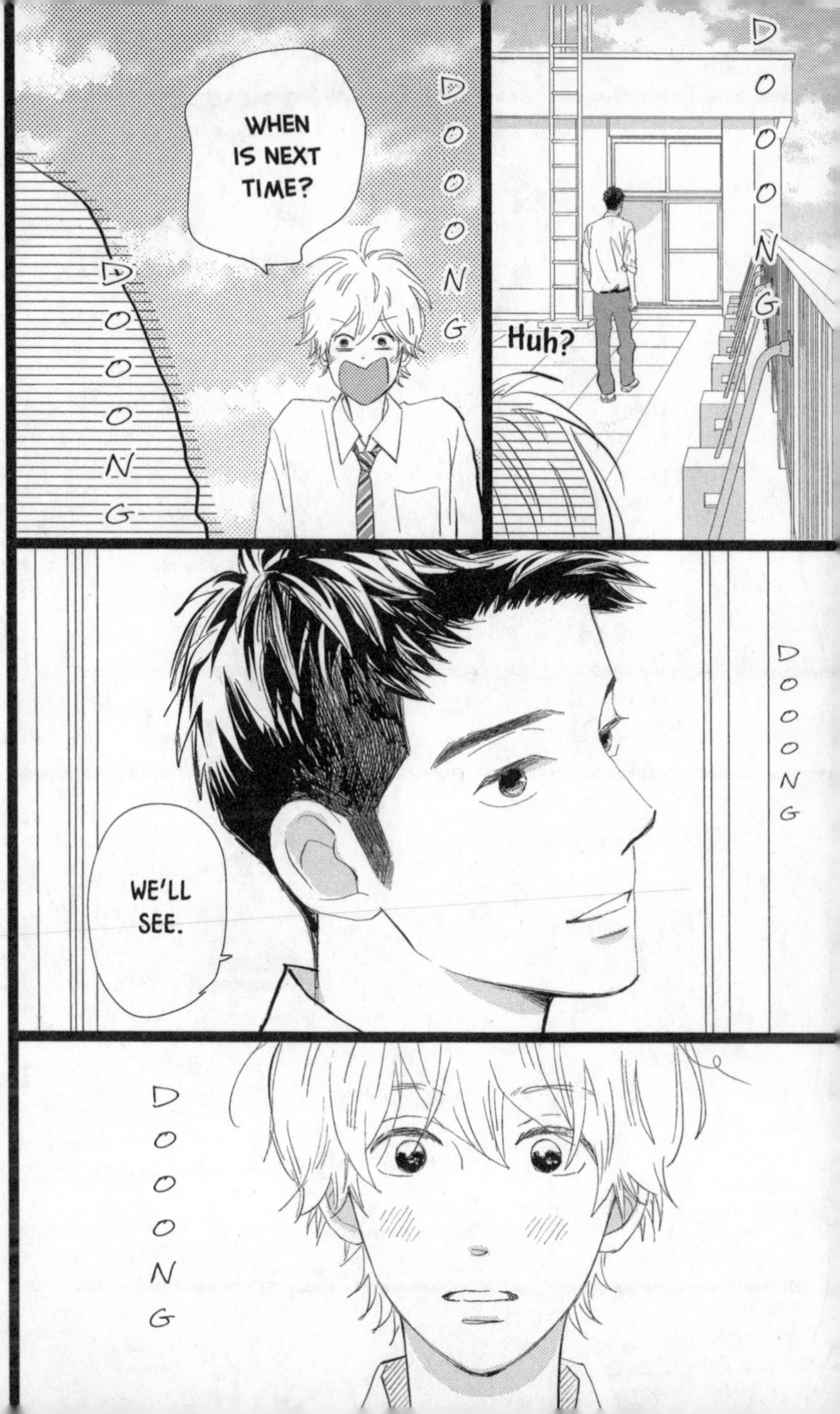
DOOOONG
Huh?
DOOOONG
WHEN IS NEXT TIME?
DOOOONG
DOOOONG
WE'LL SEE.
DOOOONG

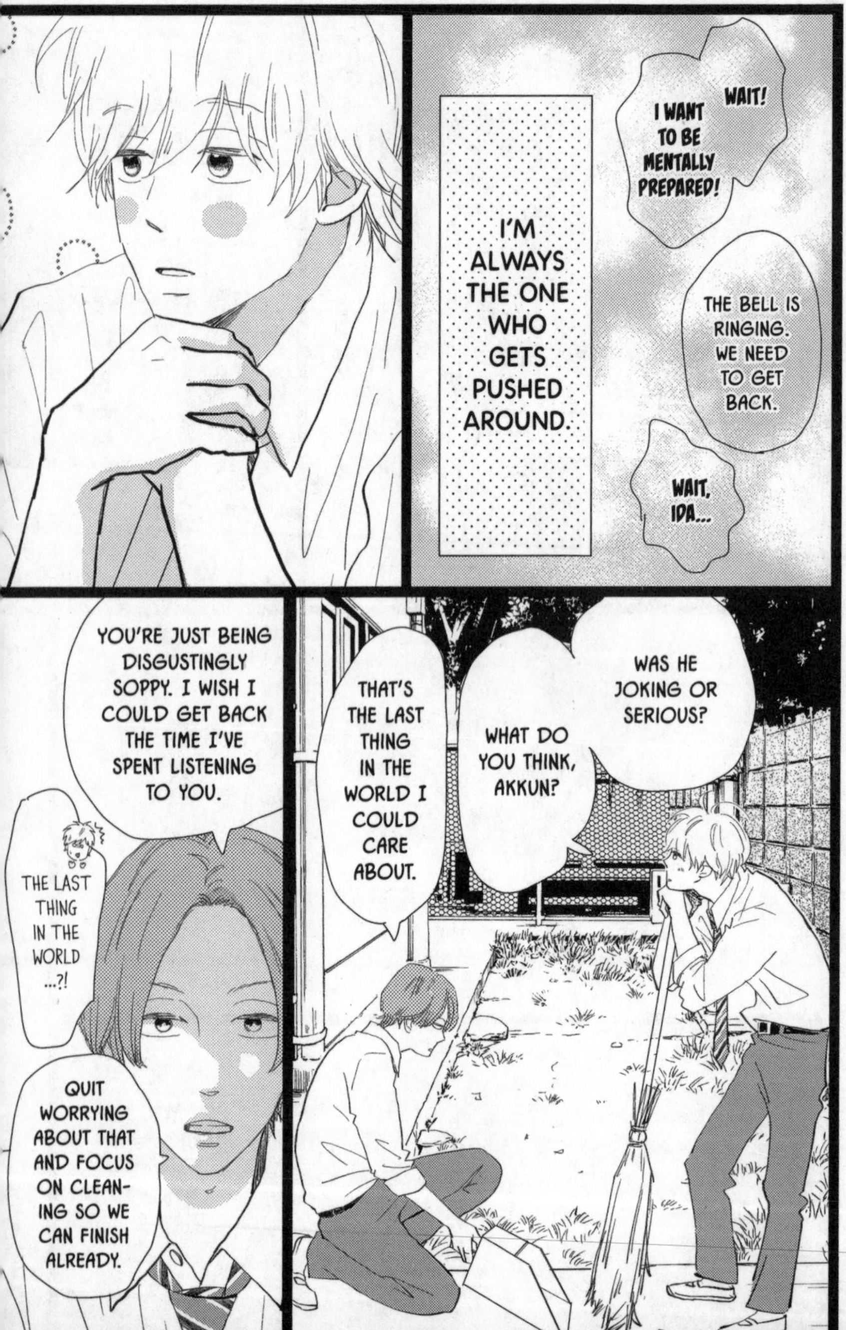
WAIT!
I WANT TO BE MENTALLY PREPARED!
THE BELL IS RINGING. WE NEED TO GET BACK.
WAIT, IDA...
I'M ALWAYS THE ONE WHO GETS PUSHED AROUND.
WAS HE JOKING OR SERIOUS?
WHAT DO YOU THINK, AKKUN?
THAT'S THE LAST THING IN THE WORLD I COULD CARE ABOUT.
YOU'RE JUST BEING DISGUSTINGLY SOPPY. I WISH I COULD GET BACK THE TIME I'VE SPENT LISTENING TO YOU.
THE LAST THING IN THE WORLD ...?!
QUIT WORRYING ABOUT THAT AND FOCUS ON CLEAN-ING SO WE CAN FINISH ALREADY.

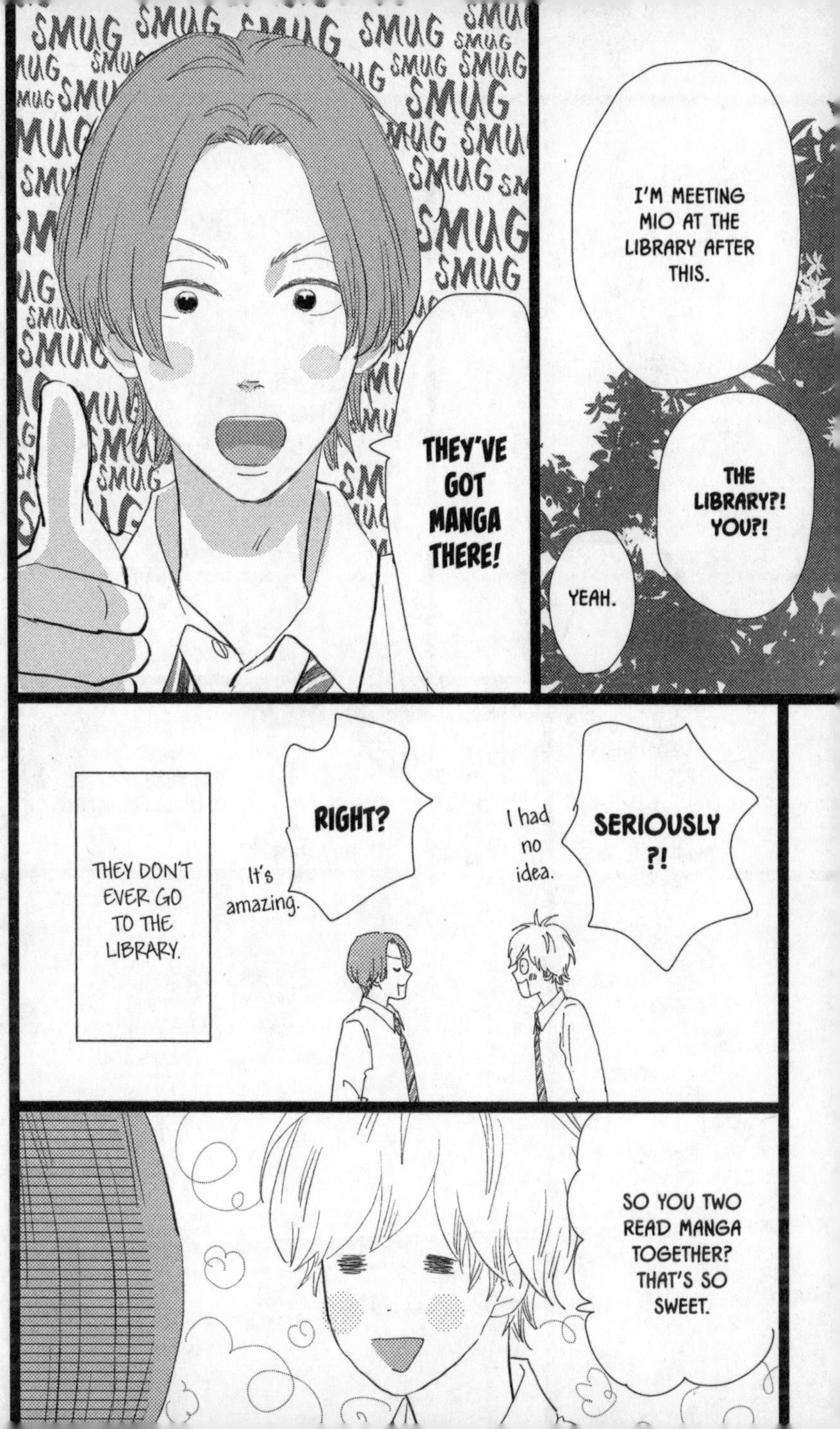
I'M MEETING MIO AT THE LIBRARY AFTER THIS.
THE LIBRARY?! YOU?!
YEAH.
THEY'VE GOT MANGA THERE!
SMUG SMUG SMUG SMUG
SERIOUSLY?!
I had no idea.
RIGHT?
It's amazing.
THEY DON'T EVER GO TO THE LIBRARY.
SO YOU TWO READ MANGA TOGETHER? THAT'S SO SWEET.

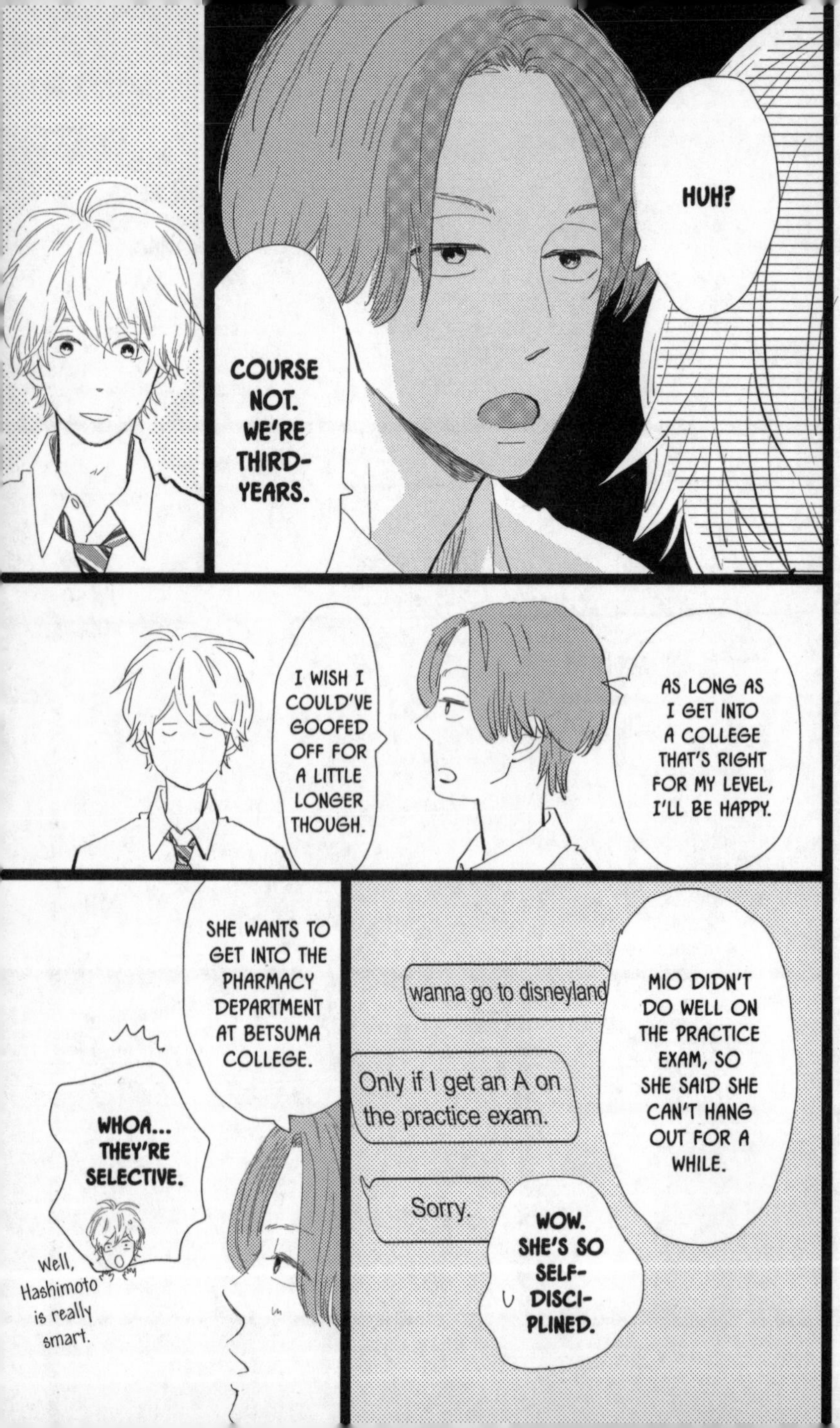
HUH?
COURSE NOT. WE'RE THIRD-YEARS.
AS LONG AS I GET INTO A COLLEGE THAT'S RIGHT FOR MY LEVEL, I'LL BE HAPPY.
I WISH I COULD'VE GOOFED OFF FOR A LITTLE LONGER THOUGH.
MIO DIDN'T DO WELL ON THE PRACTICE EXAM, SO SHE SAID SHE CAN'T HANG OUT FOR A WHILE.
wanna go to disneyland
Only if I get an A on the practice exam.
Sorry.
WOW. SHE'S SO SELF-DISCI-PLINED.
SHE WANTS TO GET INTO THE PHARMACY DEPARTMENT AT BETSUMA COLLEGE.
WHOA... THEY'RE SELECTIVE.
Well, Hashimoto is really smart.

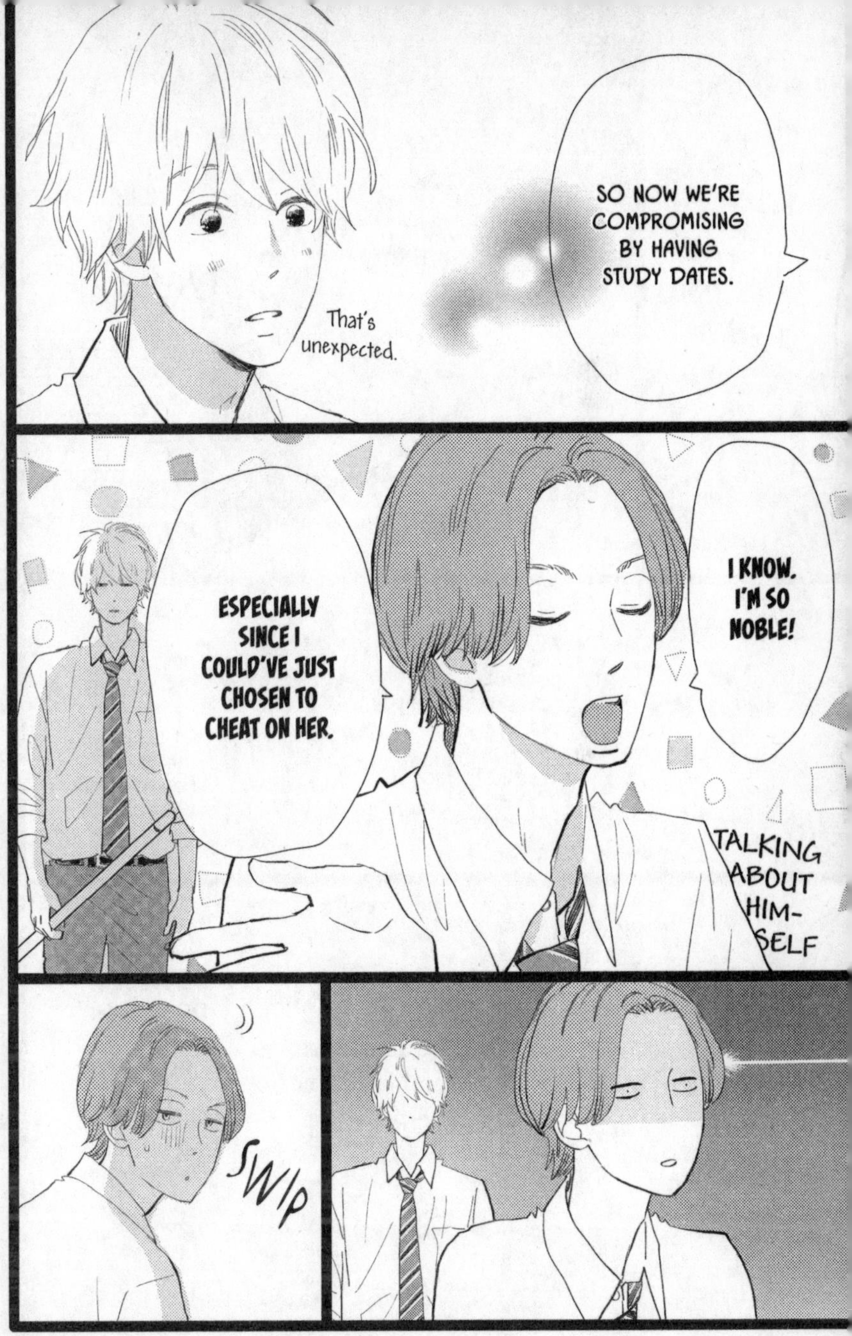
SO NOW WE'RE COMPROMISING BY HAVING STUDY DATES.
That's unexpected.
I KNOW. I'M SO NOBLE!
ESPECIALLY SINCE I COULD'VE JUST CHOSEN TO CHEAT ON HER.
TALKING ABOUT HIM-SELF
SWIP

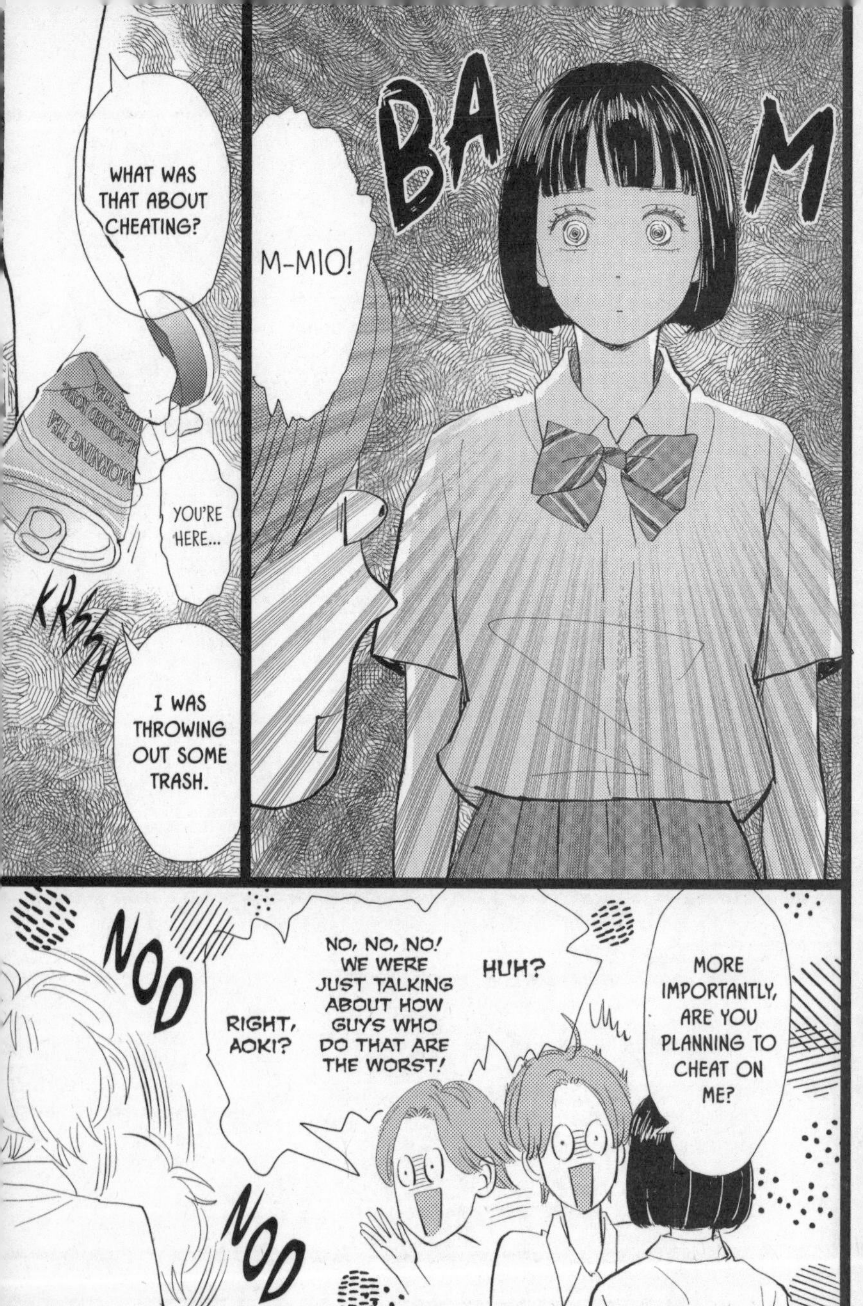
BAM
M-MIO!
WHAT WAS THAT ABOUT CHEATING?
YOU'RE HERE...
KRSSH
I WAS THROWING OUT SOME TRASH.
MORE IMPORTANTLY, ARE YOU PLANNING TO CHEAT ON ME?
HUH?
NO, NO, NO! WE WERE JUST TALKING ABOUT HOW GUYS WHO DO THAT ARE THE WORST!
RIGHT, AOKI?
NOD
NOD

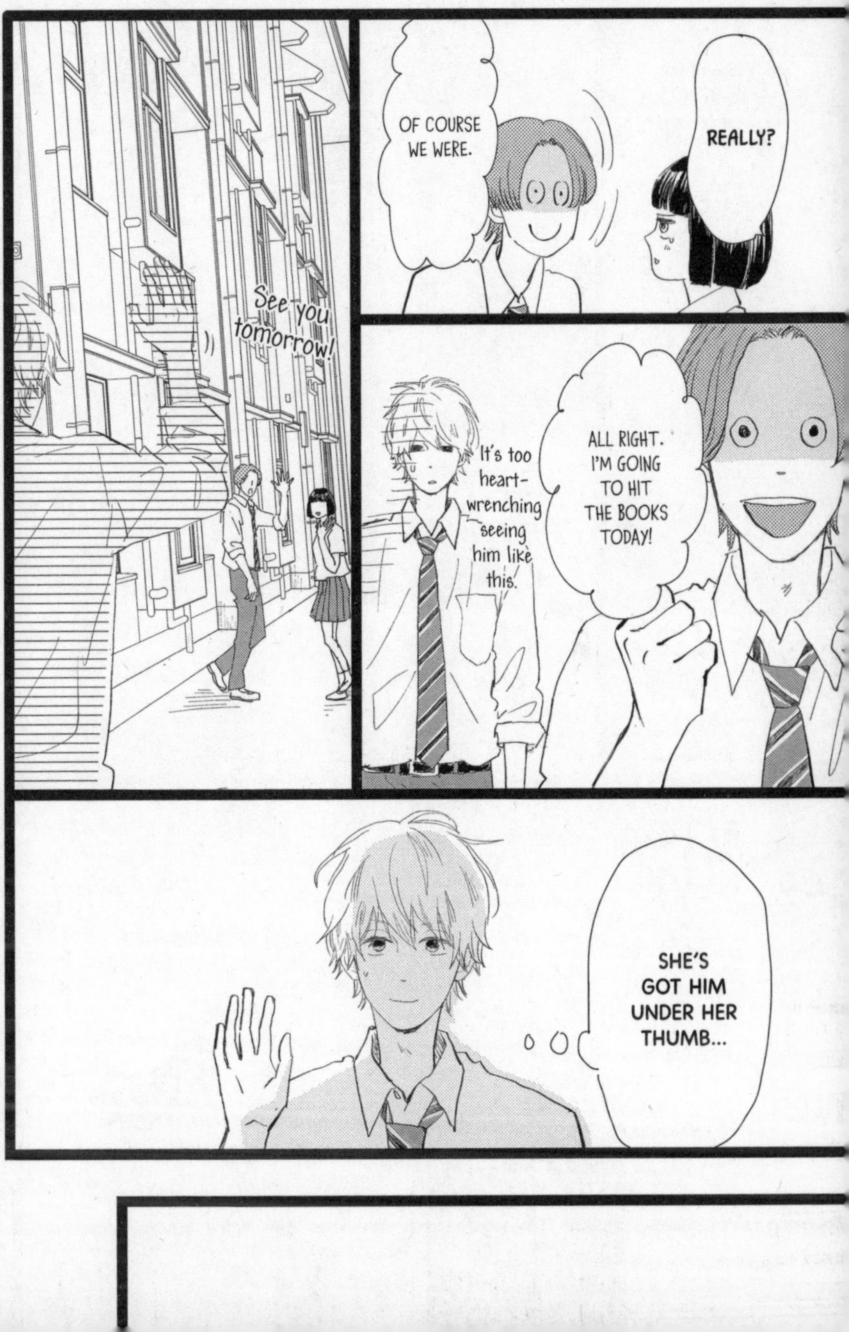
REALLY?
OF COURSE WE WERE.
ALL RIGHT. I'M GOING TO HIT THE BOOKS TODAY!
It's too heart-wrenching seeing him like this.
See you tomorrow!
SHE'S GOT HIM UNDER HER THUMB...

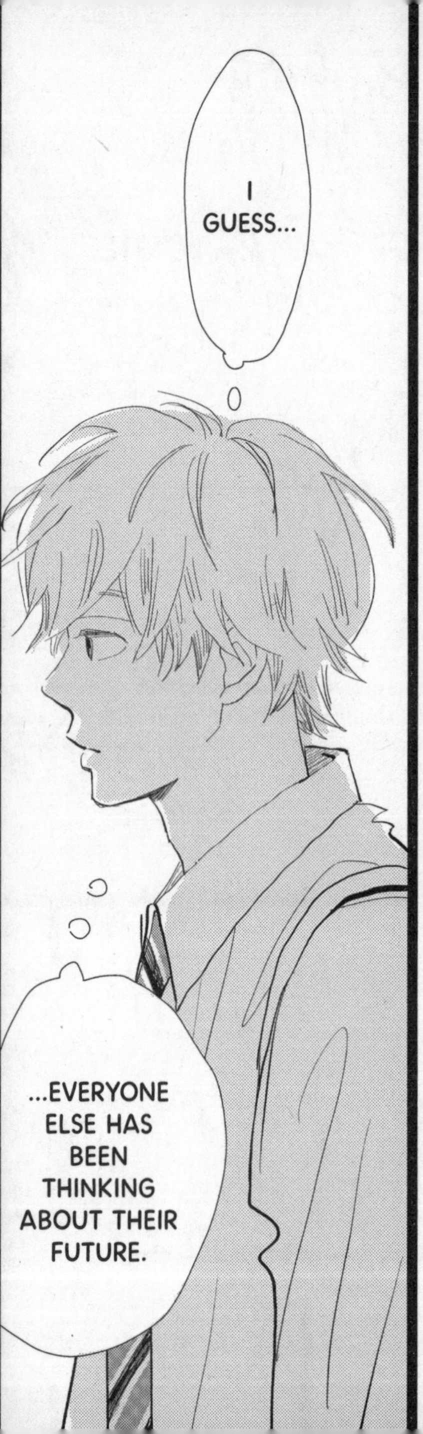
I GUESS...
...EVERYONE ELSE HAS BEEN THINKING ABOUT THEIR FUTURE.

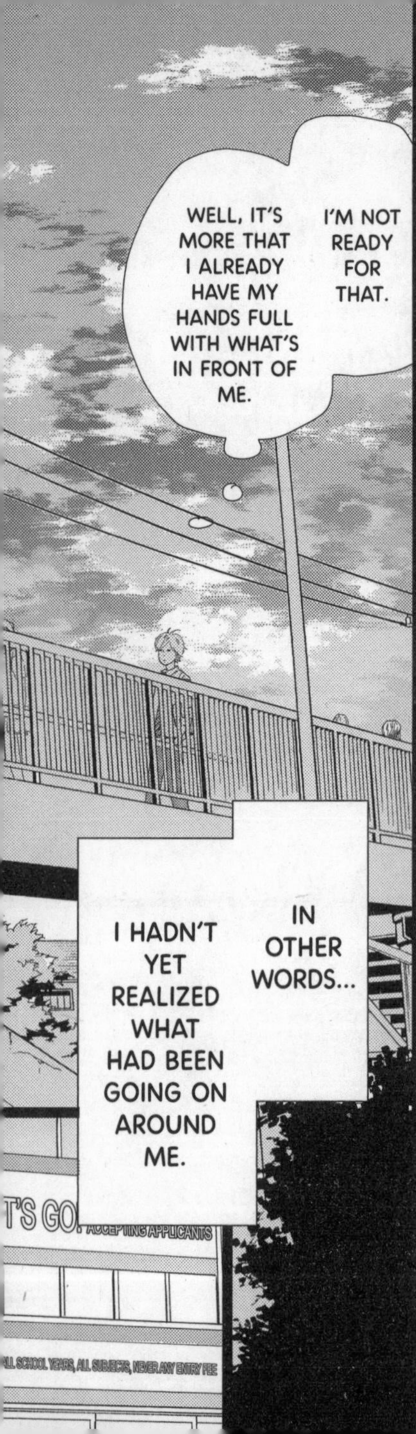
I'M NOT READY FOR THAT.
WELL, IT'S MORE THAT I ALREADY HAVE MY HANDS FULL WITH WHAT'S IN FRONT OF ME.
IN OTHER WORDS...
I HADN'T YET REALIZED WHAT HAD BEEN GOING ON AROUND ME.
T'S GO
ACCEPTING APPLICANTS
LL SCHOOL YEARS, ALL SUBJECTS, NEVER ANY ENTRY FEE

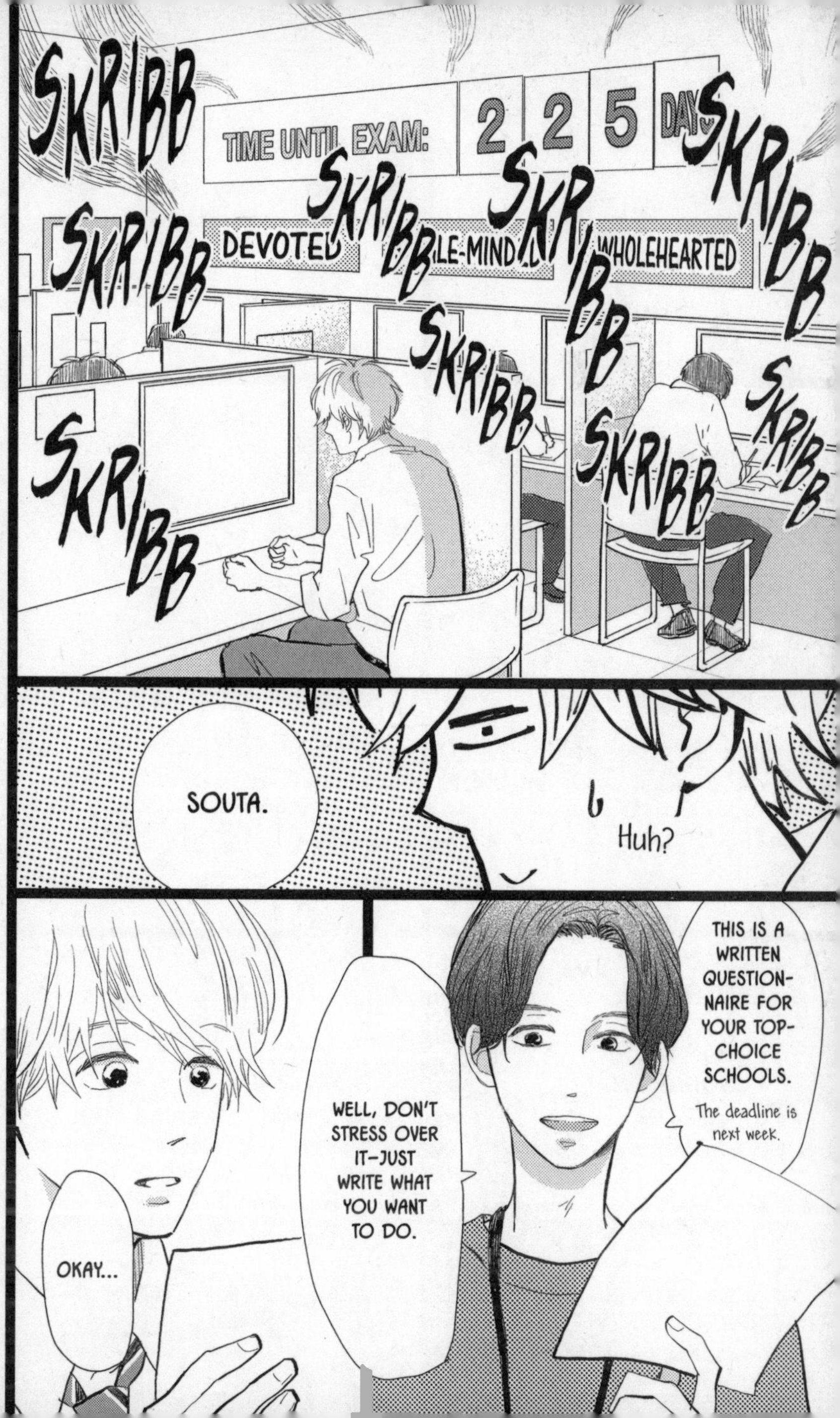
SKRIBB
TIME UNTIL EXAM:
2 2 5
SKRIBB
SKRIBB
SKRIBB
SKRIBB
DEVOTED
WHOLEHEARTED
SKRIBB
SKRIBB
SKRIBB
SKRIBB
SOUTA.
Huh?
THIS IS A WRITTEN QUESTIONNAIRE FOR YOUR TOP-CHOICE SCHOOLS.
The deadline is next week.
WELL, DON'T STRESS OVER IT—JUST WRITE WHAT YOU WANT TO DO.
OKAY...

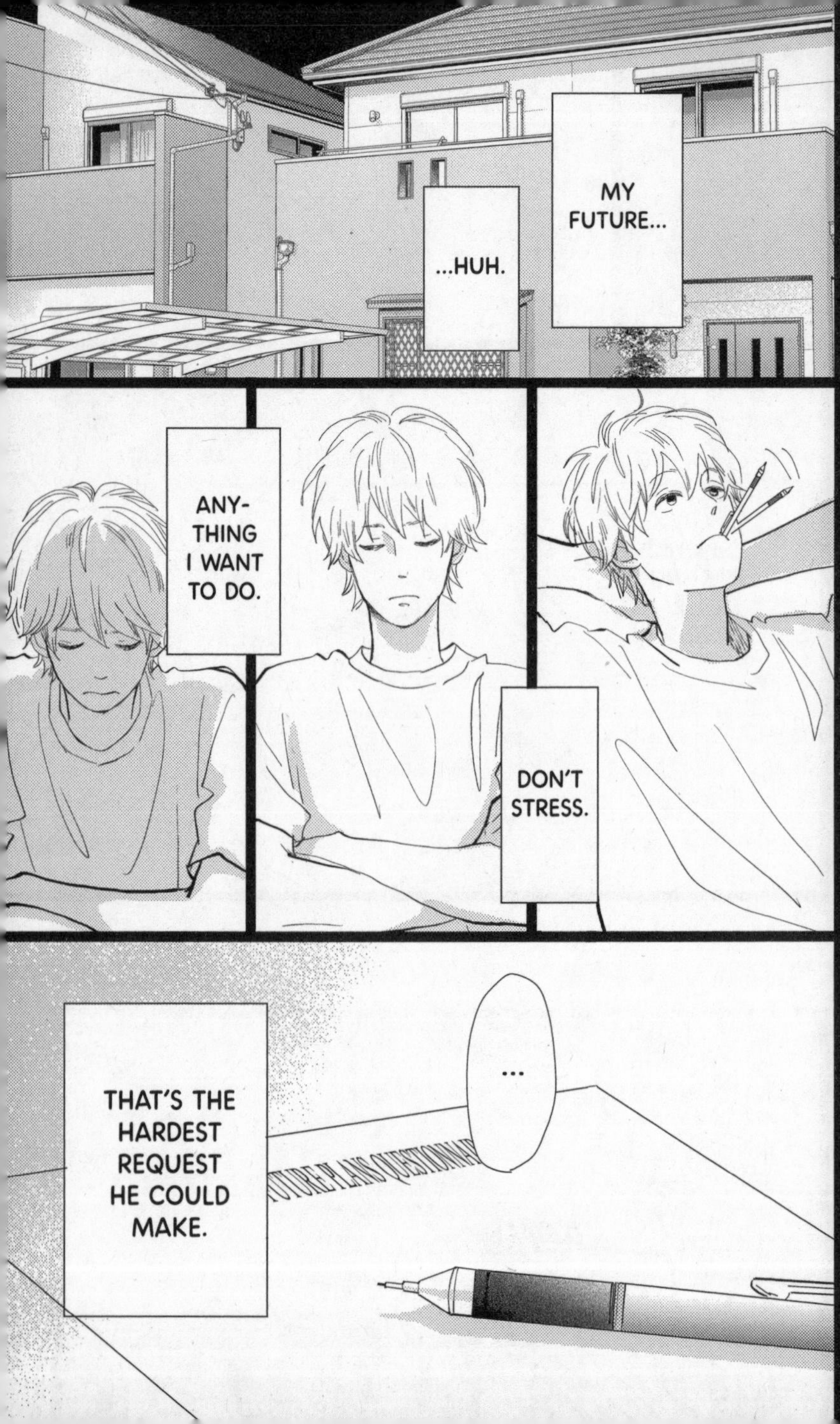
MY FUTURE...
...HUH.
DON'T STRESS.
ANY-THING I WANT TO DO.
...
THAT'S THE HARDEST REQUEST HE COULD MAKE.

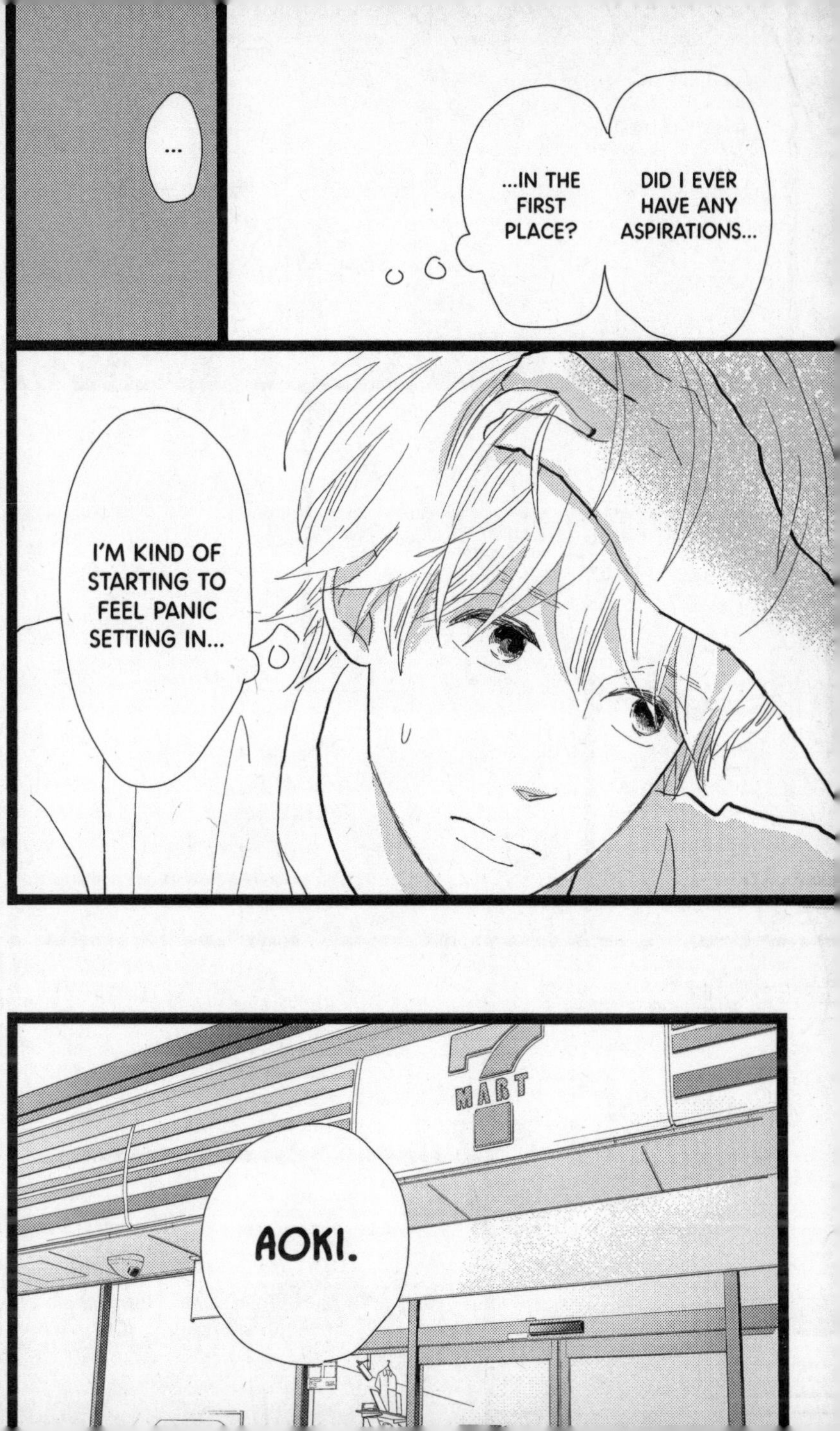
DID I EVER HAVE ANY ASPIRATIONS... ...IN THE FIRST PLACE?
...
I'M KIND OF STARTING TO FEEL PANIC SETTING IN...
MART
AOKI.

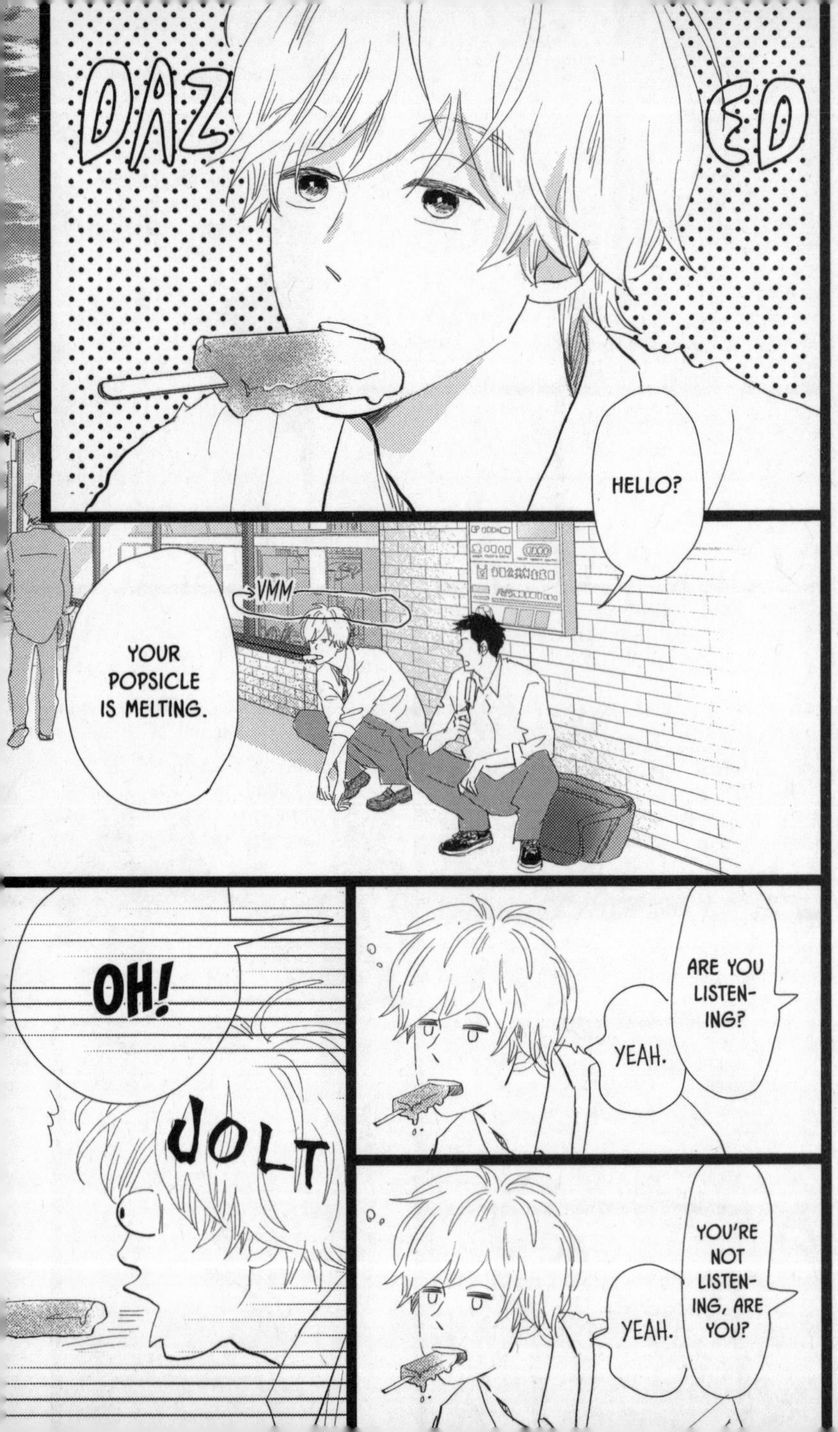
DAZED
HELLO?
VMM
YOUR POPSICLE IS MELTING.
ARE YOU LISTENING?
YEAH.
YOU'RE NOT LISTENING, ARE YOU?
YEAH.
OH!
JOLT

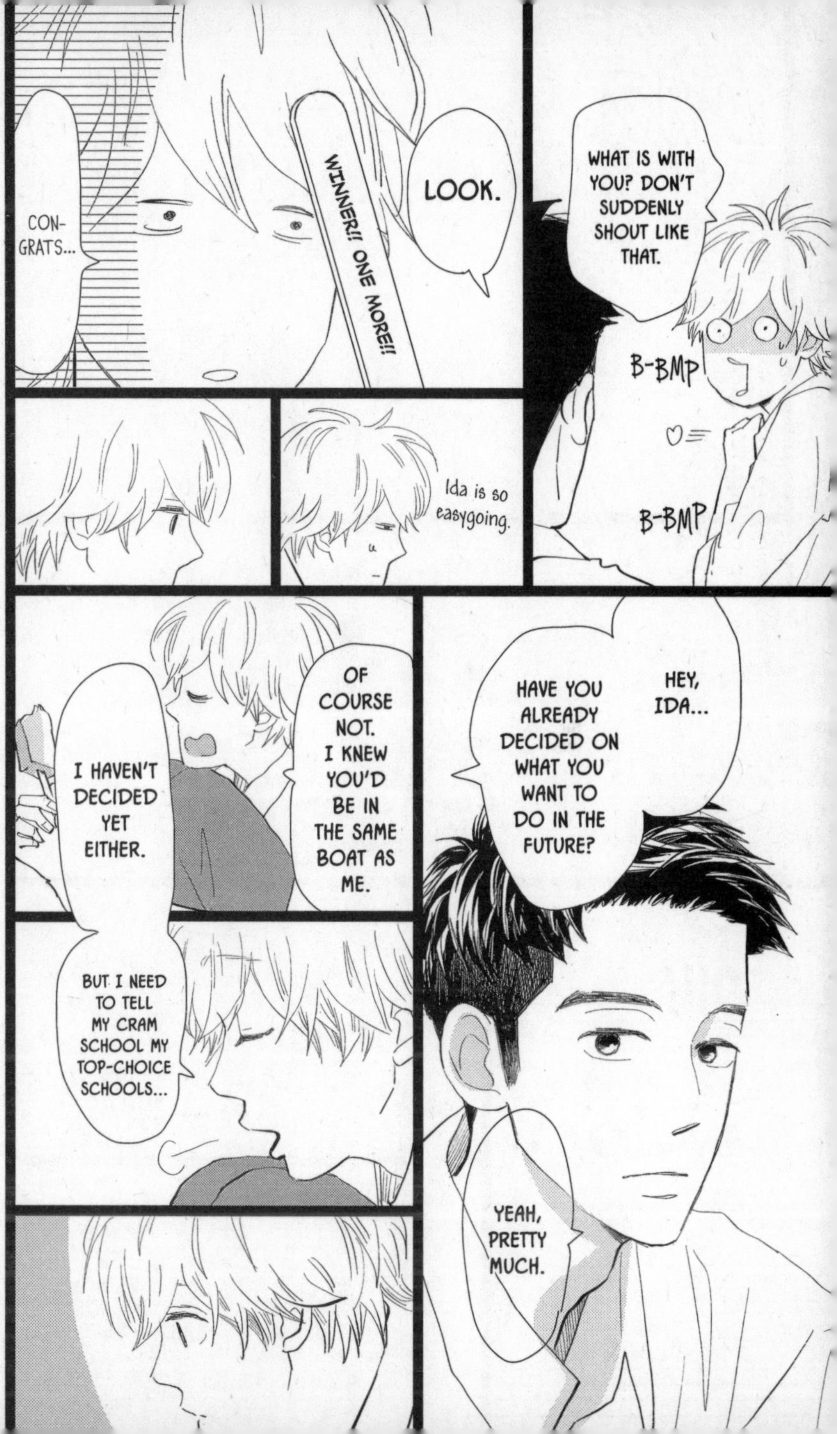
WHAT IS WITH YOU? DON'T SUDDENLY SHOUT LIKE THAT.
B-BMP
B-BMP
LOOK.
WINNER!! ONE MORE!!
CON-GRATS...
Ida is so easygoing.
HEY, IDA...
HAVE YOU ALREADY DECIDED ON WHAT YOU WANT TO DO IN THE FUTURE?
YEAH, PRETTY MUCH.
OF COURSE NOT. I KNEW YOU'D BE IN THE SAME BOAT AS ME.
I HAVEN'T DECIDED YET EITHER.
BUT I NEED TO TELL MY CRAM SCHOOL MY TOP-CHOICE SCHOOLS...

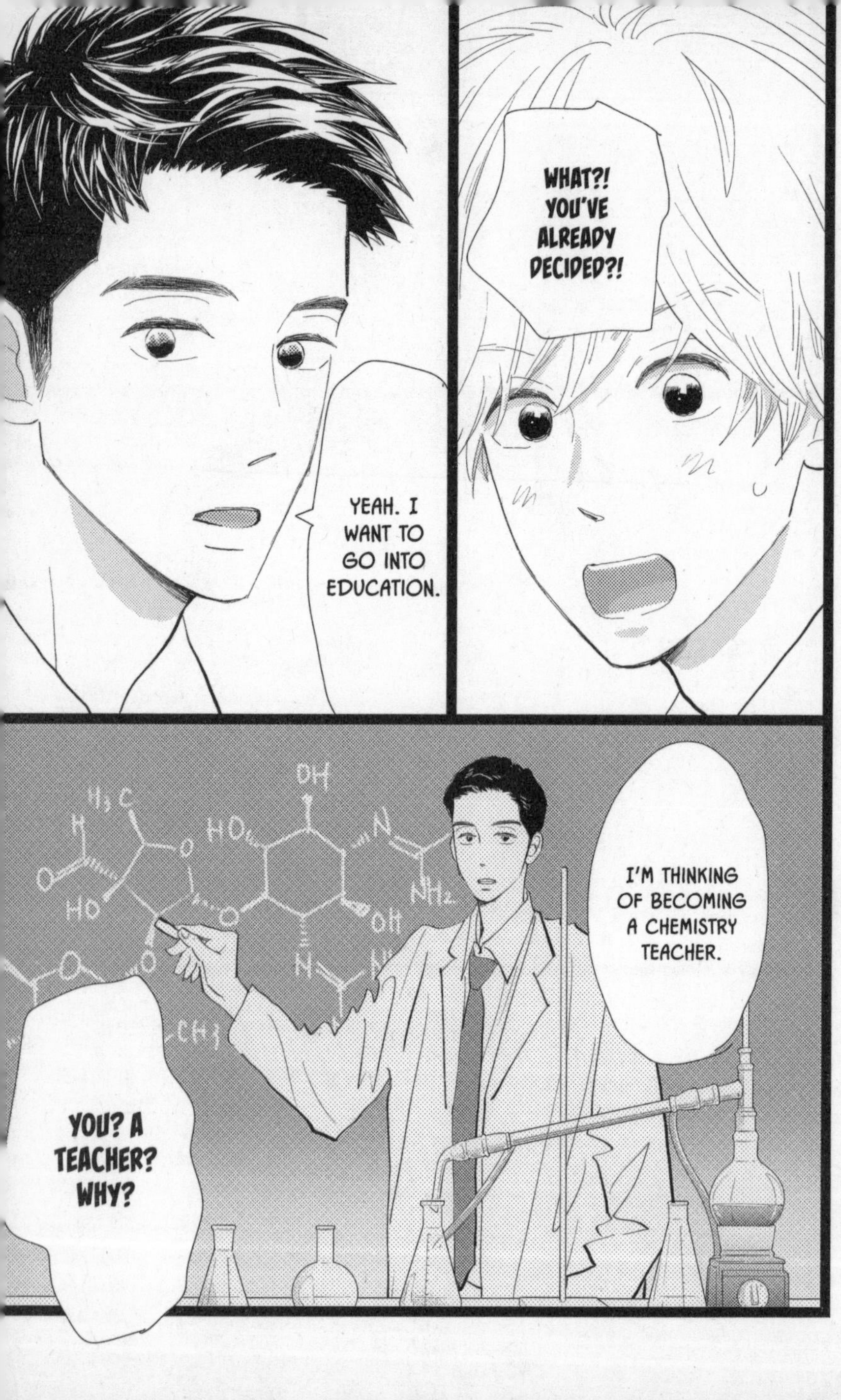
WHAT?! YOU'VE ALREADY DECIDED?!
YEAH. I WANT TO GO INTO EDUCATION.
I'M THINKING OF BECOMING A CHEMISTRY TEACHER.
YOU? A TEACHER? WHY?

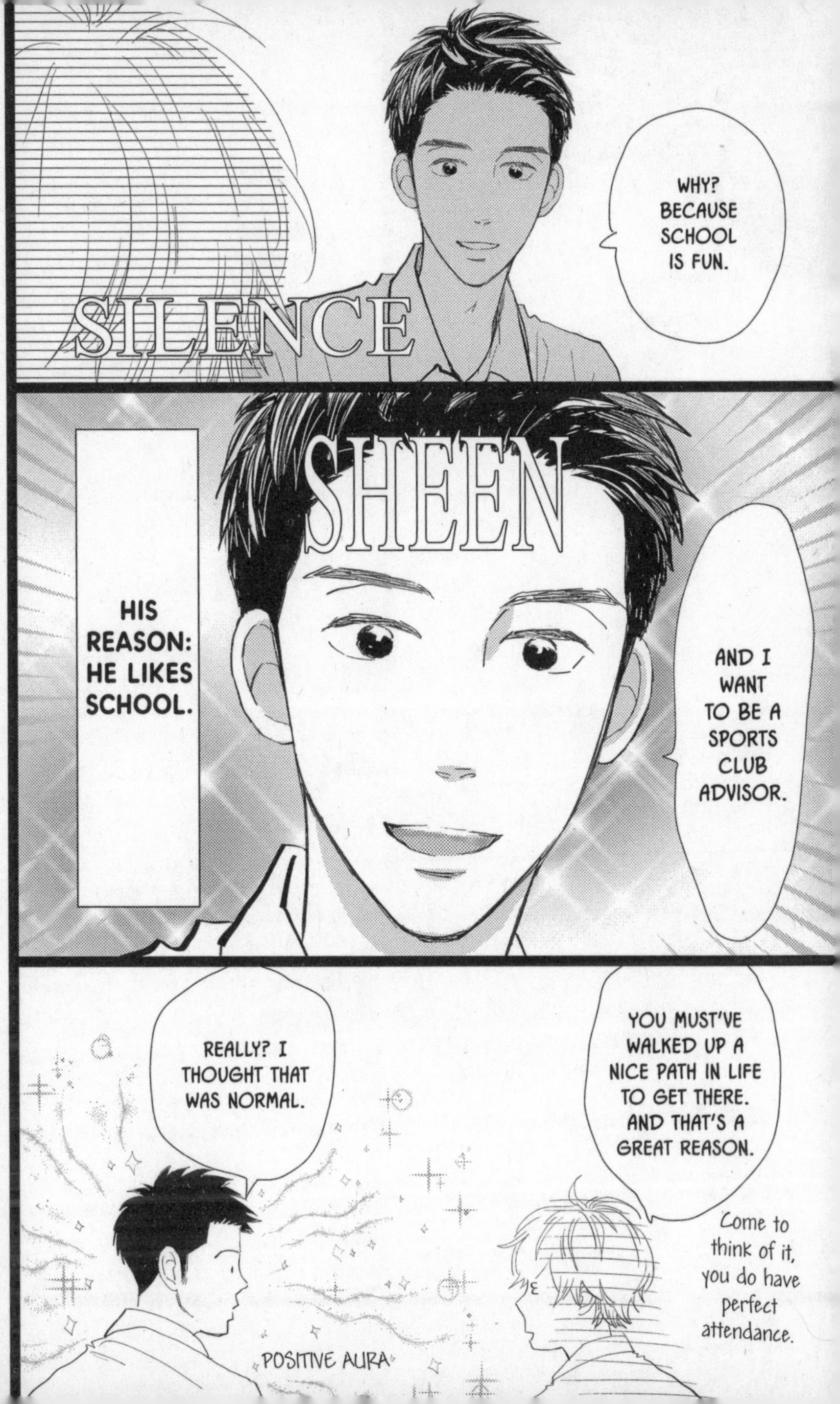
WHY? BECAUSE SCHOOL IS FUN.
SILENCE
AND I WANT TO BE A SPORTS CLUB ADVISOR.
SHEEN
HIS REASON: HE LIKES SCHOOL.
YOU MUST'VE WALKED UP A NICE PATH IN LIFE TO GET THERE. AND THAT'S A GREAT REASON.
REALLY? I THOUGHT THAT WAS NORMAL.
Come to think of it, you do have perfect attendance.
POSITIVE AURA

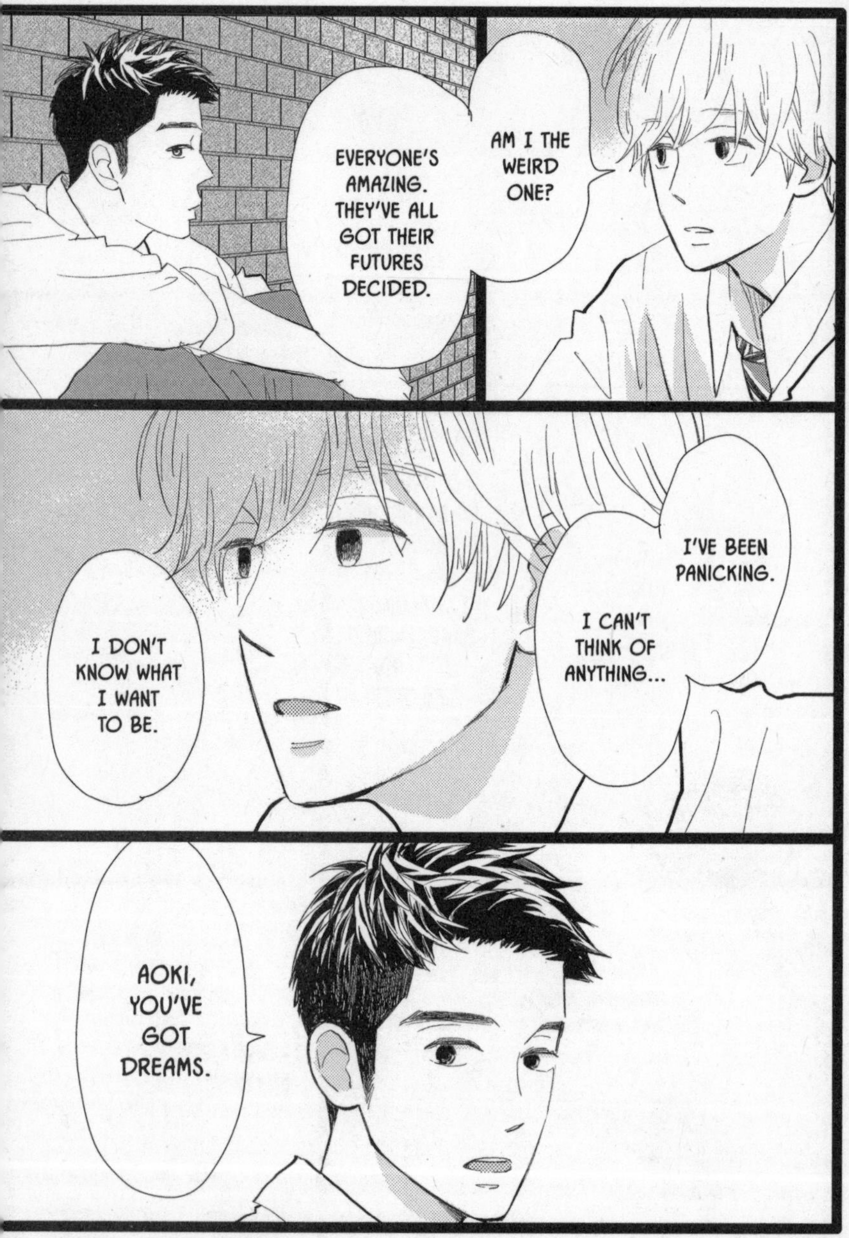
AM I THE WEIRD ONE?
EVERYONE'S AMAZING. THEY'VE ALL GOT THEIR FUTURES DECIDED.
I'VE BEEN PANICKING.
I CAN'T THINK OF ANYTHING...
I DON'T KNOW WHAT I WANT TO BE.
AOKI, YOU'VE GOT DREAMS.

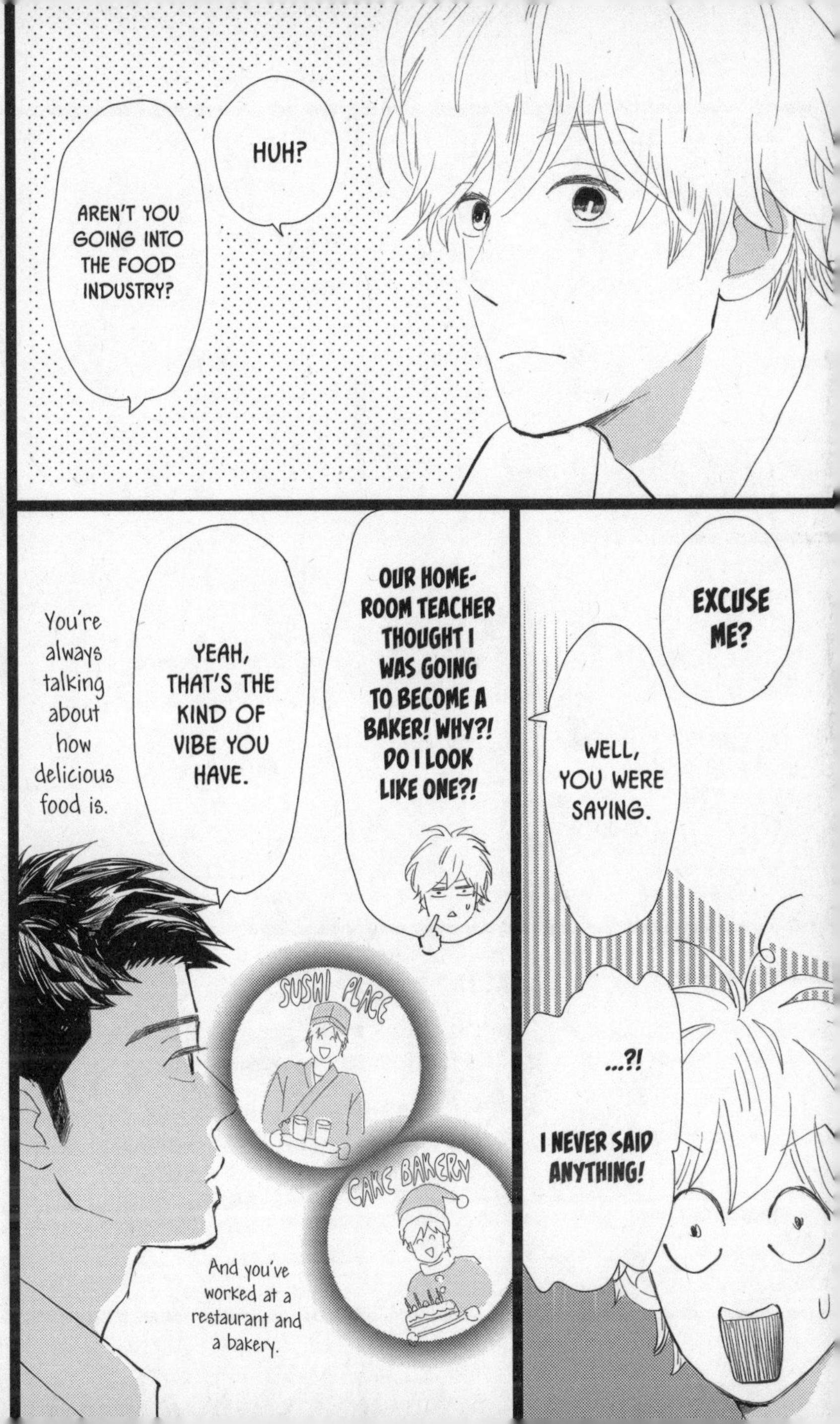
HUH?
AREN'T YOU GOING INTO THE FOOD INDUSTRY?
EXCUSE ME?
WELL, YOU WERE SAYING.
...?!
I NEVER SAID ANYTHING!
OUR HOME-ROOM TEACHER THOUGHT I WAS GOING TO BECOME A BAKER! WHY?! DO I LOOK LIKE ONE?!
YEAH, THAT'S THE KIND OF VIBE YOU HAVE.
You're always talking about how delicious food is.
SUSHI PLACE
CAKE BAKERY
And you've worked at a restaurant and a bakery.

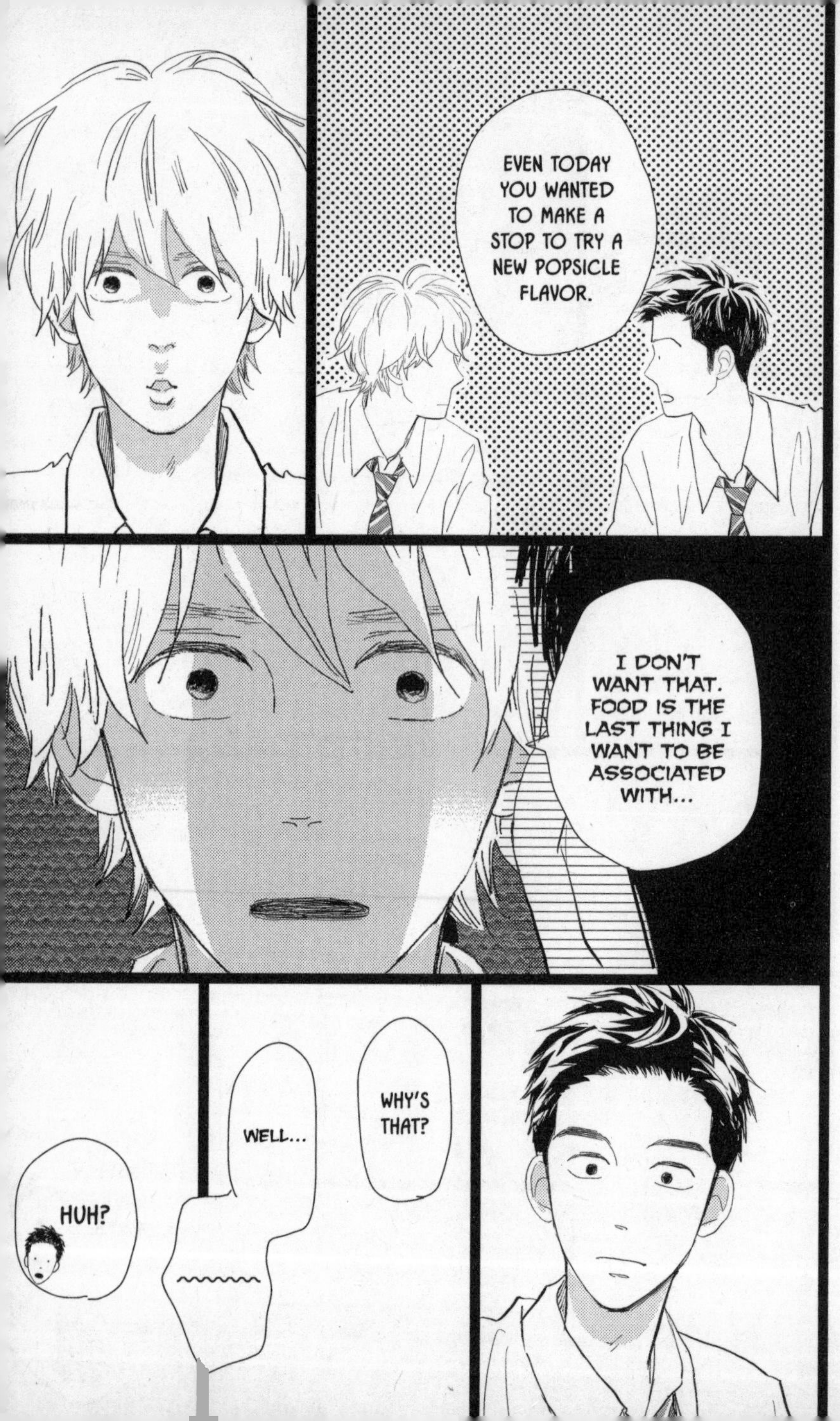
EVEN TODAY YOU WANTED TO MAKE A STOP TO TRY A NEW POPSICLE FLAVOR.
I DON'T WANT THAT. FOOD IS THE LAST THING I WANT TO BE ASSOCIATED WITH...
WHY'S THAT?
WELL...
HUH?

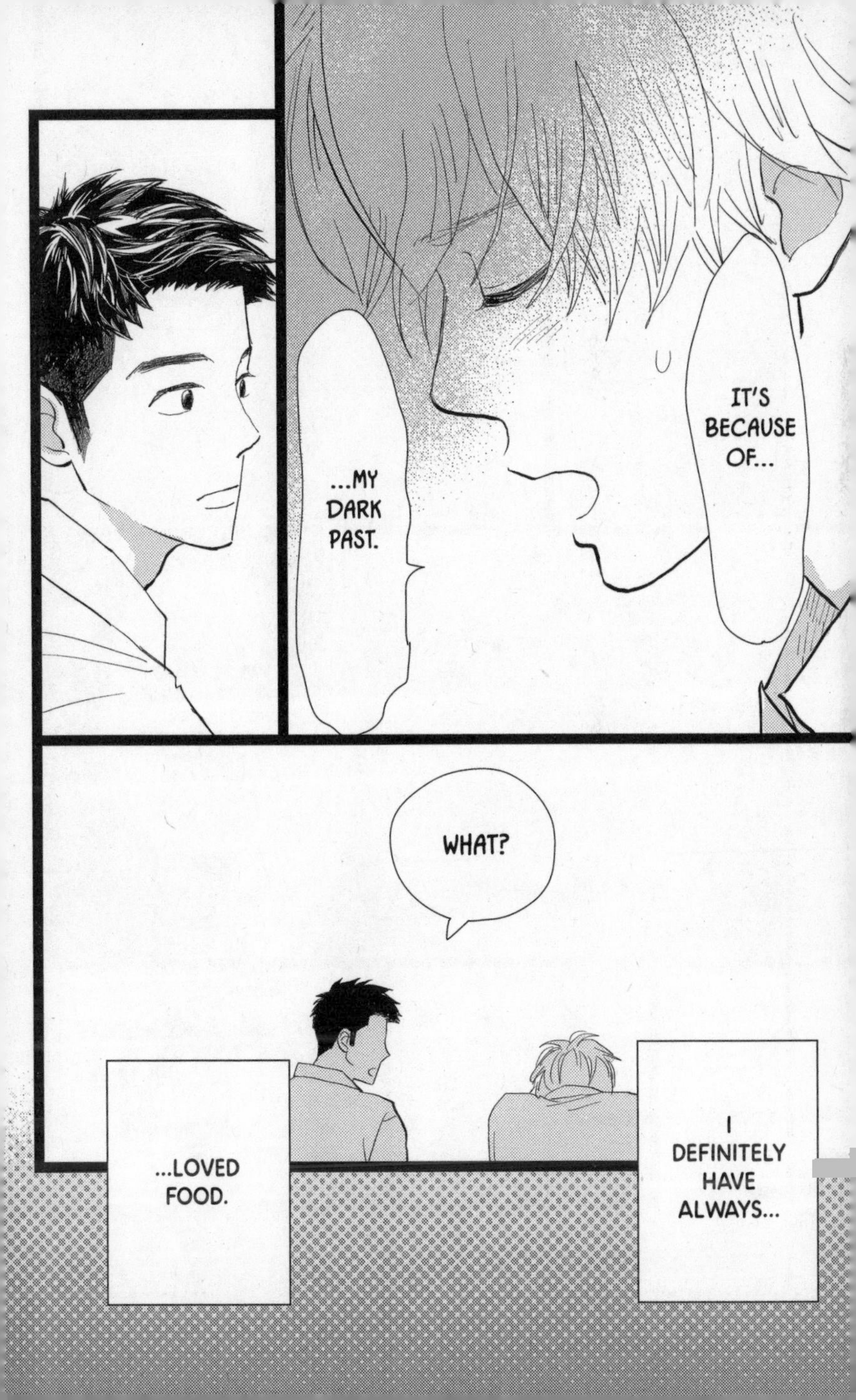
IT'S BECAUSE OF...
...MY DARK PAST.
WHAT?
I DEFINITELY HAVE ALWAYS...
...LOVED FOOD.

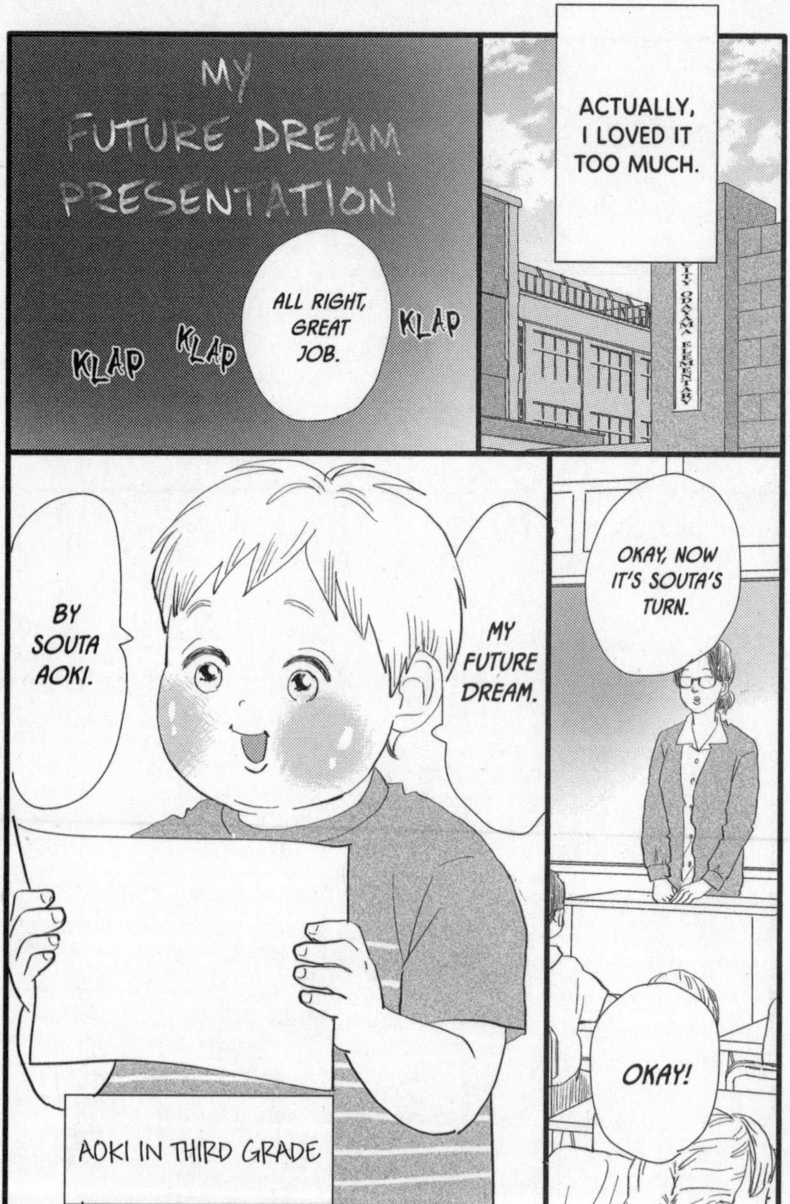
ACTUALLY, I LOVED IT TOO MUCH.
ODAYAMA ELEMENTARY
MY FUTURE DREAM PRESENTATION
KLAP
ALL RIGHT, GREAT JOB.
KLAP
KLAP
OKAY, NOW IT'S SOUTA'S TURN.
OKAY!
MY FUTURE DREAM.
BY SOUTA AOKI.
AOKI IN THIRD GRADE

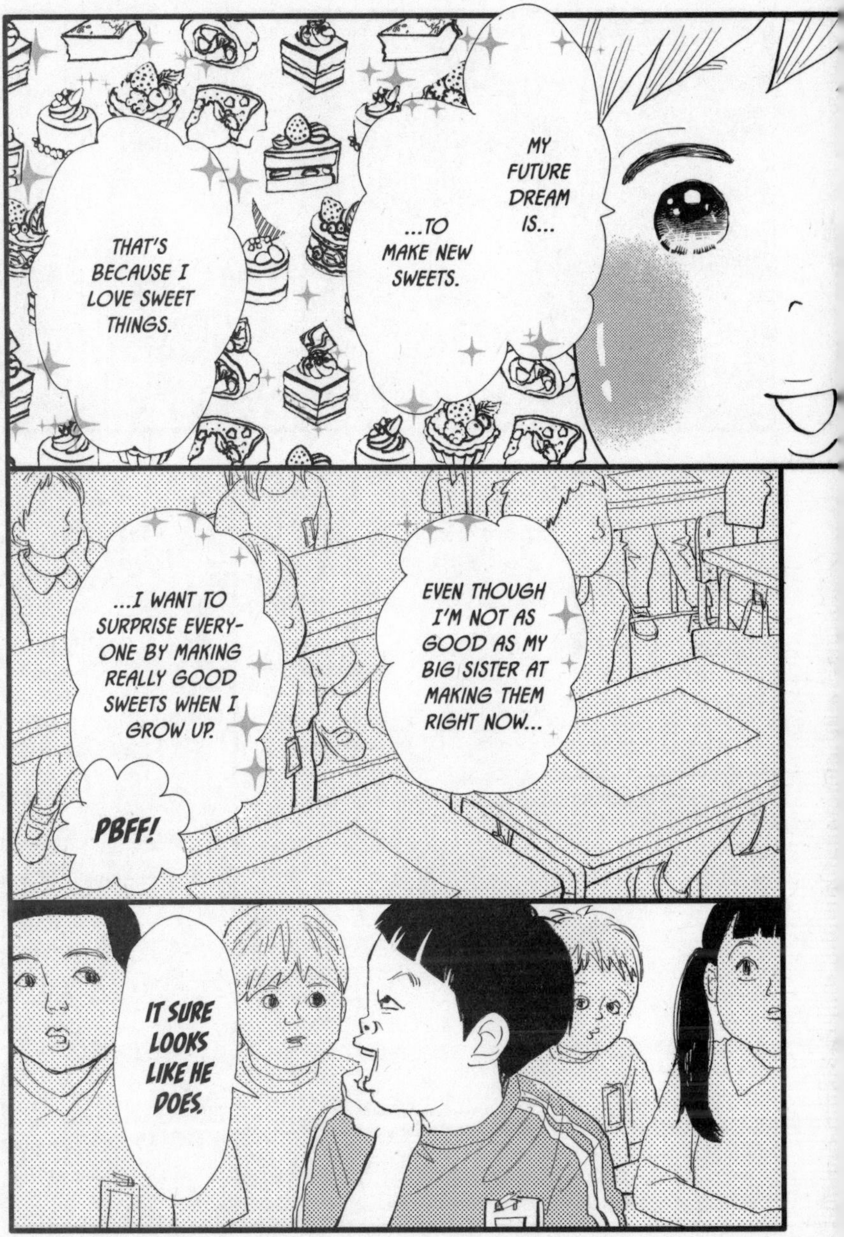
MY FUTURE DREAM IS...
...TO MAKE NEW SWEETS.
THAT'S BECAUSE I LOVE SWEET THINGS.
EVEN THOUGH I'M NOT AS GOOD AS MY BIG SISTER AT MAKING THEM RIGHT NOW...
...I WANT TO SURPRISE EVERY-ONE BY MAKING REALLY GOOD SWEETS WHEN I GROW UP.
PBFF!
IT SURE LOOKS LIKE HE DOES.

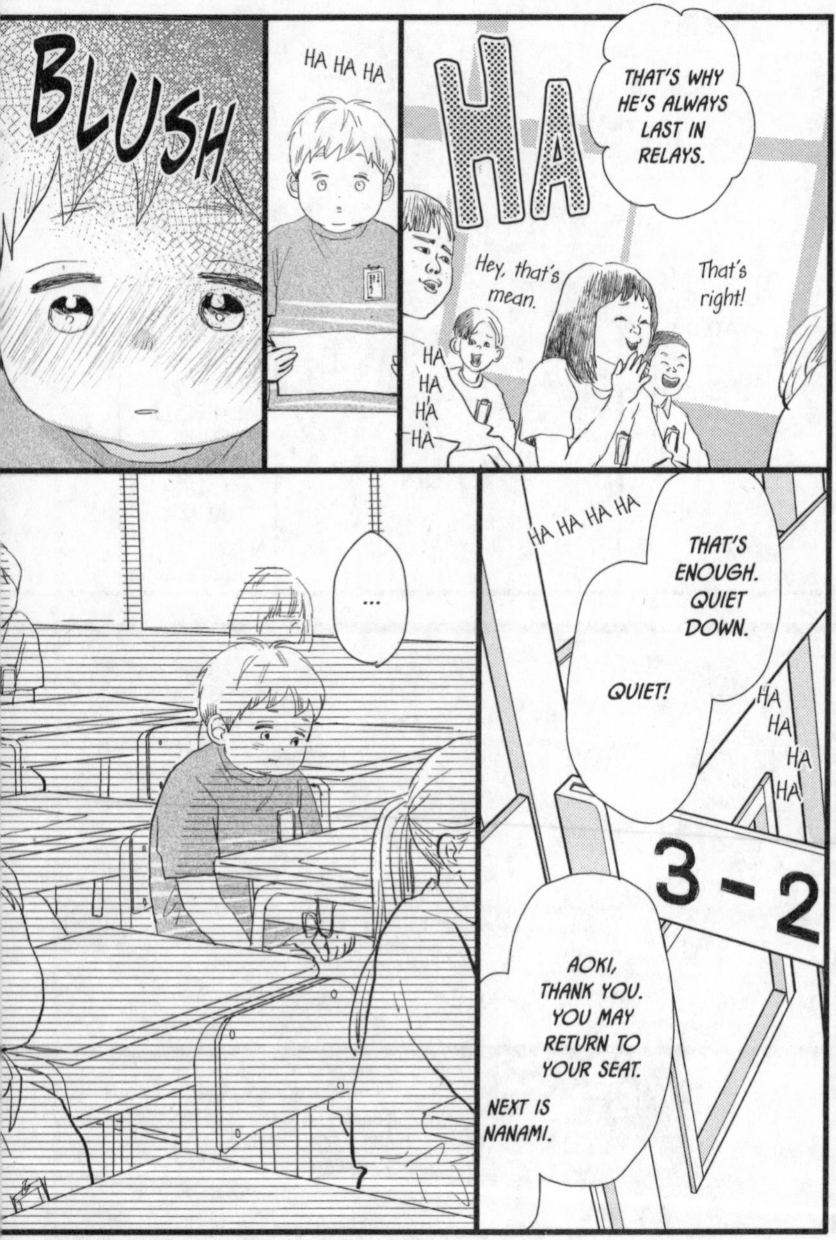
THAT'S WHY HE'S ALWAYS LAST IN RELAYS.
HA
That's right!
Hey, that's mean.
HA HA HA HA
HA HA HA
BLUSH
HA HA HA HA
THAT'S ENOUGH. QUIET DOWN.
QUIET!
HA HA HA HA
3-2
AOKI, THANK YOU. YOU MAY RETURN TO YOUR SEAT.
NEXT IS NANAMI.
...

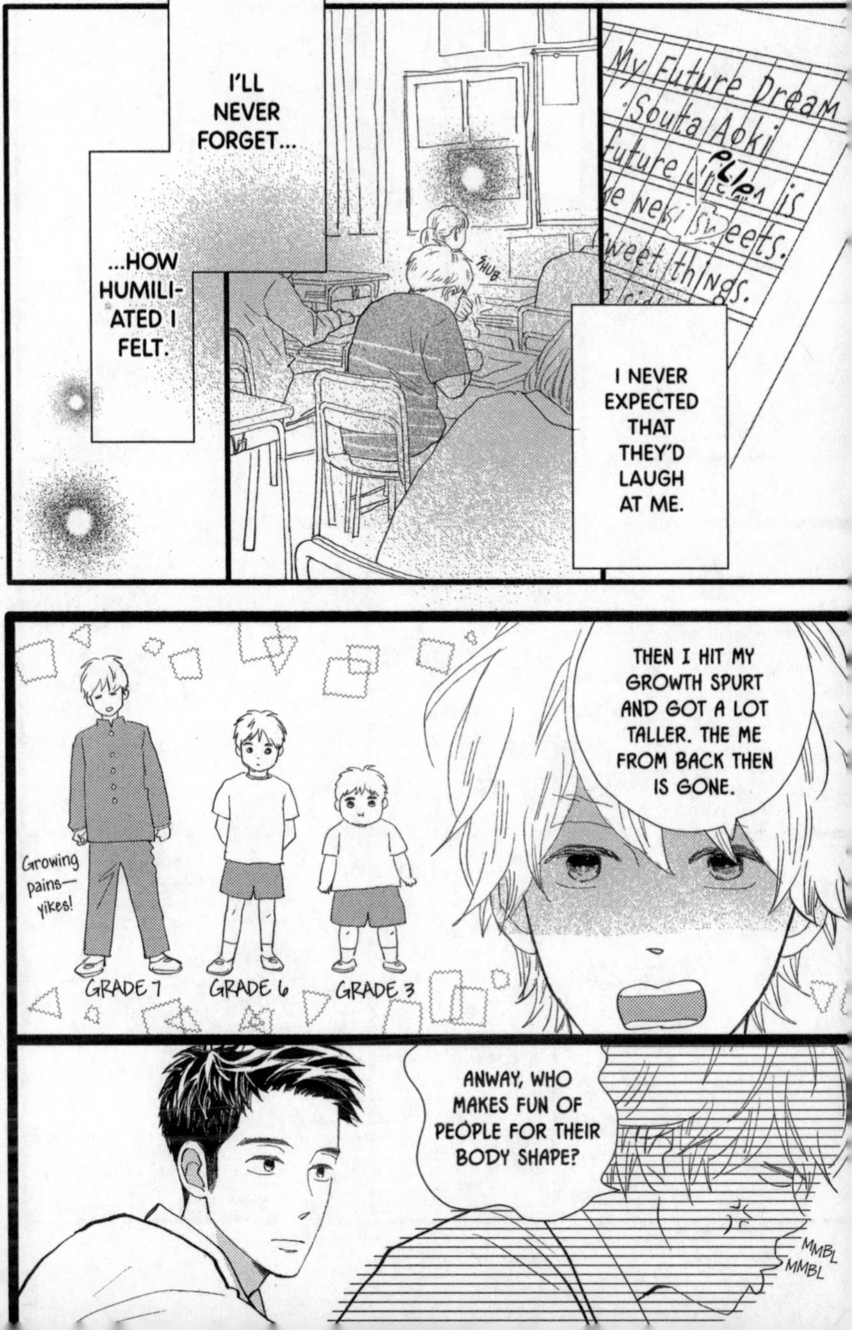
My Future Dream
Souta Aoki
sweet things.
PLIP
I NEVER EXPECTED THAT THEY'D LAUGH AT ME.
SHUB
I'LL NEVER FORGET...
...HOW HUMILIATED I FELT.
THEN I HIT MY GROWTH SPURT AND GOT A LOT TALLER. THE ME FROM BACK THEN IS GONE.
GRADE 3
GRADE 6
GRADE 7
Growing pains—yikes!
MMBL MMBL
ANWAY, WHO MAKES FUN OF PEOPLE FOR THEIR BODY SHAPE?

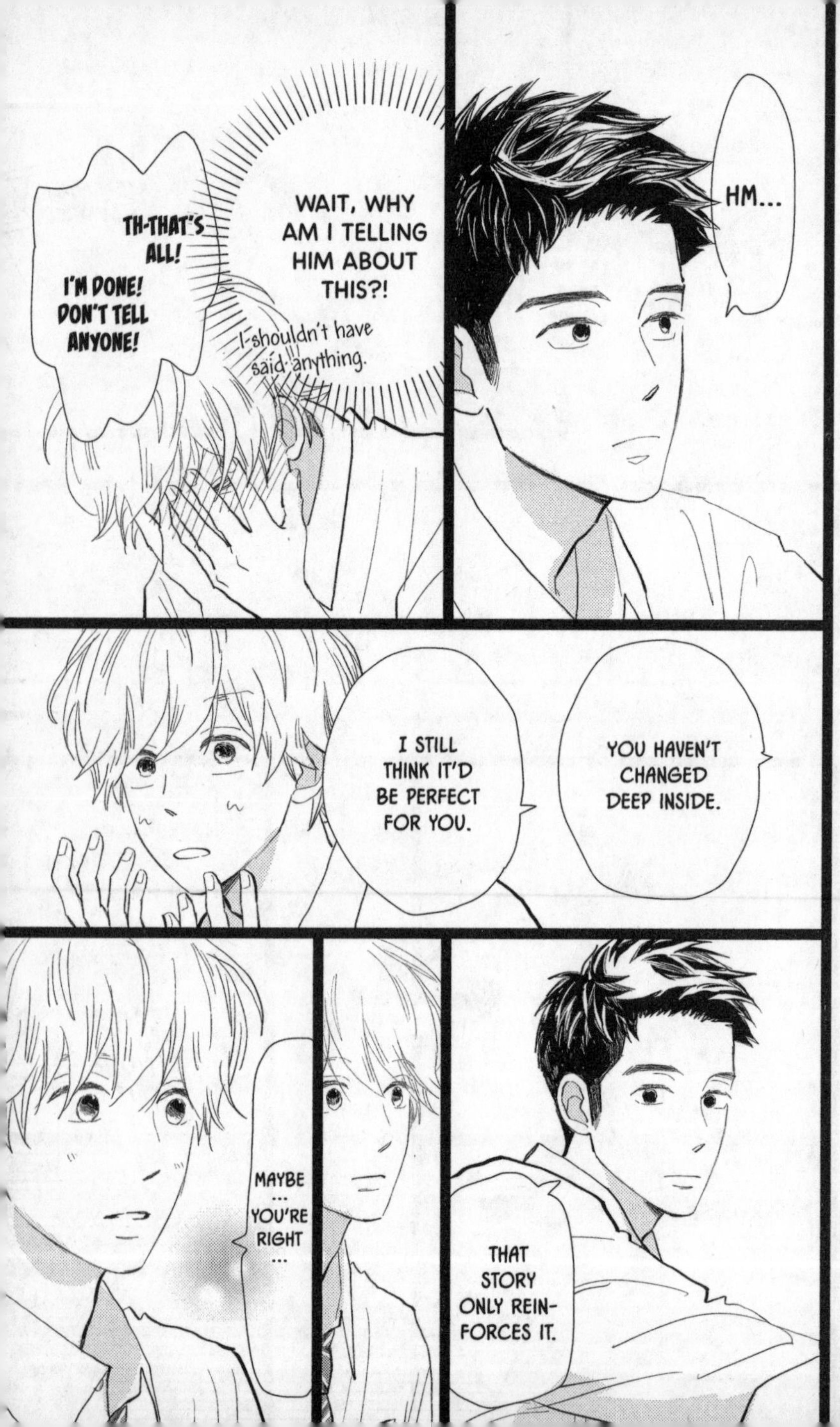
HM...
WAIT, WHY AM I TELLING HIM ABOUT THIS?!
I-shouldn't have said anything.
TH-THAT'S ALL!
I'M DONE! DON'T TELL ANYONE!
YOU HAVEN'T CHANGED DEEP INSIDE.
I STILL THINK IT'D BE PERFECT FOR YOU.
THAT STORY ONLY REIN-FORCES IT.
MAYBE ... YOU'RE RIGHT ...

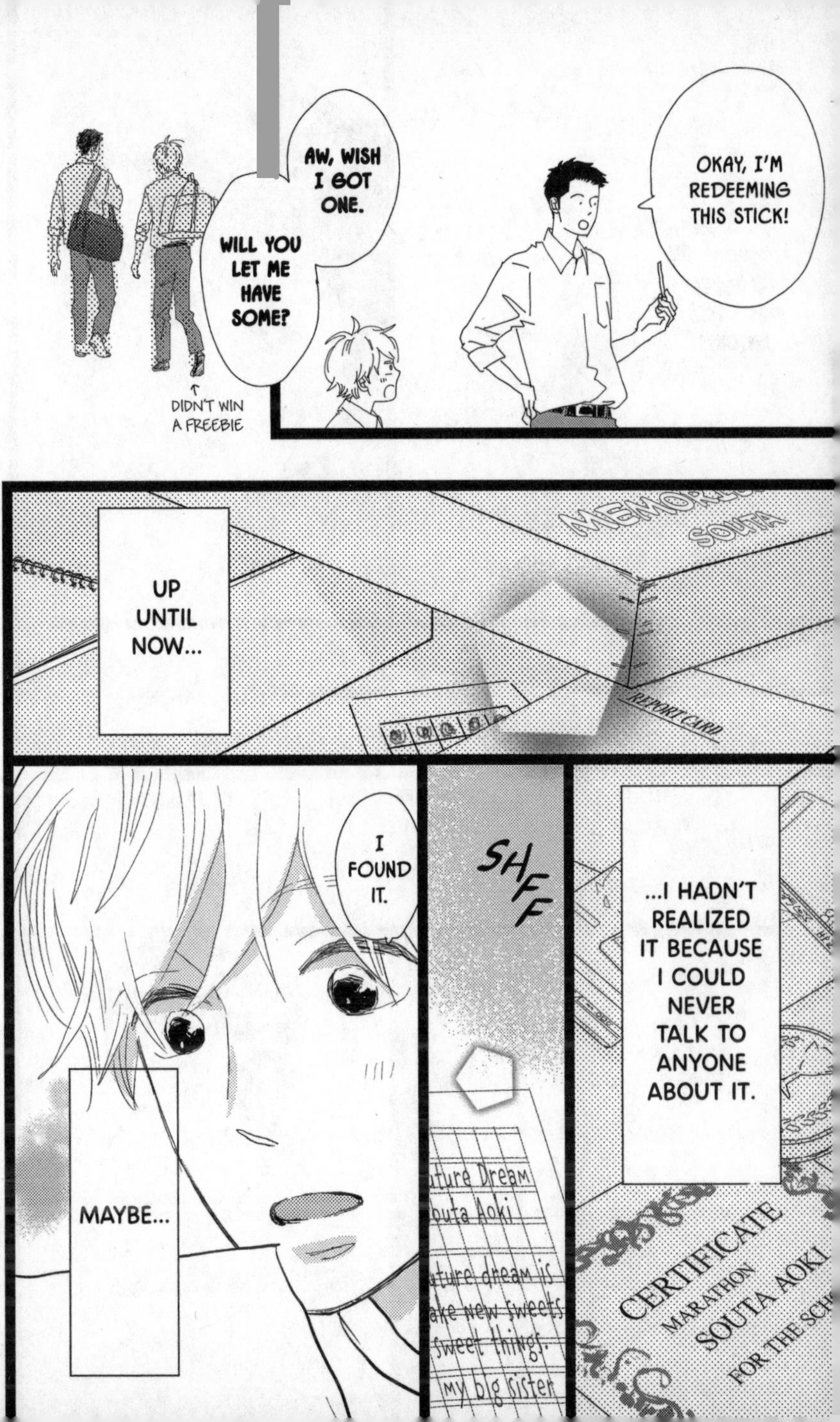
OKAY, I'M REDEEMING THIS STICK!
AW, WISH I GOT ONE.
WILL YOU LET ME HAVE SOME?
DIDN'T WIN A FREEBIE
SOUTA
REPORT CARD
UP UNTIL NOW...
...I HADN'T REALIZED IT BECAUSE I COULD NEVER TALK TO ANYONE ABOUT IT.
CERTIFICATE
MARATHON
SOUTA AOKI
SHFF
I FOUND IT.
MAYBE...

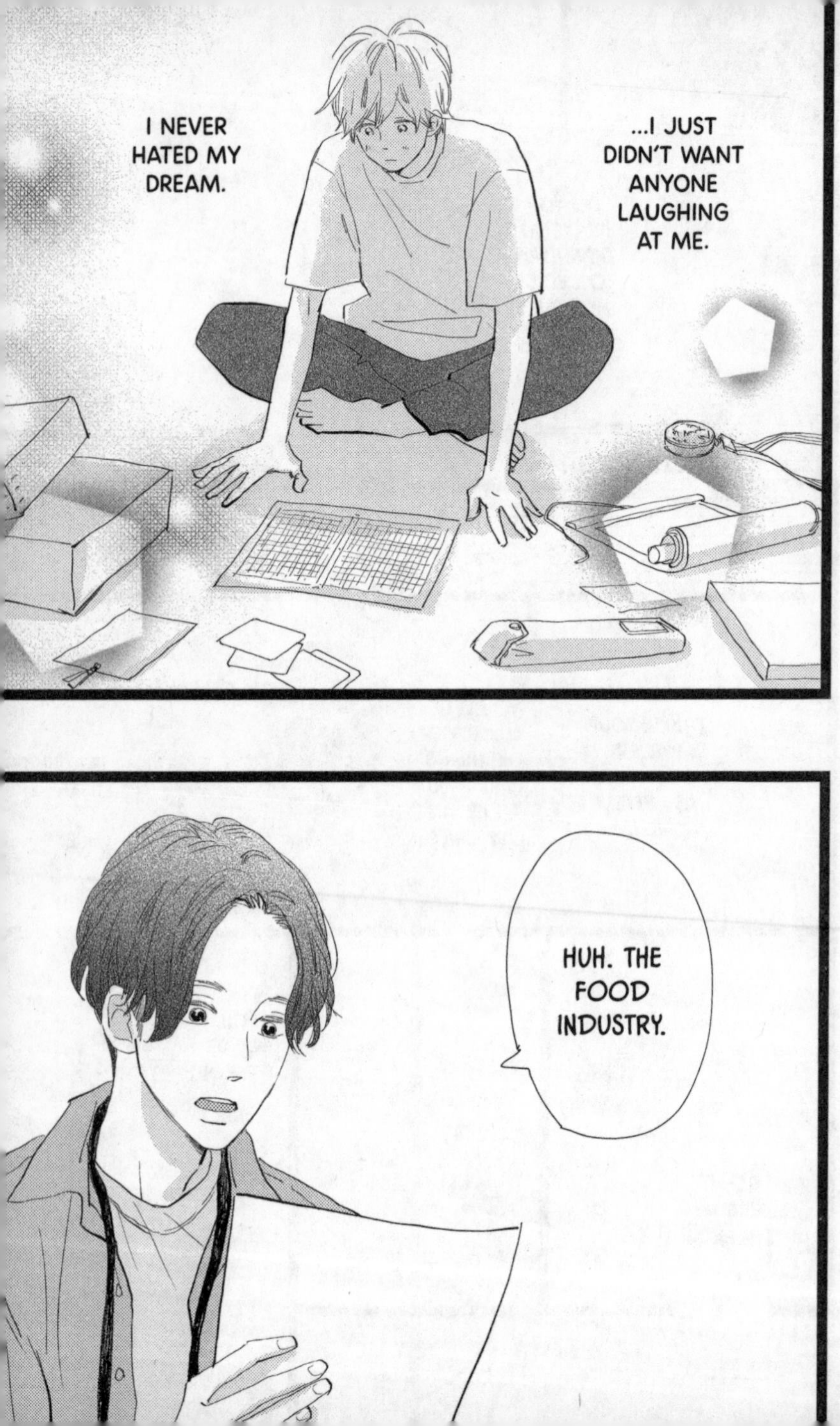
...I JUST DIDN'T WANT ANYONE LAUGHING AT ME.
I NEVER HATED MY DREAM.
HUH. THE FOOD INDUSTRY.

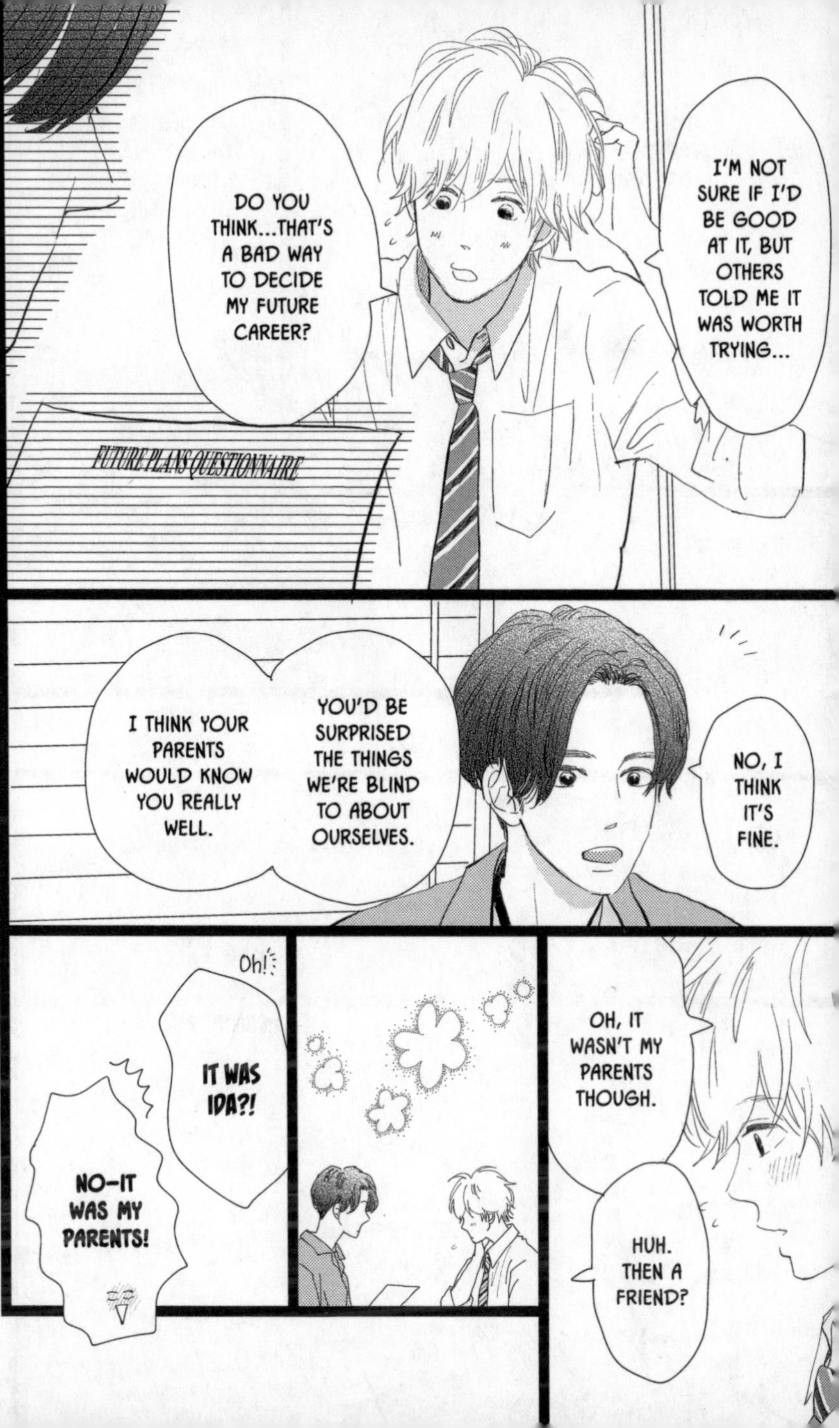
I'M NOT SURE IF I'D BE GOOD AT IT, BUT OTHERS TOLD ME IT WAS WORTH TRYING...
DO YOU THINK...THAT'S A BAD WAY TO DECIDE MY FUTURE CAREER?
FUTURE PLANS QUESTIONNAIRE
NO, I THINK IT'S FINE.
YOU'D BE SURPRISED THE THINGS WE'RE BLIND TO ABOUT OURSELVES.
I THINK YOUR PARENTS WOULD KNOW YOU REALLY WELL.
OH, IT WASN'T MY PARENTS THOUGH.
HUH. THEN A FRIEND?
Oh!
IT WAS IDA?!
NO—IT WAS MY PARENTS!

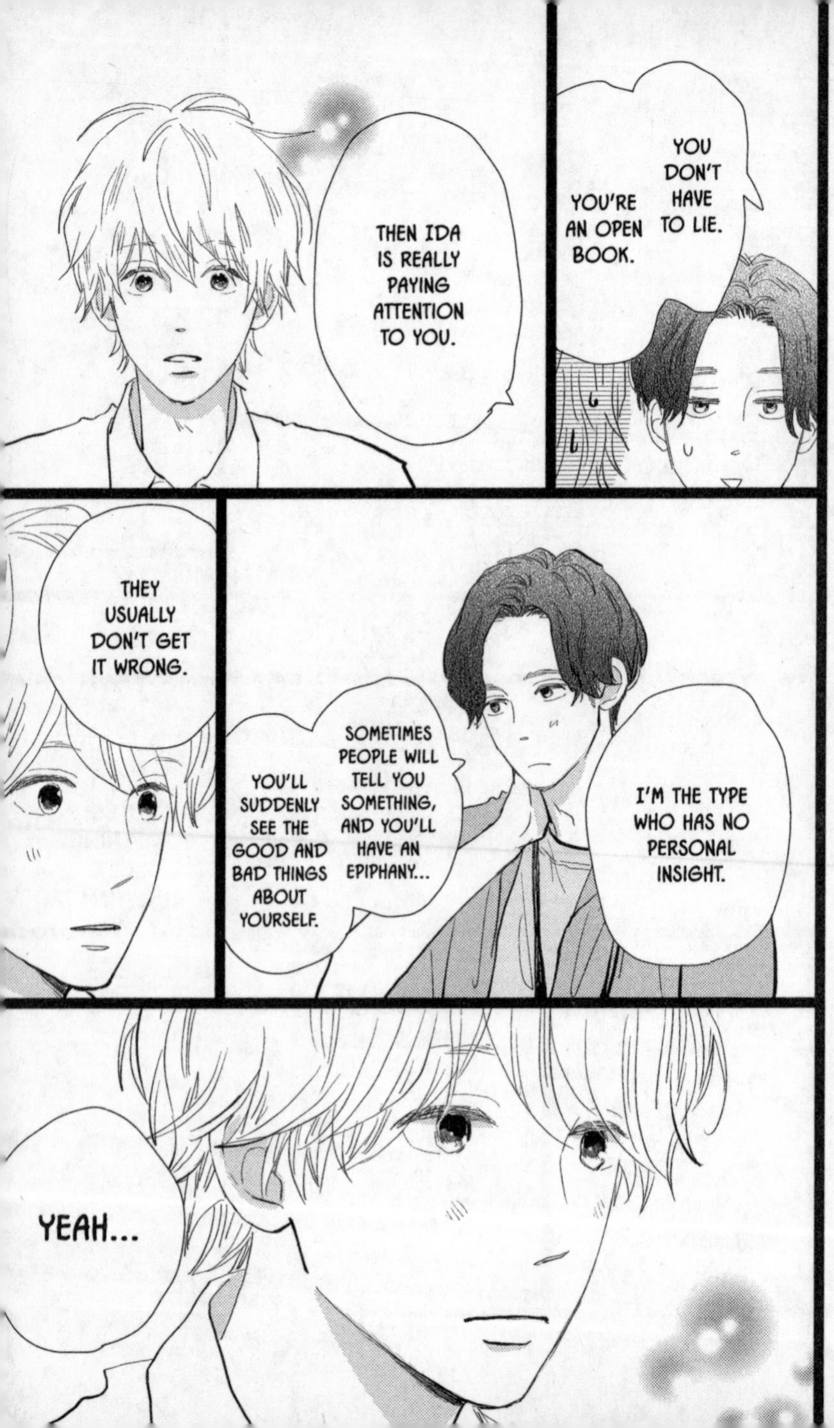
YOU DON'T HAVE TO LIE.
YOU'RE AN OPEN BOOK.
THEN IDA IS REALLY PAYING ATTENTION TO YOU.
I'M THE TYPE WHO HAS NO PERSONAL INSIGHT.
SOMETIMES PEOPLE WILL TELL YOU SOMETHING, AND YOU'LL HAVE AN EPIPHANY...
YOU'LL SUDDENLY SEE THE GOOD AND BAD THINGS ABOUT YOURSELF.
THEY USUALLY DON'T GET IT WRONG.
YEAH...

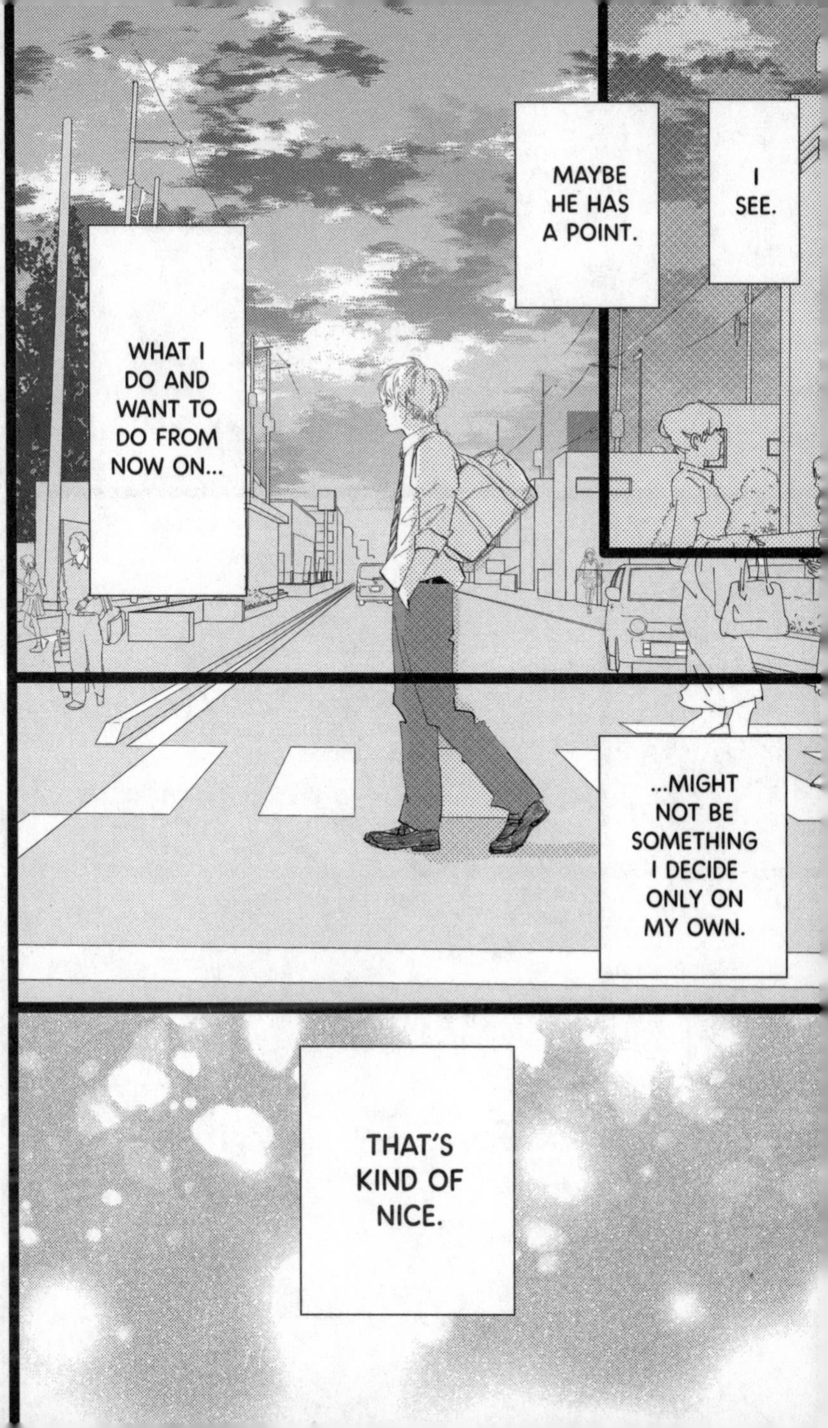
I SEE.
MAYBE HE HAS A POINT.
WHAT I DO AND WANT TO DO FROM NOW ON...
...MIGHT NOT BE SOMETHING I DECIDE ONLY ON MY OWN.
THAT'S KIND OF NICE.

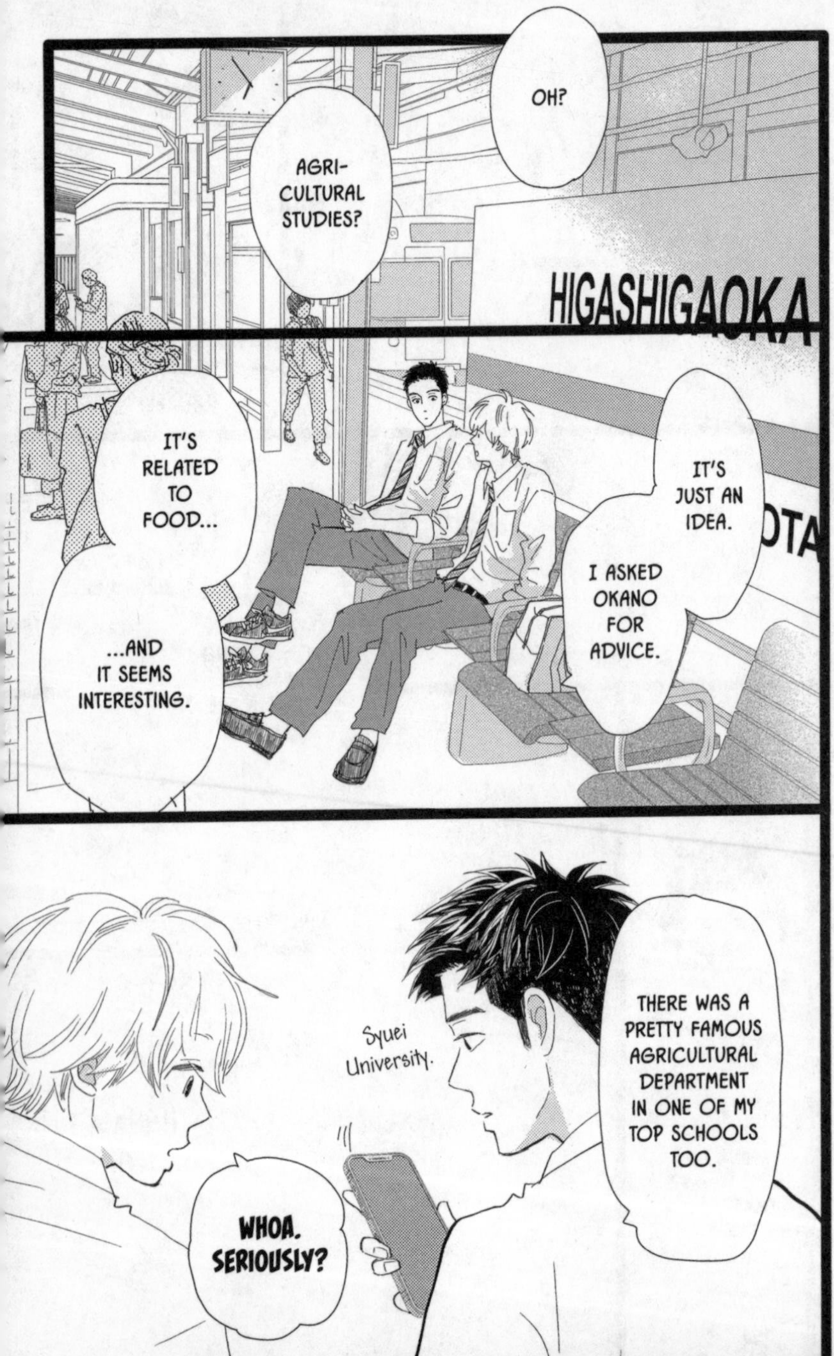
OH?
AGRI-CULTURAL STUDIES?
HIGASHIGAOKA
IT'S JUST AN IDEA.
I ASKED OKANO FOR ADVICE.
OTA
IT'S RELATED TO FOOD...
...AND IT SEEMS INTERESTING.
THERE WAS A PRETTY FAMOUS AGRICULTURAL DEPARTMENT IN ONE OF MY TOP SCHOOLS TOO.
Syuei University.
WHOA. SERIOUSLY?

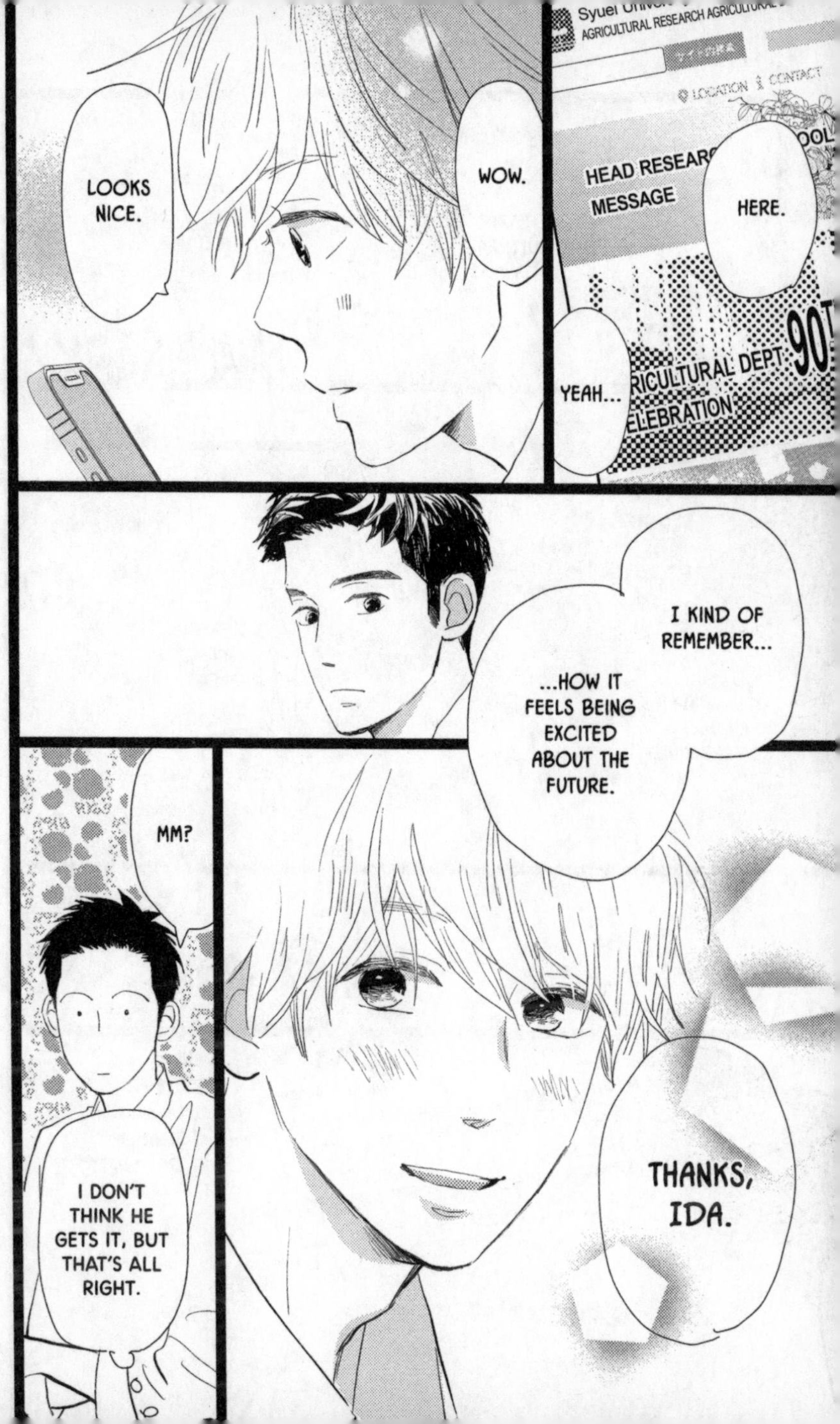
AGRICULTURAL RESEARCH AGRICULTURAL
LOCATION
CONTACT
HEAD RESEAR
MESSAGE
HERE.
RICULTURAL DEPT.
ELEBRATION
YEAH...
WOW.
LOOKS NICE.
I KIND OF REMEMBER...
...HOW IT FEELS BEING EXCITED ABOUT THE FUTURE.
THANKS, IDA.
MM?
I DON'T THINK HE GETS IT, BUT THAT'S ALL RIGHT.

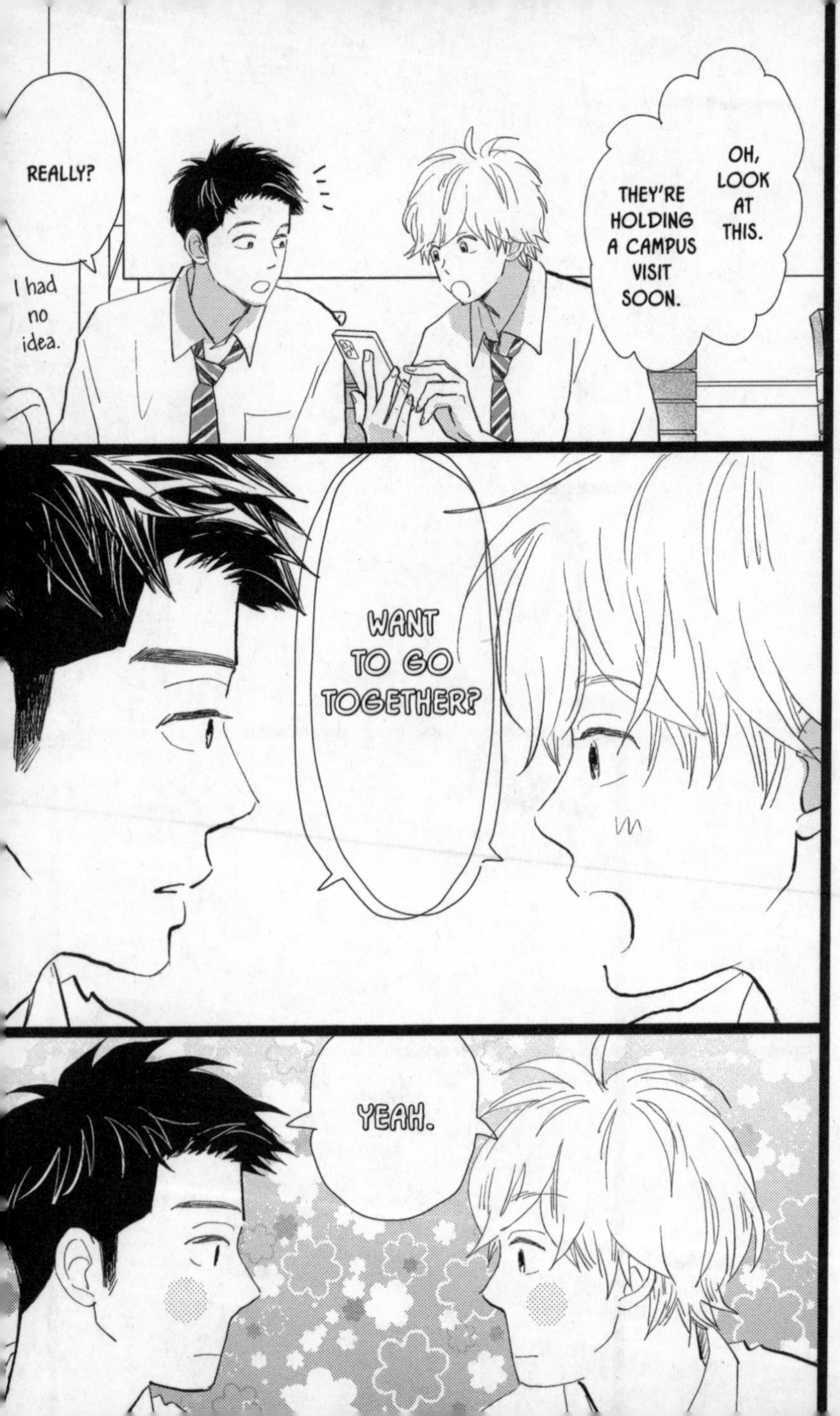
OH, LOOK AT THIS.
THEY'RE HOLDING A CAMPUS VISIT SOON.
REALLY?
I had no idea.
WANT TO GO TOGETHER?
YEAH.

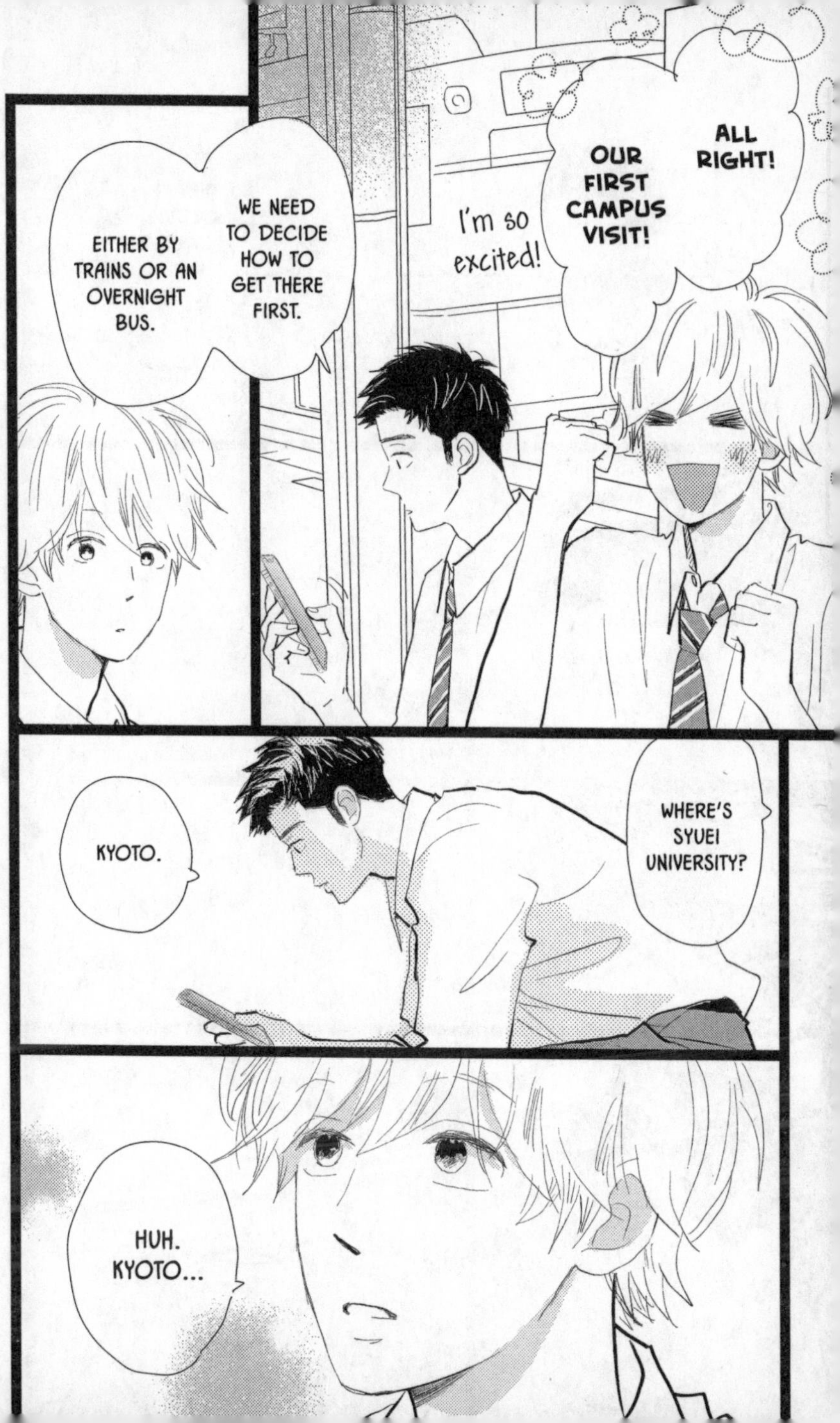
ALL RIGHT!
OUR FIRST CAMPUS VISIT!
I'm so excited!
WE NEED TO DECIDE HOW TO GET THERE FIRST.
EITHER BY TRAINS OR AN OVERNIGHT BUS.
WHERE'S SYUEI UNIVERSITY?
KYOTO.
HUH. KYOTO...

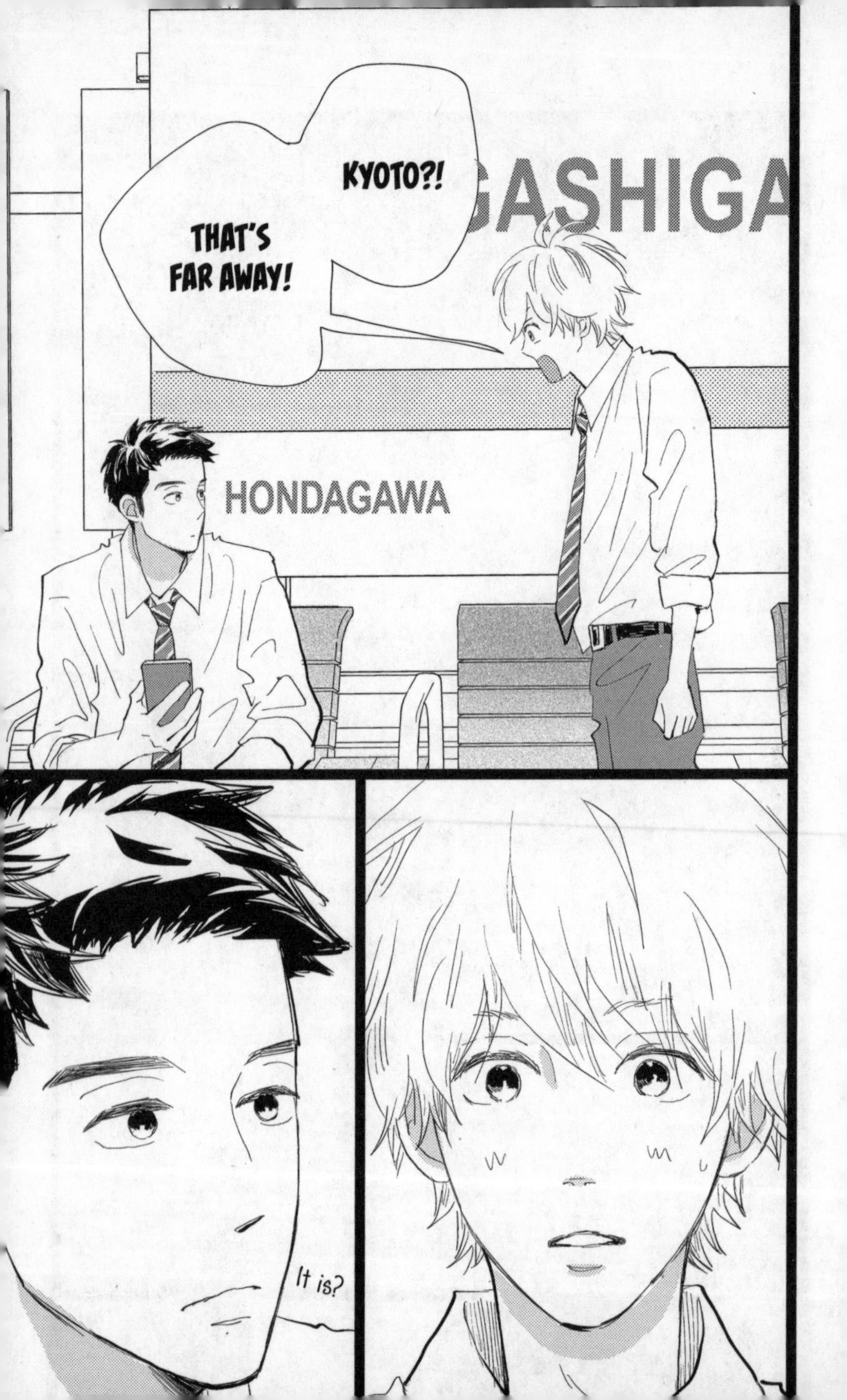
GASHIGA
KYOTO?!
THAT'S FAR AWAY!
HONDAGAWA
It is?

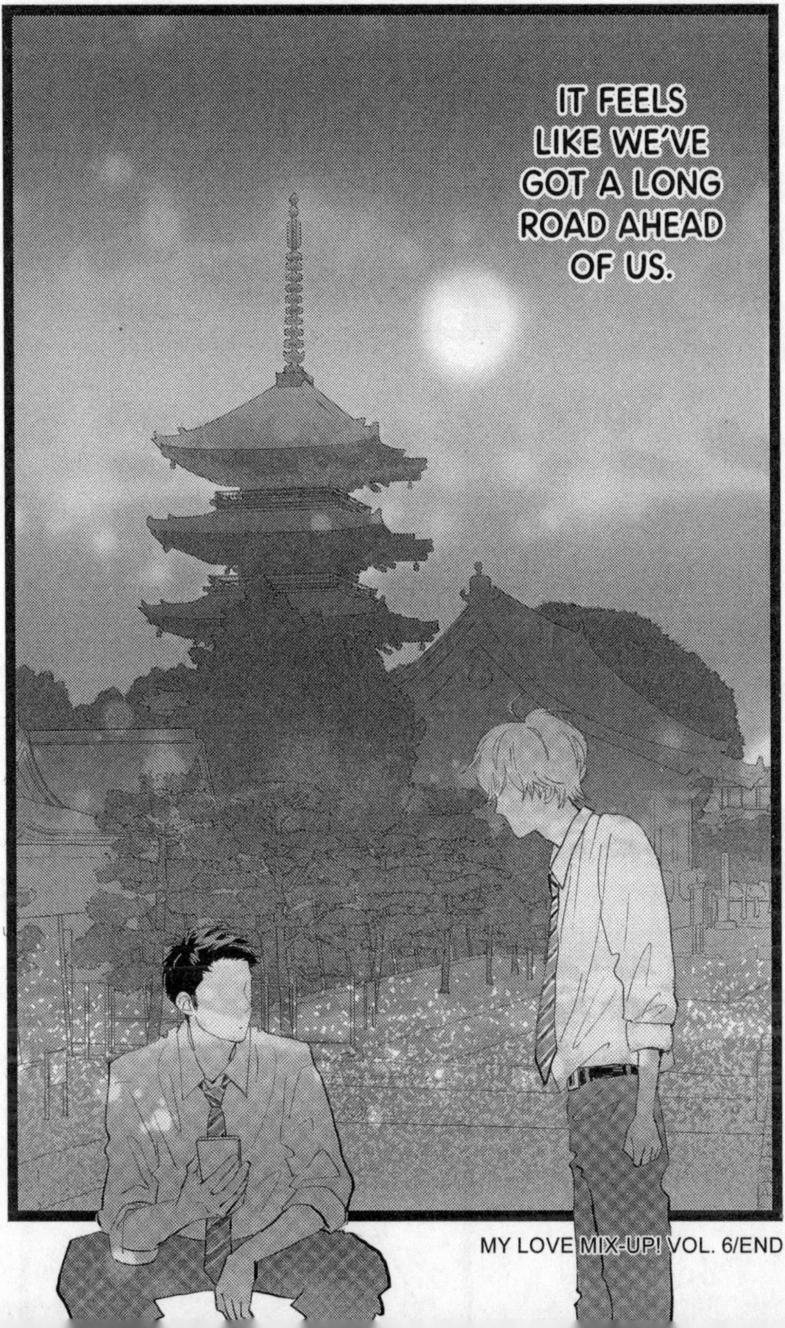
IT FEELS LIKE WE'VE GOT A LONG ROAD AHEAD OF US.

MY LOVE MIX-UP! VOL. 6/END

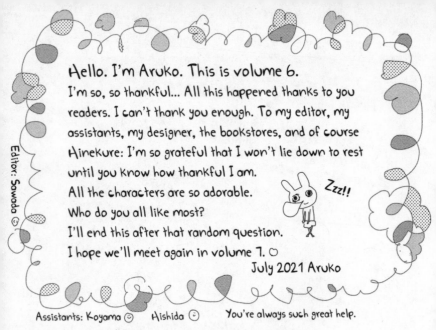

Hello. I'm Aruko. This is volume 6.

I'm so, so thankful... All this happened thanks to you readers. I can't thank you enough. To my editor, my assistants, my designer, the bookstores, and of course Hinekure: I'm so grateful that I won't lie down to rest until you know how thankful I am.

All the characters are so adorable.

Who do you all like most?

Zzz!!

I'll end this after that random question.

I hope we'll meet again in volume 7. ○

July 2021 Aruko

Editor: Sawada ☺

Assistants: Koyama ☺ Hishida ☺ You're always such great help.

Thank you for picking up *My Love Mix-Up!* volume 6.

Aruko Sensei, our editor, and all the readers—you've supported us continuously for two years of serialization. I'm so happy you're still with us and reading the manga even now. Thank you for everything. I'm going to work even harder. Also, Aoki and his friends are already in their last year of high school. I feel the same as I would seeing my own grandchildren grow up. Ida in particular seemed taciturn to me, so I had trouble getting him at first, but as I read Aruko Sensei's draft I low-key realized his gestures and expressions are lovely. Now I really like him a lot. I'm excited for you to see how charming the characters are in lots of different ways, like in the little theaters coming up. I hope to see you in the next volume.

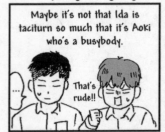

Maybe it's not that Ida is taciturn so much that it's Aoki who's a busybody.
That's rude!!
...

I like summer because daylight lasts longer. But then I get exhausted really quickly. What to do?!

Aruko

Time keeps moving on, and volume 6 is already here. The change in the distance between the two on the cover is riveting and deeply poignant at the same time. Aruko Sensei, our editor, and all our readers—thank you for nurturing this story with me.

Wataru Hinekure

Aruko is from Ishikawa Prefecture in Japan and was born on July 26 (a Leo!). She made her manga debut with *Ame Nochi Hare* (Clear After the Rain). Her other works include *Yasuko to Kenji*, and her hobbies include laughing and getting lost.

Wataru Hinekure is a night owl. *My Love Mix-Up!* is Hinekure's first work.

My Love Mix-Up!

Vol. 6
Shojo Beat Edition

STORY BY
Wataru Hinekure
ART BY
Aruko

Translation & Adaptation/Jan Mitsuko Cash
Touch-Up Art & Lettering/Inori Fukuda Trant
Design/Yukiko Whitley
Editor/Nancy Thistlethwaite

Printed in the U.S.A.

Published by VIZ Media, LLC
P.O. Box 77010
San Francisco, CA 94107

10 9 8 7 6 5 4 3 2 1
First printing, January 2023

ratings.viz.com RATED T TEEN

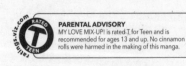

PARENTAL ADVISORY
MY LOVE MIX-UP! is rated T for Teen and is recommended for ages 13 and up. No cinnamon rolls were harmed in the making of this manga.

VIZ MEDIA
viz.com

Shojo Beat
shojobeat.com

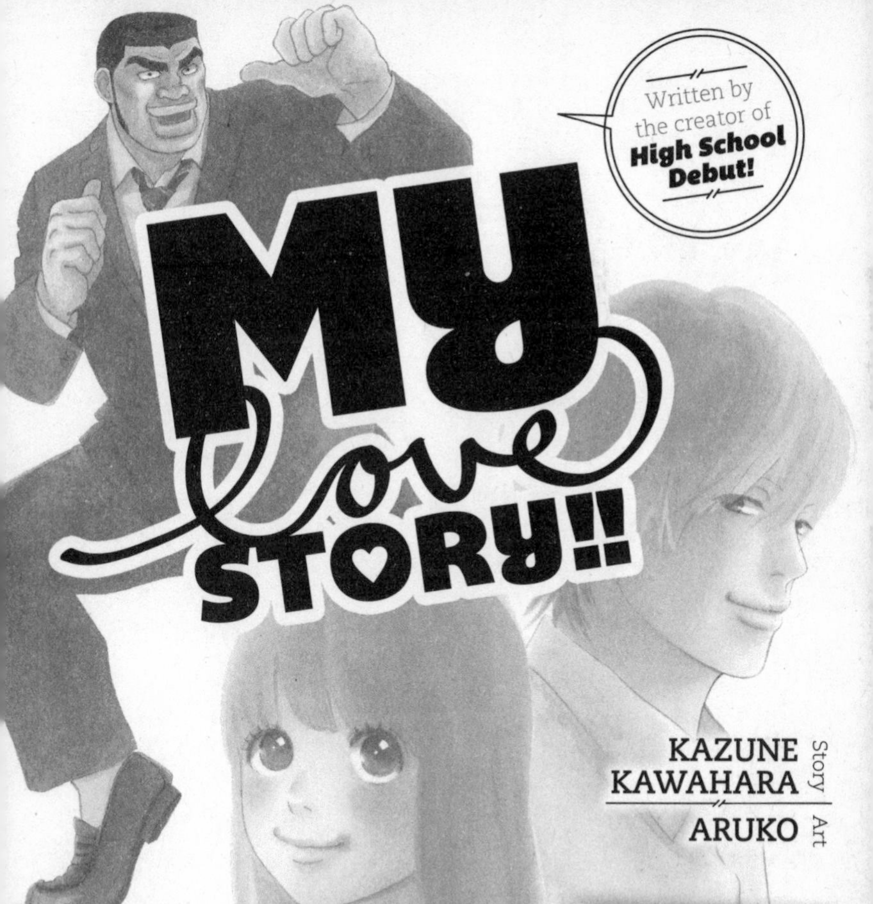
Written by the creator of High School Debut!
MY love STORY!!
KAZUNE KAWAHARA Story
ARUKO Art

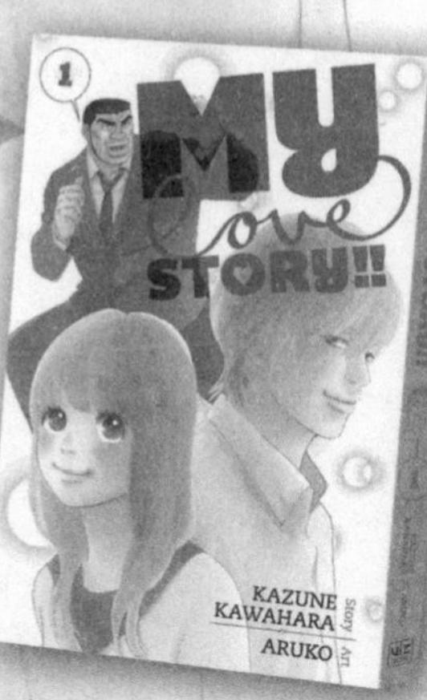
1
MY love STORY!!
KAZUNE KAWAHARA Story
ARUKO Art

Sometimes the greatest romantic adventure isn't falling in love— it's what happens after you fall in love!

IMA KOI

Now I'm in Love

STORY & ART BY
Ayuko Hatta

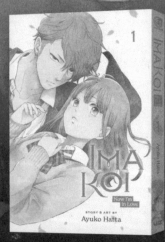

After missing out on love because she was too shy to confess her feelings, high school student Satomi blurts out how she feels the next time she gets a crush—and it's to her impossibly handsome schoolmate Yagyu! To her surprise, he agrees to date her. Now that Satomi's suddenly in a relationship, what next?

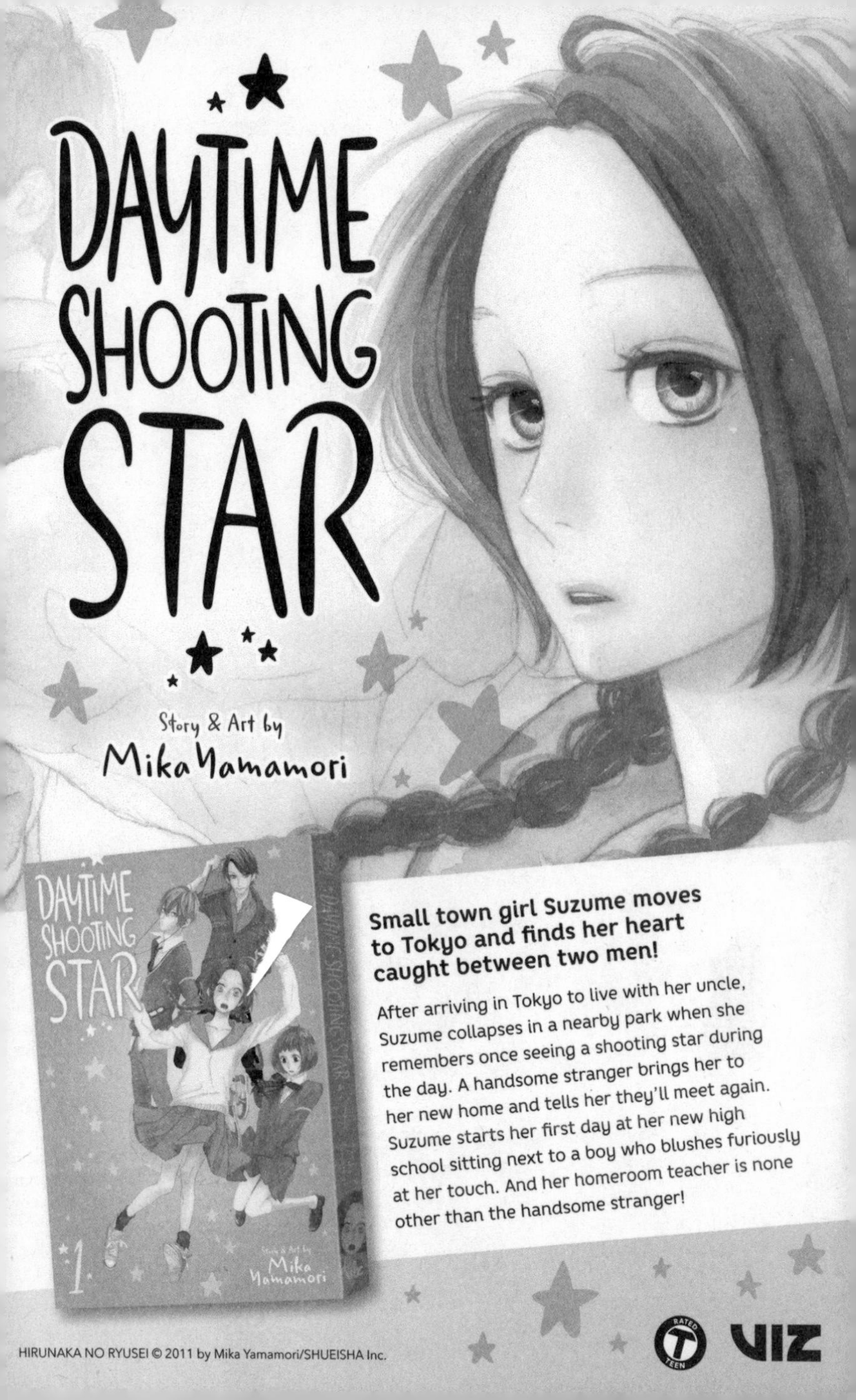
DAYTIME SHOOTING STAR
Story & Art by
Mika Yamamori
DAYTIME SHOOTING STAR
1
Story & Art by Mika Yamamori
Small town girl Suzume moves to Tokyo and finds her heart caught between two men!
After arriving in Tokyo to live with her uncle, Suzume collapses in a nearby park when she remembers once seeing a shooting star during the day. A handsome stranger brings her to her new home and tells her they'll meet again. Suzume starts her first day at her new high school sitting next to a boy who blushes furiously at her touch. And her homeroom teacher is none other than the handsome stranger!
RATED T TEEN
VIZ
HIRUNAKA NO RYUSEI © 2011 by Mika Yamamori/SHUEISHA Inc.

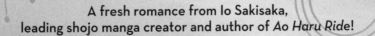
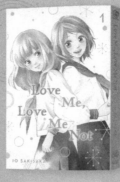

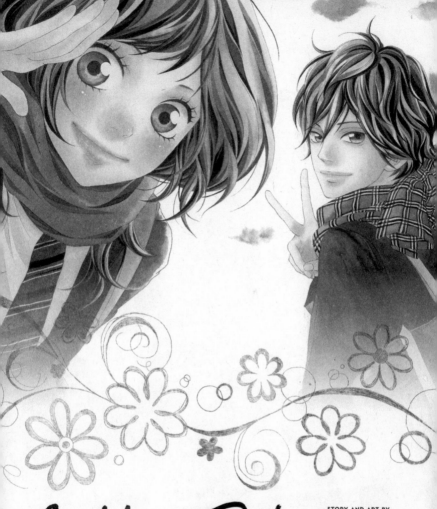

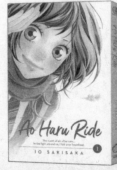

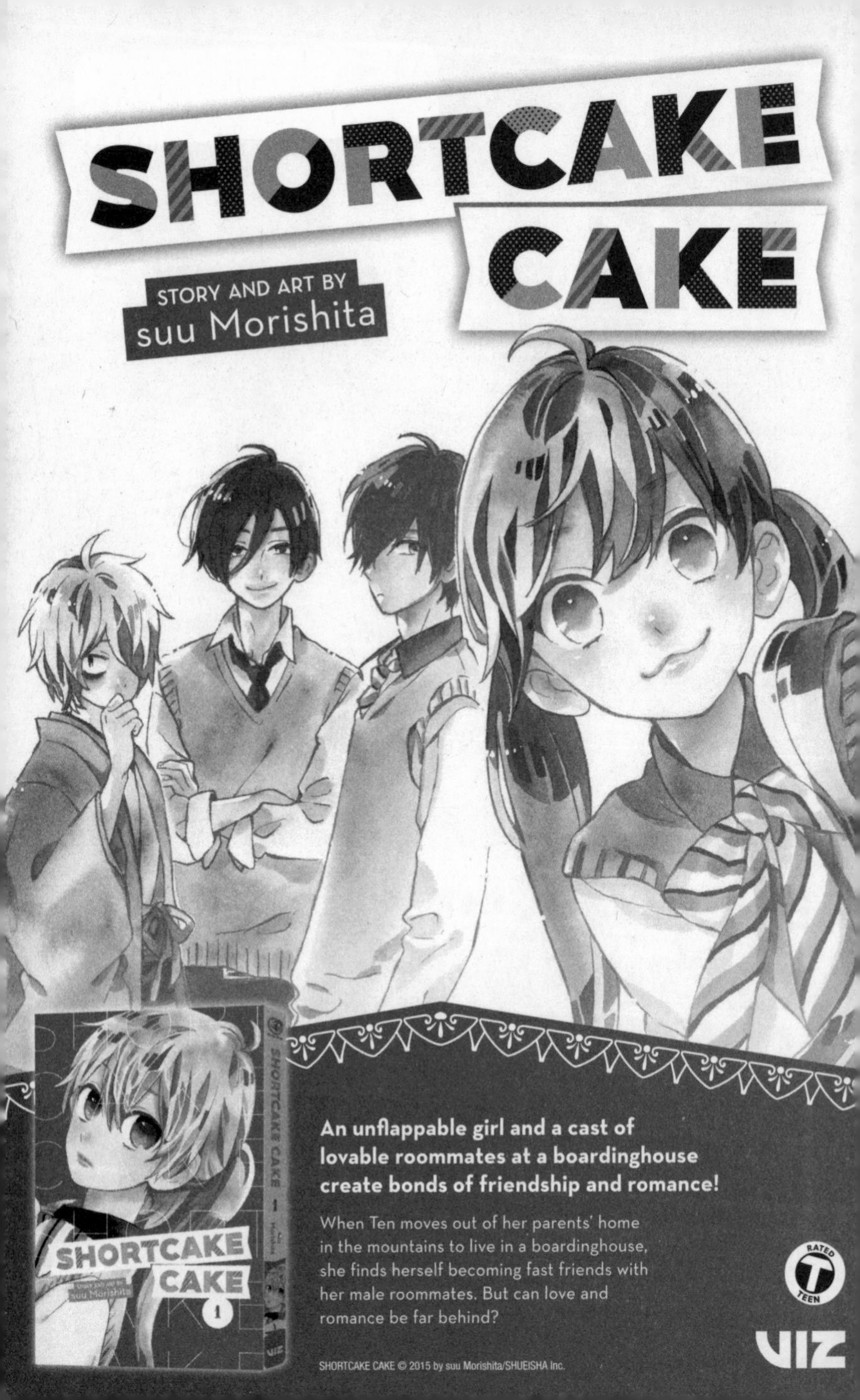
SHORTCAKE CAKE
STORY AND ART BY
suu Morishita
SHORTCAKE CAKE
SHORTCAKE CAKE
suu Morishita
1
An unflappable girl and a cast of lovable roommates at a boardinghouse create bonds of friendship and romance!
When Ten moves out of her parents' home in the mountains to live in a boardinghouse, she finds herself becoming fast friends with her male roommates. But can love and romance be far behind?
RATED T TEEN
VIZ
SHORTCAKE CAKE © 2015 by suu Morishita/SHUEISHA Inc.

Stop!

You may be reading the wrong way.

In keeping with the original Japanese comic format, this book reads from right to left—so action, sound effects, and word balloons are completely reversed to preserve the orientation of the original artwork. Check out the diagram shown here to get the hang of things, and then turn to the other side of the book to get started!

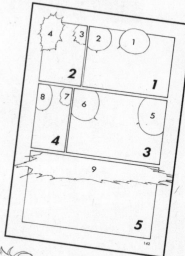

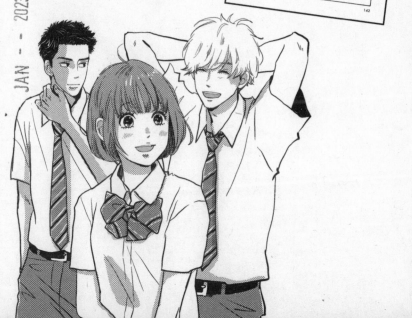